CORPORATE GOVERNANCE

Corporate Governance

Practices, procedures and powers in British
companies and their boards of directors.

R.I. TRICKER
The Corporate Policy Group,
Oxford

Gower

R.I. Tricker
The Corporate Policy Group,
Oxford

© R.I. Tricker 1984

Published by Gower Publishing Company Limited,
Gower House, Croft Road, Aldershot,
Hants GU11 3HR England

Gower Publishing Company,
Old Post Road, Brookfield, Vermont 05036, U.S.A.

British Library Cataloging in Publication Data
Tricker, R.I.
Corporate governance.
1. Directors of corporations – Great Britain.
I. Title
658.4'22   HD2745

ISBN 0-566-00749-5

Library of Congress Cataloging in Publication Data
Tricker, R. Ian (Robert Ian)
Corporate governance.

"Based on the work of the Corporate Policy Group, Oxford."
Bibliography: p.
Includes index.
1. Directors of corporations – Great Britain.
2. Corporations – Great Britain.
3. Corporation Law – Great Britain.   I. Title.
HD2745.T77 1984   658.4'22'0941   84-4071

ISBN 0-566-00749-5

Typeset by FD Graphics, Fleet, Hampshire

Printed and bound in Great Britain
by Billings & Sons Limited, Worcester.

Contents

Acknowledgements

This book is based on studies, from 1979 to 1983, by The Corporate Policy Group into the direction, supervision and accountability of the modern corporation — the processes of corporate governance.

There are four groups of people without whose help this work could not have been completed:

The Trustees and Sponsors of The Corporate Policy Group
  — for funding and facilitating the research,

The Warden and Fellows of Nuffield College, Oxford
  — for providing the Group with a congenial academic home,

The Director and Council of the Oxford Centre for Management Studies
  — for enabling the author to undertake the work,

and all the chairmen and directors of companies who have taken part in the studies, and particularly those who provided data on corporate structures, often involving considerable effort.

To them all gratitude is warmly expressed.

I would also like to acknowledge the contributions of my doctoral students, Joachim Mueller and Simon Murray, to my knowledge and thinking during many tutorials: and to thank Constance Wells, the Administrator of The Corporate Policy Group, for her unflagging enthusiasm and commitment to the work.

Of course the responsibility for the research and its conclusions lies with the author, and the proposals do not necessarily represent the views of the Trustees or Sponsors of The Corporate Policy Group.

R.I. Tricker
Oxford 1984

Chapter 1

The Principal Features, Issues and Ideas

A remark of Lord Caldecote, made when he was Chairman of the Delta Metal Group[1], captures the essential point of this book.

"The trouble with British companies", he said, "is that the directors mark their own examination papers."

There have been many criticisms of the way British companies are run: and yet some continue to be remarkably successful. There are numerous proposals for change — two-tier boards, non-executive directors, worker participation, audit committees, shareholder committees, institutional investor action, a British Securities & Exchange Commission and many more; but in truth the activities of boards of directors in Britain seem very varied and little is known about them.

The studies, on which this book is based, set out to learn more about the nature of corporate direction and supervision at board level. The genesis of the work lies in research undertaken for Deloitte Haskins & Sells in 1977. At that time the British accountancy profession and various City institutions were interested in the potential of the audit committee. The report[2] argued that, in the British context, the audit committee was a North American concept in search of relevant European problems: the real issue was the composition of boards, their activities and the use of independent directors.

Interviews with company directors and chairmen, undertaken for this early study, showed how diverse were the practices and how inadequate the conventional ideas about boards of directors in modern business. To understand more about corporate direction, control and governance *The Corporate Policy Group* was formed in 1979[3].

What We Have Learned

Two different strands emerged from our work, that have been

interwoven in this book. On the one hand, there are opportunities to improve board level effectiveness; and, on the other, there are challenges to the way in which business entities operate in society and, consequently, a need to rethink the underlying conceptual framework.

The Company in Society

The joint-stock company, with limited liability for its shareholders was an elegantly simple and eminently successful development of the mid-nineteenth century. It facilitated the provision of capital, encouraged business growth, secured employment, provided innovation in industry and commerce, and created wealth.

The model of the incorporated, limited liability company proved to be robust, flexible and enormously adaptable. But the flowering of the corporate concept produced the seeds of subsequent confusion.

In the corporate idea a legal entity is created, quite separate from its owners and its managers, with statutory rights and responsibilities. Directors are elected by the shareholders and required to report to them.

Ownership is the basis of power, and is exercised through meetings of the shareholder-members of the company.

It is an idea that has become over-successful. Companies no longer, necessarily, reflect this underlying concept. Consequently practices designed to reflect the original model do not relate to the actual situation in many companies today.

Firstly there has been an enormous proliferation of companies in recent years – well over 800,000 incorporated in Britain now. Many of them are tiny and dominated by the owner-manager. Others are vast, with huge resources, operating internationally in many businesses and markets.

Then there is the considerable complexity of groups of companies. The original corporate concept did not envisage one company owning another. Now major companies can have hundreds of subsidiaries and associate companies in their group: moreover, they may be held at many levels of sub-subsidiaries. A typical company in the top 50 has 230 subsidiaries ranged down to the fifth level; the largest has over 800 down to eleven levels.

Further complexity arises where there is a divorce between

the corporate structure of subsidiary companies and the organisation structure adopted for running the business, taking management decisions and measuring performance. We found many examples of such structures, in which subsidiaries had a fiscal, regulatory and liability limiting role; but not a managerial one. Yet each company has its directors, with a duty to direct, and a perception in company law as the accountable business entity.

The underlying theme of this book is that the practices and structures of modern business no longer reflect the ideas that brought about the original joint-stock, limited liability company. Consequently there is a need to rethink the conceptual framework for enterprise in modern society and to develop our knowledge of the reality of the directors' task.

We have discovered how the power to govern differed between companies; in some cases still residing with the owners, in others being assumed by the incumbent top management. Financial institutions occasionally took a role; whilst in groups of companies the management stream often exercised power over and above the corporate structure.

Consequently, to understand the reality of the direction and control of companies, we felt it was essential to distinguish different types of company. Four categories are suggested, based not on the present legal model, but on the actual basis of power to affect company affairs. These are: —

The *Proprietary* Company — with common owners, directors and managers,

The *Private* Company — with some divorce between ownership and management, but no public investment,

The *Public* Company — those with external public investment, but not themselves dominated, and

The *Subordinate* Company — a company dominated by another.

The original Victorian concept emphasised structure and ownership: these proposals reflect business processes and the reality of power today.

This four part framework has been adopted, throughout the book, as the basis for discussing, and differentiating the work of directors. It also forms the basis for proposals made at the end for rethinking the way in which companies are regulated.

The first part of the book (chapters 2 — 6) covers this material on the corporation in society. We see how the original idea was derived and how it has evolved. The research evidence on the proliferation, concentration and diversification of companies is marshalled; and the material on the complexity of groups of companies is explored. This leads to the development of the alternative conceptual framework.

This first part will be most relevant to those concerned with the regulation of the company in society — the company lawyer, company secretary, government regulator and the institutions of corporate self-regulation like the Stock Exchange and the Accounting Standards Committee. Essentially it is for all interested in, and wanting to influence, the development of social and political policy about companies.

The following policy issues — which will all be explored subsequently — demonstrate the current concerns with matters of governance from those outside the enterprise: —

1. Proposals to rethink the *supervision* of executive management
   - two tier boards proposed by the original European Community draft 5th directive[4]
   - encouragement to increase the use of non-executive directors[5,6,7]
   - the suggestion that non-executive directors should be totally independent of the company[7]
   - the idea of non-executive directors' reports to the members[8]
   - criticisms of directors by Department of Trade Inspectors[9]
   - encouragement of audit committees[10]
2. Ideas about *representation* on the board
   - boards representing capital, labour and the public interest, suggested by the Bullock Committee[11] and considered in the draft 5th directive[12]
   - suggestions for representative directors to reflect consumer interests or the interests of other groups[13]
   - the use of nominating committees made up of independent directors to propose board appointments[14]
3. Questions about *accountability*
   - the whole debate about the role and nature of accounting standards — what is their purpose, who is responsible for setting them, how are they to be policed?[15]

- disclosure of information to stakeholder groups, other than the members, as proposed in The Corporate Report[16]
- ideas about employee communication and consultation, found in many sectors and advocated in the Vredeling proposals[17]

4. Challenges to the *limitation of shareholders' liability*
   - the need to rethink the protection of the interests of creditors, consumers and others, as rehearsed by the Cork Committee[18]
   - questioning the right of subsidiary companies in a group to be totally cocooned by limited liability and proposing the right of creditors, employees and others to attack the directors and the assets of the dominant group − as proposed in the draft 9th directive[19]
   - ideas about alternative forms of corporate structure, such as the proposals for a new form of incorporation for small firms[20]

5. Increasing *corporate regulation* and the intention of the European Community to seek the *harmonisation* of company laws in the member states[21]

6. Ideas about *corporate democracy*, sometimes called industrial democracy[22]

7. Concerns about the *legitimacy* of the large company in society and ideas about *corporate social responsibility*[23]

In the past there seemed little challenge to management's prerogative to run the company unimpeded, no demand for independent supervision or disclosure, no intervention in matters of accountability, no questioning of corporate power and legitimacy, little interest in involvement or participation in management decisions. Today there is a concern with matters of governance from those external to the enterprise, on matters of corporate accountability, regulation and public policy.

Company chairmen, chief executives and other directors, whose interests are in improving board level effectiveness rather than policy formulation, may skip Part 1. In doing so they must accept the conceptual framework for the different types of company, which is adopted in the subsequent discussion.

In Part 2 of the book (chapters 7 − 9) we look at the constraints of corporate power and think through the nature of corporate accountability. We also review the nature of limited liability in groups and the implications of the 9th directive. A set of proposals is made for holding the actual business units in a group accountable, where there is a mismatch with the corporate structure.

The Governance of the Company

The third part of the book (chapters 10 – 14) is concerned with what directors actually do; and with rethinking the work of directors. This is the section of immediate concern to the practising director and chairman. Whilst management processes have been widely explored, relatively little attention has been paid to the processes by which companies are governed. There is a paucity of thought about the basis of power in the modern corporation and of the prerogative to manage. Practices have run ahead of the underlying procedural and legal ideas.

None of the mainstreams of management thought recognise governance as a specific area of interest. The traditional, functional focus is on the work that managers do – the planning, organising, motivating, controlling and coordinating[24]. The behavioural and structural schools are interested in achieving results through people and organisations, whilst systems theories focus on information and decisions, and contingency theory recognises the ambiguity of the entire process.

But issues of governance that might arise are considered to be external to the pursuit of managing, and properly in the field of corporate jurisprudence or of bureaucratic, regulatory mechanisms.

It is apparent from the mainstream of management literature, that the management role has been primarily perceived as running the business operations efficiently and effectively – the product design, procurement, personnel, management, production, marketing and finance functions, and so on within the boundaries of the company under which it trades. Activities are often referred to as internal or external to the company. The focus is on managing the business.

By contrast, the governance role is not concerned with running the businesses of the company, per se, but with giving overall direction to the enterprise, with overseeing and controlling the executive actions of management and with satisfying legitimate expectations for accountability and regulation by interests beyond the corporate boundaries.

If management is about running business; governance is about seeing that it is run properly. All companies need governing as well as managing.

In the third part of the book we depict corporate governance superimposed on management.

Fig. 1 The activities of governance and management compared

This process of corporate governance can usefully be thought of as having four principal activities: —

Direction	formulating the strategic direction for the future of the enterprise in the long term,
Executive Action	involvement in crucial executive decisions,
Supervision	monitoring and oversight of management performance, and
Accountability	recognising responsibilities to those making a legitimate demand for accountability.

The European Commission, in the draft 5th directive, has raised the possibility of separating the executive, managerial role from a supervisory role to be undertaken by the upper tier of a two-tiered board, the current practice in Germany. Walter Goldsmith, Director-General of the Institute of Directors[25], has made a different distinction between the roles of management and company direction. The board, he argued, is concerned with direction of the business and the development of longer term strategy, and with seeing that the management is running the business properly.

A similar distinction was drawn by Professor Eilon[26], who argued that the functions of the board include the formulation of policy and objectives, the selection of strategies and the evaluation of corporate performance. "It is sometimes convenient", he writes, "to distinguish between direction and management, the former being concerned with policy and objectives, the latter with planning, execution and control".

In the framework to be adopted later in this book we combine both ideas into a model of corporate governance.

The Nature of Governance

All human societies need governing, wherever power is exercised to direct, control and regulate activities that affect people's interests. Governance involves the derivation, use and limitation of such powers. It identifies rights and responsibilities, legitimises actions and determines accountability.

Governance is necessary whether the body of people is a nation state, a town community, a professional society or a business corporation. Corporate governance is concerned with the processes by which corporate entities, particularly limited liability companies, are governed; that is with the exercise of power over the direction of the enterprise, the supervision and control of executive actions, the concern for the effect of the entity on other parties, the acceptance of a duty to be accountable and the regulation of the corporation within the jurisdiction of the states in which it operates.

In Britain it seems that there is some difficulty with the word "governance" when applied to companies. Some executives fear an attack on their perceived rights and duties to manage the enterprise, an erosion of their managerial prerogative, by even recognising the concept. Others, executives and civil servants alike, would prefer to identify governance solely with the government at the state level, as in Harold Wilson's[27] "The Governance of Britain". However, the word "governance" has totally valid, indeed Chaucerian[28], roots. More to the point, it pertinently and appropriately covers processes which every corporate entity has to undertake and which need to be distinguished from managing and management.

The origins of the word can be found in the Latin "gubernare" meaning to rule or to steer, and the Greek Κυβερ$ζτζ$ς which means steersman. Norbert Wiener[29] used the Greek root as the basis for cybernetics – the science of control in man and machine. The idea of steersman – the person at the helm – is a particularly helpful insight into the reality of governance.

Why Corporate Governance is Important

Scant attention has been paid to governance in the British company. Inevitably, in the early days of a newly incorporated company, if ownership, direction and management all vest in the same entrepreneurial individual, there is little opportunity for a distinction between management and governance. Similarly, if a company is dominated by a single person, as can happen even in public companies, managing and governing will be subsumed under the combined chief executive and chairman's role. Likewise if a board of directors is comprised wholly of executives the focus is likely to be on the management of the business. But, the expectations and demands of the modern, complex corporation necessitate a differentiation between governance and management. Consider some of the issues that can arise: –

1. Who exercises power of appointment to the board – members, institutional investors, the incumbent board, the chairman?
2. How are the chairman and the chief executive to be appointed? Who makes the nomination – the retiring chairman, the non-executive directors, the board, or major shareholders?
3. Should the roles of chairman and chief executive be separate? If so, what *are* their respective roles, and how do they interact? If not, who is to monitor and oversee the performance of the top executive? Who provides for succession?
4. Where is strategy formulated in a complex group? What are the responsibilities of the boards of subsidiary companies for strategy? How much autonomy should they have for business decisions? Can they allocate funds

they have themselves created; or are they subservient to the management of their parent company? Do the directors really direct: or do they approve management's plans?

5. Why have subsidiary companies at all: could not the same benefits be achieved with business divisions, and executive managers rather than boards of directors? Are the directors of subsidiaries really the apex of the management pyramid, called "director" for reasons of recognition, reward and status, rather than to direct the company in a de jure sense?

6. Can business performance be adequately monitored and controlled if the board is dominated by the same people who are running the business? How is accountability to be demonstrated?

7. What should be the membership of the board? Should there be non-executive directors, and in what proportion to the executive directors? Should non-executives be totally independent outsiders: if so, can they ever know enough about the business to contribute?

8. Should non-executive directors be responsible for supervising the executives or would this be divisive? How can they exercise such control? Should they ever meet together separately from the board? Should there be an audit committee of non-executives?

Summary

There are two reasons for rethinking corporate governance: −
- for the regulation of companies in society: preventing abuses of corporate power without necessarily inhibiting flexibility, innovation and entrepreneurial risk taking
- for improving the quality of board activities, and making boards more effective.

Governance is different from management; and involves setting the corporate direction, involvement in executive action, supervision and accountability.

Part 1 –

The Corporation in Modern Society

Chapter 2

The Notion of the Company
– what it is conceptually and legally

The Underlying Concepts

The key idea, in the classical concept of the joint-stock, limited liability company, is the creation of an autonomous corporate entity, incorporated under the law, quite separate from its shareholders. The company has a legal persona, may contract and own property in its own right, and may sue and be sued.

The shareholders are the members of the company and their liability to contribute to the debts of the company is limited to the sums they have agreed to risk when investing in the company. Unsatisfied creditors of an insolvent company may not pursue their debts with the shareholders.

The company also acquires perpetuity, since its shares may be transferred, thus giving it a life beyond that of its founders and facilitating succession. In the words of the nineteenth-century hymn, it is immortal, invisible.

The members, having financed the equity capital, acquire the rights to nominate and to elect the directors. This board oversees the running of the business and reports regularly to the members on the stewardship exercised by the directors over the corporate assets. Independent auditors, themselves appointed by the members, report whether the directors' report and accounts show a true and fair view of the company's performance and position. State intervention is limited, requiring the keeping of certain records, fulfilling various duties and filing information which is open to public inspection.

Power to govern the company is derived from ownership, as depicted in figure 1.

This classical concept of the corporation is neat, simple, enshrined in company law and rooted in nineteenth-century ideology. Unfortunately it bears about as much resemblance to

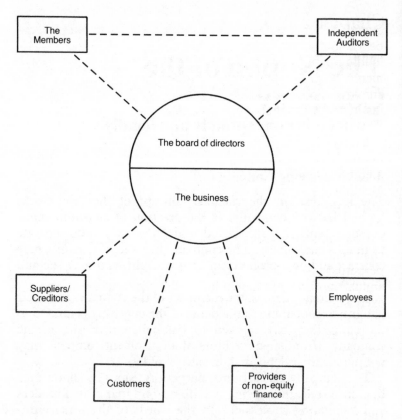

Fig. 1 The de jure concept of the corporation

the reality of the modern corporation as a hang-glider does to Concorde.

The De Facto Reality of Corporate Governance

Let us consider the de facto reality of governance in public companies, subsidiary companies and private companies.

1. Public companies

Public companies, that is those which may invite the public to subscribe for shares, now account for less than 1% of all companies registered in Britain. Yet their significance in terms of size, turnover and contribution to wealth creation has never been greater, as we shall see in chapter 4.

In the modern, public corporation the legal model inadequately reflects the governance processes. Shareholders may be geographically dispersed, have widely differing sizes of holding, and have various expectations of the company. The members may well include individual private investors, employees of the company, nominees for blocks of shares and institutional investors, such as pension funds and unit trusts. What is good for one shareholder may not be good for another.

The institutional shareholders may be able to influence matters directly, without the involvement of the whole body of members, not necessarily acting in the interests of the whole. Meetings of members are felt by many to be inadequate and inappropriate vehicles for exercising governance, as we shall see.

Considerable power vests in the board, and particularly its chairman. Some argue that boards can become self-perpetuating and inadequately accountable, because the annual meeting of shareholders is an inadequate forum for exercising governance. Others look for alternative forms of governance such as supervisory boards, independent non-executive directors or audit committees. These are matters to be explored in detail later. But it is apparent that, rather than the de jure model of figure 1, a more realistic representation of governance in the public company is shown in figure 2 as seen below. The shareholders are perceived as investors; with rights, certainly, but viewed alongside other stakeholder interest groups.

The board of directors is typically able to exercise considerable power. Even the auditors seem to accept a duty beyond that of reporting to the members; finding themselves protecting the interests of all who might rely on the published accounts. Others have questioned the independence of auditors[1], emphasising their identification with management.

The development of the unlisted securities market in London has added a new dimension to matters of governance in the public company.

> For example, a growth orientated company, in a high technology aspect of electronics, made a relatively small placement of shares through the USM. Less than 35% of the total equity was traded; the remainder being retained by the founder entrepreneurs. The shares are now selling at a considerable premium and significant blocks are held by a few major funds.

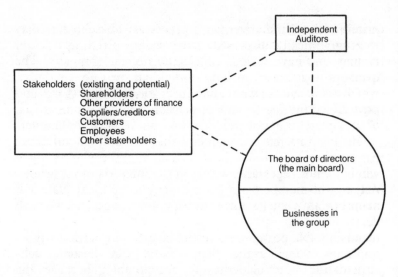

**Fig. 2   The de facto reality of the corporate concept:
in the public company**

Such a disposition of shareholdings raises some interesting
questions of governance that we shall deal with later.
European Community initiatives to encourage wider holdings
in companies and to facilitate the trading in shares would
compound the issue.

2. Subsidiary companies
Another aspect, of fundamental significance in the evolution
of corporate governance, has been the rise of large, complex
groups of companies. This was a matter totally overlooked by
the pioneers of the corporate concept. Having created a legal
persona, capable of contracting, buying and selling in its own
name, the legislators had created an entity which could
acquire shares in other corporate entities.

In the early days of corporate mergers, the companies that
were merged together to form a new, larger corporation,
tended to be submerged and disappear as separate entities.
Not so in more recent years. Research evidence, marshalled in
chapter 5, shows how groups of companies can now be vast
and impressively interconnected. There may be hierarchical
nestings of companies, with many levels of subsidiaries; or the
companies may form a network with interconnected holdings.
Some subsidiaries will be wholly-owned; others may have

minority outside shareholder interests, perhaps left over from the time of acquisition or the result of a joint venture. Some may have governmental stakes, particularly when registered in overseas countries. Others may be associate companies, in which the dominant company is able to exercise managerial power over the business, without holding an absolute majority of the voting shares.

The de facto reality of governance in a subsidiary company has different dimensions from that of the public company. In a wholly-owned subsidiary the dominant shareholder, the parent company, acts not only in the ownership role, but in the managerial one, as well. Moreover the organisation and decision-making structure adopted for management control may be different from the corporate structure. The important implications for the exercise of power over governance, in such cases, is inadequately developed in the law. Figure 3 attempts to depict the reality of governance in a wholly-owned subsidiary.

The board of a wholly-owned subsidiary may, effectively, be the top management team of that business; wholly responsible for executive actions. There may be a chairman or a minority of other directors drawn from the head office of the group or from other group companies to exercise co-ordination and objective supervision.

But the executive directors of the subsidiary, far from being independent, may rely on the management structure throughout the group for their own remuneration levels, rewards, promotion and terms of service. Likewise the company may be strongly guided and constrained by group policies, powers and controls. Strategy must be consistent with group thinking and resources will be provided according to group criteria. In other cases, of course, a holding company may grant considerable autonomy to its subsidiaries, acting rather like a major institutional shareholder or investment banker; but the right to exert managerial control nevertheless exists.

A wholly-owned subsidiary does not, automatically, enjoy the autonomy enshrined in the classical corporate concept – except in the limitation of liability on the part of the owners. There is a duality of governance through the corporate, legal channel and the management channel.

Where there are minority interests in a subsidiary company, or it is far removed geographically or in activity from the

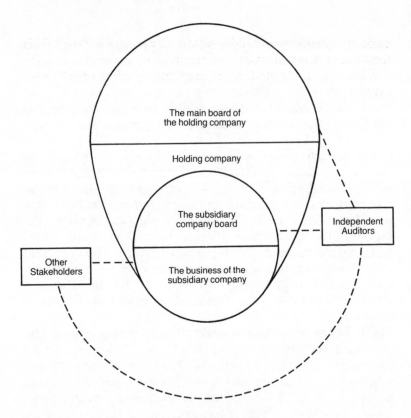

Fig. 3   The de facto reality of governance:
the wholly-owned subsidiary company

central authority, one may find independent directors on the board, drawn from outside the group. Nevertheless, if there are executive directors — as is nearly always the case — the duality of governance remains.

3. Private companies

The third set of companies, which cannot invite public subscription for their shares and which are not themselves subsidiary to another company, form a diverse group of private companies.

Some private companies are small, with few members and little, if any, separation between the owners and the top managers of the business. These are the owner-managed companies. Obviously governance can be exercised by direct involvement of the owners in management. Truly these are cases in which the top management are, legitimately, able to treat the company as their own, subject to the law.

Figure 4 attempts to represent this close affinity between owners, directors and the business.

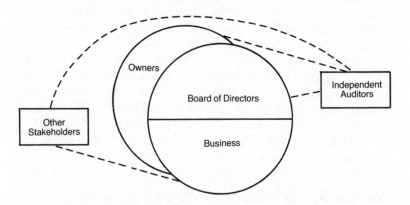

Fig. 4 The de facto reality of governance:
the closely-held, private company

In other private companies a separation between owners and managers occurs. As we shall see later, this evolution of corporate control has been plotted over many years[2], and often happens in a family company on succession into second and subsequent generations, of the founder's family; also as additional capital is introduced to facilitate growth from outside sources.

Then there has been the more recent experience of corporate formations and restructuring brought about by the availability of venture capital.

> The Business Start-Up Scheme[3] and the subsequent Business Expansion Scheme[4] have provided a unique fiscal incentive to individuals paying UK tax at the higher rates to invest in unlisted trading companies, by making such investments (up to £40,000 per annum) allowable for tax purposes. Such a stimulus to investment has succeeded in channelling the savings of rich individuals into smaller, innovative companies.

Venture Capital Funds have been created to raise such money and to invest in a portfolio of high growth companies. Clearly there are important implications for governance in such cases, particularly where the venture capital fund, or a major individual investor, wants to exercise close supervision over his investment. In some cases an investor may bring added value to the business by offering know-how, business introductions or guaranteed orders in addition to his cash. Again there are governance implications in such partners.

Some large public companies have also been investing part of their own research and development budgets in external venture companies; seeking corporate rejuvenation through collaboration in outside ventures. Typically such investments in venture capital "glass houses", intended to stimulate and nurture new developments, are financed under a deal which guarantees the investor company appropriate benefits from the products and technologies developed. Again there are matters of governance to be determined.

Modern British Company Law

At the time of writing (1983) the Companies Act 1948[5] provides the underpinning of company law (although a further consolidating act is in draft). The '48 Act, with 363 pages, was the most comprehensive expression of the statutes regulating companies to date. There have been amending Acts in 1967, 1976, 1980 and 1981, with a very minor amending Act in 1983.

The 1967 Companies Act[6] abolished the status of the exempt private company, thus removing certain exemptions which closely held private companies had enjoyed under the 1948 Act on the appointment of auditors, making loans to directors and filing accounts for overseas companies. The 1967 Act also required for the first time the publication of information on the names and place of incorporation of subsidiary companies, director's emoluments, salaries of highly paid employees, the profitability and turnover of different classes of business carried on, the number and wages of employees, and political and charitable contributions.

A further Companies Act in 1976[7], introduced the concept of the accounting reference period, with a duty to prepare, lay and deliver accounts on specific dates, and procedures for changing the reference date. There were also clauses on the content of accounting records, the qualifications, appointment, resignation and removal of auditors, and some miscellaneous provisions on returns and the registered office.

Corporate mergers in the 60's brought a new focus on the comparability of company accounts. Company failures, and the advent of business news pages in the quality newspapers to comment on them, focused public opinion on the role of boards. The accountancy profession became more interventionist in the work of its members, demanding higher standards of work and requiring conformance to accounting standards[8].

Some corporate failures led to the appointment of Department of Trade Inspectors, whose reports, though lacking the force of law, being addressed to the Department, nevertheless were frequently highly critical of the work of company directors.

> "The lesson is that a company needs a board that can be providing an independent check on its executive, that is fully and fairly informed of the group's affairs, that is in a position to monitor the actions of the executive and that, in consequence, is in a position in the event of some unexpected happening..... to give shareholders an immediate and convincing account of the situation[9]."

> "Mr. M. although only devoting part of his time to the company was Chairman and Chief Executive throughout the period with which we are concerned. As Chairman it was for him to settle policy..... as Chief Executive it was for him at least to supervise the implementation of these policies."

> "The impression we have gained during the course of hearing evidence is that Mr. M. expected his executives to carry out his instructions to the letter and nothing more, and not to doubt or question the wisdom of their instructions. It is difficult to envisage how any worthwhile executive could operate for long under such conditions[10]."

> "The non-executive directors took an insufficient part in deciding the policy of the group and, through excessive confidence (in the Managing Director) were content to leave to him matters which the board as a whole should have been deciding. Some of the non-executive directors had been directors of the group for many years, yet they were ill-informed about many important transactions of the group. They did not question the executive directors sufficiently."

> "The non-executive directors did not sufficiently recog-

nise that directors should behave as reasonably conscientious persons, aware of their responsibilities to investors, and the fact that investors are rightly relying on them, and that they must be very careful in placing their reliance on others[11]."

The Companies Act of 1980[12] added another 150 pages to the principal Act of 1948. For the first time the formal classification of 'public company' was introduced, requiring every company that wishes to invite the public to subscribe for shares to be so registered and to add the words 'Public Limited Company' or 'PLC' to their name. Some companies which previously had been considered to be public companies changed their status to private. A 'private company' is any company other than a public company, under the '80 legislation.

The Act also included clauses on the issue of share capital, class rights and the payment for and maintenance of share capital. Restrictions were placed on the distribution of profits and assets. Particulars were required of substantial contracts with directors and loans were prohibited to directors and people connected with them, except in specific, carefully delineated circumstances. Insider dealing, that is trading on the Stock Exchange in securities about which one has privileged, price sensitive information, was prohibited: indeed it was made a criminal offence leading to imprisonment or a fine, or both.

An interesting feature of the Act was the confirmation[13] that directors owe a fiduciary duty to the company and the company alone, (i.e. to the members who form the company): but it also stated that "the matters to which the directors of a company are to have regard in the performance of their functions shall include the interests of the company's employees in general as well as the interests of its members".

The case of Prudential Assurance Co. Ltd. v Newman Industries Ltd.[14] in 1980 was of major importance in determining the rights of shareholders. Previously it had been thought that any damage to the company was not a damage to the shareholders personally. Consequently any right of action by an individual member lay through the meeting of members of the company, not by an individual action against the company or members of its board.

In the Newman case the Prudential, a minority shareholder,

with 3.2% of the shares, alleged that officers of the company had conspired to use company monies to acquire another business on a valuation which concealed relevant information. Unusually the Prudential proceeded with three actions simultaneously: 1) claiming damages from the defendant, 2) seeking representative action on behalf of all other shareholders and 3) a derivative action on behalf of Newman.

The decision is of major importance in company law. First because it makes clear that a minority shareholder can bring an action on behalf of the company (called a *derivative* action because the shareholder sues on behalf of the company and derives the claim from it) for damage caused by the company. Second, the case decides that a minority shareholder can bring an action (called a *representative* action) on behalf of himself and other shareholders in regard to *personal damage* suffered by shareholders as a result of the alleged wrongdoing of the directors, so long as the shareholders have at least a common interest and a common grievance.

In 1981 the Companies Act[15] primarily introduced the requirements of the European Community's 4th directive on company accounting and reporting into British company law. The provisions on the form and content of the accounts and the notes to the accounts represent some of the most detailed and prescriptive requirements in British company law.

The '81 Act introduced a size classification for companies[16], allowing some companies to deliver modified accounts to the Registrar, exempting them from the requirements for full disclosure, but still requiring them to produce full accounts to shareholders.

Other matters covered in the 185 pages of the '81 Act included the registration of company and business names, linked to the closing of the Register of Business Names; the maintenance of share capital, and allowing companies to purchase their own shares; the disclosure of interests in voting shares in public companies, associated with 'dawn raids' on some companies by predator companies previously not known to be interested in acquiring substantial interests; and various supplemental matters on registration, investigation and disclosure.

Merger movements since the early 1900's, and particularly in the 1960's and 1970's, have led to the formation of complex groups of companies which were not envisaged by those who developed the original corporate concepts. Company legislation has evolved and expanded to cope with new situations as they arise: but the original conceptual framework has not changed.

Summary

The classical ideas of the joint stock company remain: viz
- .. an autonomous legal entity incorporated under the law,
- .. limitation of liability of members for corporate debts,
- .. ownership as the basis of power, through the ability to nominate and elect the directors, and to require accountability[17],
- .. the meeting of members as the vehicle for exercising such power,
- .. regulation under the Acts, requiring the keeping of records and disclosure and filing of specific matters,
- .. supervision of executive actions through the board and with auditors, appointed by the members, to report whether the accounts provided by the directors show a true and fair view.

In the next chapter we see how these ideas have evolved and then we shall see how the reality of corporations no longer fits on this framework.

Chapter 3

The Evolution of the Company
— how the idea has changed

The dramatic evolution of the company concept in Britain stems from the mid-nineteenth-century, in particular from the Companies Acts of 1855 and 1862. At the beginning of the century to limit the liability of businessmen for the debts they incurred seemed immoral, and to separate ownership from management control foolhardy. By the end of the century both had become commonplace.

The developments that led to the corporate concept are threaded far back through the evolution of British trade and industry: indeed back to medieval England with the importance of individualism, freedom and self-regulation, contrasting with the more prescriptive rule of law in continental European countries. These contrary precedents become important in understanding some of the difficulties in harmonising company law today between member states of the European Community.

For the first half of the nineteenth-century there were four basic forms of corporate business activity: —

- Sole proprietorships — the sole trader contracting personally.
- Partnership — business proprietors working together and sharing profits, losses and liabilities.
- the unincorporated company, operating under a trust deed and perhaps having non-executive "sleeping" partners providing finance. All members, however, bore a liability for corporate debts.
- the incorporated company, operating under Royal Charter or an Act of Parliament, under which it was incorporated and which may well have limited the liability of members for corporate debts.

By the end of the century the joint-stock, limited liability company was well established. But to appreciate the evolution of the idea, to appreciate its significance today, and to contrast continental European developments which are reflected in present day proposals, we need to trace the history far back. Back indeed before the nineteenth-century, before the industrial revolution, to the very beginnings of trade in Britain.

Trade and Industry in Medieval England

The Romans left a heritage of roads, towns and ideas that undoubtedly influenced their successors; but the story of British corporate regulation is rooted in Anglo-Saxon, not Roman, thinking.

England of the eleventh-century, as the Domesday Book shows, was predominantly agricultural. Trades ancillary to agriculture and village life were practised locally – pottery, iron goods, milling and so on – by individual traders and their families. But the bulk of medieval trade and industry was professionalised and largely confined to communal towns[1].

In the twelfth and thirteenth centuries the development of Flemish commercial society led to the export of English wool and the growth of foreign trade across the shores. In the commercial towns both manufacturers and merchants traded under the aegis of craft gilds. Mercers, grocers, fishmongers and vintners amongst the mercantile traders; and saddlers, tailors, weavers, shearers and goldsmiths were typical of the manufacturers and suppliers of services.

The gilds were essentially associations for the regulation and control of the local market – which was a regulated monopoly. Gilds did not trade in their own right: they were not marketing organisations, neither were they devices for co-ownership, investment or profit sharing. Their role was essentially regulatory, enforcing the collective monopoly, ensuring standards of workmanship and product quality, often limiting entry with long apprenticeships.

The gilds safeguarded the rights of individual members by stopping interlopers and by ensuring a fair share of the market to each member, for example by limiting the hours to be worked. A growth in one member's market share, at the expense of others, was prevented: private profit and competition set brother against brother and was considered an evil.

As Tawney[2] explains:–

"The medieval theorist condemned as a sin precisely that

effort to achieve a continuous and unlimited increase in material wealth which modern societies applaud as meritorious, and the prices for which he reserved his most merciless denunciations were the more refined and subtle of the economic virtues..... The essence of the argument was that payment may properly be demanded by the craftsmen who made the goods or by the merchants who transport them..... the unpardonable sin is that of speculator or middleman who snatches private gain by the exploitation of public necessities."

As well as protecting their members, gilds also served to protect the public by regulating standards. In Britain the notion of self-regulation by professional and businessmen has ancient roots.

So successful were the gilds in London that their membership evolved into the rich and politically powerful livery companies that survive, at least in tradition, to this day. 'Yeoman' gilds of lower status workers, contributing to the livery gilds, also emerged; the forerunners of modern unions of employees.

From time to time the Crown would authorise the incorporation of an entity, recognising the rights and duties of a group of citizens involved in the corporation, as in the case of towns with a Royal Charter. The Crown also chartered The Company of Merchant Adventurers, for traders dealing in the export and import of goods. Through their charter the members were granted a monopoly to govern shipping matters and to act against non-members. The Company of Merchant Adventurers was a corporate organisation bringing together members with shared interests. The Company did not trade in its own right; like the gilds it was a regulatory mechanism to maintain a monopoly and to rule the activities of its members, not a company of members trading together for profit — that was a development of the Elizabethan age.

However, in medieval European countries corporate ventures for growth and profit *were* emerging. In addition to the Flemish merchants, great trading firms and banking houses, significant mercantile and financial units, developed during the fifteenth-century in Italy and Southern Germany. Such ideas did not catch on in medieval England.

Postan[3] tells how, in the first half of the fourteenth-century, several large enterprises emerged in England which might have developed into major commercial or banking houses. A few great merchants, acting in syndicates with joint stock partners did develop major businesses. But, inevitably, in England, they had to trade with Kings – and ended in bankruptcy or worse.

> "The promise of precious commercial and financial capitalism never materialised..... The beginnings of English commercial capitalism were nipped in the bud and the place of the capitalists was taken by regulated companies which for all the commercial and financial power they collectively represented, were still redolent with the medieval spirit of regulation and monopoly."[4]

But notice that the regulation involved was self-regulation by the members, for the benefit of themselves and those they served, not state regulation at either the national or the local level.

English Individualism

There was a rising by labourers in 1381. Trevelyan[5] commented that:–

> "the spirit that had prompted the rising was one of the chief reasons why serfdom died out in England, as it did not die out on the continent of Europe. Personal freedom became universal at an early date in our country..... self-help and self-government were for long centuries taught to the English in the school of town life..... there were no rights without duties."

The conventional chronology accepted by most scholars, including Marx and Weber, was of a medieval England which underwent a fundamental transition from peasant, feudal society to the basis of a capitalist one. A society rooted in the stable norms of kinship and the village community gave way to an impersonal, fragmented and changing world characterised by market, urbanisation and, eventually, industrialisation.

But Macfarlane[6], having studied legal treatises and local history, as well as personal diaries of the time, demonstrates that such views on the nature of property, inheritance practices, household and kinship structures and of business practices may be misfounded. Since the thirteenth-century, he argues:–

> "England has been inhabited..... by a people whose social, economic and legal system was in essence different, not only from that of peoples in Asia or Eastern Europe,

but also in all probability from the Celtic and Continental countries of the same period[7]."

Recognition of rights of the individual, enshrined in Magna Carta, the approach to personal ownership of property, and power based on such ownership, suggest that ideas in England had been significantly different from continental European thinking, for far longer than many historians accept.

"... England in the thirteenth-century was a far more sophisticated market than Marx (recognised)[8]."

England's early transition, towards the market economy, and concomitant interest in business, was founded in an ethic of individual rather than state regulation, based on the laws of property: and was not reflected in much continental European thinking rooted in different, Roman influenced, ideas about the proper relationship between the individual and the state.

As Macfarlane comments[9]:

"When Jefferson wrote, 'We hold those truths to be sacred and undeniable: that all men are created equal and independent, that from that equal creation they demand rights inherent and inalienable', he was putting into words a view of the individual and society which had its roots in thirteenth-century England or earlier."

Such a long standing and deeply rooted view becomes important to our present study as we consider the harmonisation of European and English company law, under the aegis of the European Community. Moreover we see the potential significance of the individual in England, when considering the appropriate balance between individual, enterprise and state.

Trade Flourishes in the 16th and 17th Centuries

Although the precedents for an individualistic approach to business, and a self-regulatory attitude to corporate governance, are to be found in medieval England, it was the sixteenth and seventeenth centuries which saw the great flowering of trade and commerce.

New countries and territories were being opened up for trade and exploitation. New trade routes and faster communications were developed. New ideas came from science. New freedoms in religion. New opportunities in business. Padua and Venice joined the Netherlands as centres of commerce and trade.

As Wright remarks, Elizabethan England represented 'a new commercial age'[10]. Freedom of trade, untroubled by state impositions and unrestrained by monopolies, now became the watchword.

Francis Bacon (1561-1627), himself more a parliamentarian than the Kings he served[11] wrote of the benefits of "free trade into all parts of both the East and West Indies"[12]. Economic liberalism was his orientation. He wrote that "trading in companies is most agreeable to the English nature": but, as Hill[13] explains, this must be taken in context as Bacon was contrasting England with the Dutch who, Bacon believed had a sense of republic which "serveth to them instead of a company"[14].

Sir Walter Raleigh (1554-1618) noted the more egalitarian nature of Dutch society, without a nobility. Dutch merchants, he wrote "more fully obtained... their purposes by their convenient privileges and settled competitors"[15]. He urged the use of state power to protect merchants' interests[16], wanting government "to allure and encourage the people for their private gain to be all workers and erectors of a commonwealth"[17]. Sir Edward Coke (1552-1654), Attorney General, strongly believed that traffic and trade were the life-blood of the country[18]. "The good bailiff of the realm", he wrote, "is the merchant[19]."

But what organisational forms were adopted in pursuit of this expanding trade and commerce?

Even in the newly competitive expansionist environment the collegiate, self-regulatory and protective form of company survived. For example the Company of Barber-Surgeons was chartered by the Crown in 1540. The Apothecaries were incorporated as a City company in 1606. But the practice of medicine had become competitive; there was considerable rivalry[20] between the College of Physicians, a self-selected body of university graduates which had the right to licence medical practicians in London, the Barber-Surgeons and the Apothecaries for the services provided to patients.

In matters of trade joint ventures between merchants, sharing investment, costs and profits on specific voyages became usual. Essentially these were partnerships for limited periods, members sharing risks with a view to profit at the end of the voyage; and sharing liabilities and loss in the event of disaster.

The Crown retained its influence, creating chartered companies to exploit the trade in the new worlds and new colonies, and appointing their governors, in, for example The East India Company, The Muscovy Company, The Virginia Company and the North West Passage Company. Authority stemmed from the sovereign, through boards or high councils in London, to groups of venturers in the colonies. This authority given to a group of peers to run an enterprise had its roots in the governance ideas of Magna Carta in 1215.

Unincorporated Companies and Bubbles in the 18th Century

Trade and commerce in England in the early eighteenth-century was, primarily, run through sole proprietorships and small partnerships. The entrepreneurs or traders were typically the owners and financed the enterprise[21].

However the need for additional capital to fund a rapidly growing business facing new opportunities, and the availability of such finance amongst successful professional men, businessmen and land owners, led to the development of unincorporated companies – co-partnerships, in which some members ran the venture, with others as financial or sleeping partners. Of course being, essentially, partnerships all members were liable for the company's debts if it ran into financial difficulties.

The attractions of investment in the commercially expanding world of the early eighteenth-century, enabled some unscrupulous promoters to sponsor companies and encourage speculation by investors with little hope of return and a significant chance of liability. The Bubble Act of 1720, a criminal statute, was enacted to protect the investor by preventing the creation of a large stock of easily transferable shares in unincorporated companies.

The Bubble Act was rather obscure and did not prevent unincorporated companies being created in the middle of the century under trust deeds which expressly circumvented the 1720 Act. However the trustees tended to be poorly rewarded for their services, and shares could still prove difficult to transfer freely[22].

In the closing years of the eighteenth-century there was a growing interest in limiting the liability of members for the debts of the company. This could only be obtained by incorporation under a charter from the Crown, or by a specific Parliamentary Act. Consequently some promoters sought, and a few obtained, Parliament's warrant to form a company with the liability of the members limited to a preagreed amount.

Two other forms of business structure are worth mentioning. Under maritime law ships could be registered with the Admiralty, with the ownership divided into transferable shares. The Bubble Act did not apply. Originally the shares tended to be held by the fisherman who worked the boat, or the master and crew of the sailing vessel: later shares were held by owners who did not go to sea.

Also, under the law of the Cornish tin-mining stannaries, companies could be created in which the group of shareholders agreed the extent of the costs they were willing to bear and entered their names in a book for their individual share, usually an eighth. Such companies were called 'cost-book' companies and were similar to the 'pay share' partnership adopted in lead-mining business in the Pennines. By the end of the eighteenth-century the main investors were middle class rentiers – land-owners, lead merchants and local business and professional men[23].

Developments in commercial law also supported business growth in England. Following the Payment of Bills Act, 1698, The Promissory Notes Act 1704 and the Payment to Bearer Act in 1765, England led continental countries in the efficiency and the flexibility of commercial finance. In the later half of the eighteenth-century the growth of country banks was also an important factor in stimulating trade.

Company Law Developments in the Early 19th Century

The nineteenth-century transformed company law and the ways in which businesses were created, incorporated, governed and regulated.

The Bubble Act was repealed in 1825: it was an ambiguous Act and widely circumvented. In the same year the Board of Trade took on the responsibility for chartering companies by Letters Patent on behalf of the Crown. This form of incorporation enabled the entity to sue and be sued in its own right, but did not bestow limited liability on the members.

This power was given to the Board of Trade in 1837. Over the next fifteen years there were 164 applications for incorporation, of which 93 were successful[24].

Sole trader, partnership and unincorporated company remained the dominant organisational forms for the first half of the century. In 1844 a Joint-Stock Companies Act[25] was passed which required the registration and regulation of all unincorporated companies. This was an act of intervention on the part of government to protect the investor from the unscrupulous and fraudulent company promoter. 970 unincorporated companies were registered and over the next fifteen years a further 910 were added to the register. Predominantly the companies were in insurance, shipping and public utilities such as water and gas undertakings and market halls. Manufacturing business accounted for less than 10%[26].

The 1844 Act called for the directors to "conduct and manage the affairs of the company", to appoint the secretary, clerks and servants, to hold meetings periodically of the company (that is of the members), and to appoint a chairman to preside at such meetings. Account books were to be kept and balanced. A balance sheet was to be produced by the directors to the shareholders. Auditors were to be appointed by the company and the appointment registered with the Registrar of Joint-Stock Companies. These auditors were to report to the members on the balance sheet. A register of shareholders was to be kept, which could be inspected.

Thirty pages long, the 1844 Act laid the foundation for the registration, incorporation and regulation of companies that has survived to this day. But the liability of members was still unlimited.

Full incorporation, with the liability of members limited to their initial equity stake, was not pursued vigorously in the first half of the nineteenth-century, although the interest had been kindled in the late eighteenth. Businessmen still tended to associate incorporation with Royal Charters and trading under monopoly power and privilege — ideas quite inconsistent with the self-help norms of Victorian England. Experience of unscrupulous company promotions also raised doubts about the propriety, indeed the morality, of taking business risks whilst limiting personal responsibility.

Fundamental New Law in the Mid 1800's

Then, dramatically, in the middle years of the nineteenth-century, between 1855 and 1862, there was a volte-face. Exactly why is unclear. Cottrell[27] argues that the granting of the right to incorporate and to limit the liability of all members for the debts of the enterprise thus created, was due to confusion and a mistaken attempt to create a continental European type of corporate structure in which the liability of financial, non-management members was limited, but in which the owner-directors who ran the business remained totally liable themselves. Jeffreys[28], on the other hand, advances a more economic view that investors were seeking outlets for accumulating wealth, without staking their personal fortunes on the future of an unincorporated company. The Society for promoting an amendment of the law argued, in an 1849 report[29] that limitation of the liability of partners was required so that "capital..... (can) be advanced by respectable persons..... to answer the wants of our increasing enterprise at home and in our foreign dependencies".

In 1854 a Royal Commission[30] on the reform of mercantile law reported, which led to a Commons resolution that:–

"The law of partnership which renders every person who..... shares the profits of a trading concern liable to the whole of its debts, is unsatisfactory and should be amended to permit such persons to contribute to the capital of such concerns on terms of sharing profits, without incurring liability beyond a limited amount....."

In the ensuing debate it was apparent that a means of protecting financial, 'sleeping' partners was being sought; not the exemption of the owner/managers from liability.

However in August 1855 an Act for limiting the liability of members of certain joint-stock companies[31] was passed. Now "any joint-stock company, with a capital divided into shares of a nominal value not less than £10 each, may obtain a certificate of complete registration with limited liability upon complying with the following conditions:–

1. The promoters state that the company is proposed to be formed with limited liability,
2. The word 'Limited' shall be the last word of the company name,
3. The deed of settlement shall state that the company is formed with limited liability,

4. The deed of settlement shall be executed by at least 25 shareholders holding at least three-quarters of the normal capital and at least 20% paid up."

Further amending Acts followed in 1857[32] and 1858[33]; then in 1862 there was a Consolidating Act[34].

The 1862 Act laid down the mode of forming a company – seven or more people by subscribing their name to a Memorandum of Association could form an incorporated company with or without limited liability. Where the liability was to be limited the Memorandum should contain the name of the company with the word 'Limited' at the end, the address of the registered office, the objectives for which the company was to be formed, the declaration that the liability of the members was limited, and the amounts of capital which the company proposed to have registered. This underlying principle of incorporation has not changed since. The Act also required a register of members to be kept and an annual list of members forwarded to the Registrar of Joint-Stock Companies. A register of mortgages and charges was also to be kept, and a register of directors and managers. The company must hold a General Meeting every year. The Board of Trade was given the right to appoint inspectors to examine into the affairs of the company on application of not less than one-fifth of the shareholders. The company itself might also by special resolution appoint inspectors to examine the affairs of the company.

Not surprisingly company incorporations boomed after such liberal, permissive legislation. Company collapses followed and there was evidence of fraudulent promotion[35]. Although the statutes emphasised the rights of the shareholders to appoint directors and oversee the governance of the company, the power of executive directors, to become a dominant issue over a hundred years later as we shall see, was not unknown. Preference shares, with preferential right to dividend and capital, but with restricted voting rights on other matters were used by some executive promotors.

The Select Committee of the House of Commons discussed such problems and reported in 1867. Later that year an Act was passed which allowed companies to be registered with limited, non-management shareholders but unlimited directors, if the promoters so wanted. Few did: why accept financial exposure when it could be limited? Short Acts in

1870[36] and 1877[37] improved the winding-up procedures and enabled companies to reduce their capital respectively.

However, the principle of limited liability was firmly established. Within less than a decade English company law had moved from an essentially regulatory, interventionist stance to become the most permissive in Europe.

In the words of Gilbert & Sullivan (Utopia Ltd.): –

> All hail, astonishing fact!
> All hail, invention new,
> The Joint-Stock Company's Act
> of Parliament Sixty two.
>
> ★★★
>
> And soon or late I always call
> for Stock Exchange quotation.
> No scheme too great, and none too small
> for companification!

Company Law in Nineteenth-Century Europe and the United States

In France the société en commandité par actions had existed since 1807, but in 1856 the regulations were tightened[38]. This form of incorporation involved unlimited directors but limited shareholders. Minimum share values were stipulated which had to be fully issued and 25% subscribed. The societes a responsabilite limitee was created in 1863 for companies up to 20m francs[39], a ceiling subsequently removed. But the basis of the legislation was the Napoleonic code of 1807, which was essentially prescriptive and regulatory, as opposed to English law based on common law evolved from statute and case.

German law, like French, followed the prescriptive pattern of Roman law, lacking the flexibility of English practices. The formation of limited companies, though permitted in 1884, was tightly regulated. A board of supervision, quite separate from the company's management board of directors, was mandatory to represent and protect the shareholders' interests. Annually it examined and reported on the accounts prepared by the directors for the members, of whom it could call meetings if necessary. Company promoters and the directors who subsequently ran the business were, thus, subject to greater scrutiny and their affairs to more visibility than their English counterparts. The difference in approach survives to this day: here is the basis for the two–tier supervisory board of the draft 5th directive.

Company law developments in the United States followed the British path more closely. Individual states passed legislation to facilitate the incorporation of companies, typically in the later years of the nineteenth-century. Governance was through the members' meeting which had the power to nominate and elect the directors and to require accountability from them. Federal incorporation was not, and is still not, available.

The Private Company is Identified – Turn of the Century

For the first fifty years, or so, of incorporated, limited liability companies they were mainly public: incorporated for the purpose of attracting external capital. Today less than 1% of all registrations are public companies.

In the 1880's depression hit British trade and industry. A Royal Commission[40] was formed to explore the situation. A number of new ideas emerged. Evidence was produced to show that the interests of creditors as well as shareholders needed protection. The Commission proposed that capital should be taken up and subscribed before a company could trade, that borrowing powers should be restricted and that more disclosure should be made in the financial accounts.

A Bill was introduced in 1888[41], which would have picked up some of these ideas and, moreover, would have created a new principle requiring directors to take up not less than 20% of all shares allotted; but the Bill failed in the House of Lords. Some small Bills in 1890[42] dealt with the alteration of a company's Memorandum of Association, winding-up procedures and making false statements by promoters in a prospectus an offence.

Significantly, the Royal Commission on the Depression of Trade and Industry, in its 1886 report[43], drew attention to a new phenomenon. Since the liberalising of company law in the mid 1800's, a few companies had been incorporated which did not, in fact, seek public subscription to their capital. In the later years of the century the number of such companies had become important: 560 were registered in the five years from 1880 to 1884[44]. These 'private' companies tended to be family businesses, and trading partnerships, often in manufacturing, led by entrepreneurs. Their growth came from the plough-back of profits and the owner's funds. For them incorporation achieved limited liability, the separation of the business from its owners, and the transferability of shareholdings – very useful on inheritance and succession.

It was suggested, in evidence to the Royal Commission, that such private companies, being closely held, need not publish balance sheets. Thus emerged the idea of different types of company – the private and the public.

In 1896 Lord Davey chaired a Board of Trade Committee on Company Law Reform[45], which drew attention to the private company status and agreed that such companies should be excluded from the provisions requiring disclosure in prospectuses – thus tacitly differentiating them. The Davey Committee also saw the need to protect creditors as well as shareholders from fraudulent promoters. It recommended widespread disclosure and publicity in prospectuses, the registration of mortgages including floating charges, more stringent requirements for keeping proper books of accounts, reporting financial accounts and statutory audit, as well as emphasising the need for directors to be careful and prudent.

Davey's proposals were strongly criticised and, in the event, the subsequent 1900 Companies Act[46] introduced relatively weak reflections of the Committee proposals. The contents of prospectuses were identified, the procedures on allotment of shares were laid down and auditors were to be appointed at every Annual General Meeting of the company. But prudence was not declared a necessity in company direction.

In 1906 yet another Committee on Company Law Reform, the Loreburn Committee, reported[47]: and this led to the 1907 Companies Act[48]. Here the private company was formally recognised for the first time. It must not have more than fifty members, not invite the public to subscribe for its shares, and, by its Articles of Association, the right to transfer its shares must be restricted. Such private companies were then exempted from much of the disclosure requirements laid on the public company.

Cottrell[49] reports that, by 1914 the proportion of private companies being registered had increased to nearly four-fifths of the whole. In 1915 46,428 out of the 63,969 limited companies on the register were private. Moreover, there was a significant growth in small companies with capital less than £5,000. The trend was to accelerate.

The Amalgamation Movement of the Early 1900's

In the early 1900's another significant development was occurring with public companies. Existing businesses, some of them private companies, were being combined into large public companies. In an increasingly competitive and technologically changing world, such mergers aimed to reduce competition and support prices within an industry, and also to achieve scale economies of manufacture and selling.

Early examples of such mergers were the Salt Union, created in 1888, combining more than sixty separate salt works, and the United Alkali Company which became a public company in 1891. Mergers in the breweries, tobacco, flour, soap, sewing cotton, coal and iron and steel industries followed.

The public companies that resulted from these mergers did not lead to 'outside' shareholders gaining control of the assets[50]. Generally the balance of voting equity remained in the hands of the founders of the original businesses. External capital was raised at the time of the consolidation, or afterwards, to provide funds for further growth. Debentures and preference shares were also widely used to provide funds, whilst leaving the voting power with the equity owners.

Technological developments in the years immediately prior to the first world war also encouraged the flotation of public companies in the manufacture of bicycles, cars, fittings for gas lamps, machine tools and similar patented specialist metal products.

In the earlier company mergers it was the businesses themselves that were acquired. The new, consolidating public company took over the assets and liabilities of each company which then ceased to exist as a legal entity.

In later mergers, in the early twentieth-century, the tendency grew for the consolidating company to buy the shares of the other companies, which thus continued to have a corporate existence. In the North of England, for example, amalgamations of heavy metal manufacturers created a number of large vertically integrated concerns, some of them with jointly controlled sponsors. Moreover, such financial inter-dependence was underpinned by interlocking directorships. Here was the beginnings of the holding company with chains of subsidiaries – which is to concern us again in our studies of corporate governance[51].

Company Law Developments 1900-1950

The body of case law concerning the governance of companies grew up substantially from the late nineteenth-century. A number of early cases on the rights and duties of directors culminated in Re City Equitable Fire Insurance[52] in 1925. Here three basic propositions were laid down, which continue to be a primary authority on the subject[53].

a) *A Subjective Test of Skill*
   A director need not exhibit in the performance of his duties a greater degree of skill than may reasonably be expected from a person of his knowledge and experience.

b) *Periodical Attendance*
   He is not bound to give continuous attention to the affairs of the company. His duties are of an intermittent nature to be performed at periodical board meetings. He is not bound to attend all such meetings though he ought to whenever he reasonably can.

c) *Delegation to Executives*
   He is entitled to trust an official to perform such duties as can properly be entrusted to him in accordance with the Articles.

As Loose[53] points out "these propositions are manifestly intended for the non-executive directors, despite their unde-manding and lenient tone..... as the qualifications of directors, and business and accounting knowledge generally, have developed, so will the subjective test (in paragraph (a)) become more severe..... this must mean that the Chartered Accountant on today's board bears a much heavier responsi-bility than the country gentleman of 1883 who, it was held, could not be expected to understand the company's accounts[54]."

A major Companies Act was passed in 1929[55] and in 1947 came a major reforming act, consolidated in 1948[56]. This

brought the legislation up to the present: the contents of the
'48 Act and subsequent developments were outlined in the last
chapter.

Summary

The joint-stock, limited liability company in Britain dates
from legislation in the mid-nineteenth century. The underlying concepts of self-regulation, though, derive from ancient
ideas rooted in English individualism, and contrast with
prescriptive law and regulation by the state found in continental Europe.

Incorporation with shareholders' limited liability was,
initially, intended to facilitate the provision of capital by
non-executive, (sleeping) co-partners and to protect their
interests from unscrupulous company promoters. The welfare
of creditors and the creation of private companies were not in
mind.

Not until the end of the nineteenth-century was incorporation used to protect the interests of owner-managers, with
public subscription precluded. Now such private companies
account for over 99% of all registrations.

The need to protect creditors was subsequently recognised,
with disclosure provisions designed to benefit them as well as
the members. Today, some argue that there is a need to
protect *all* interests affected by corporate decisions.

Chapter 4

The Corporate Take-Off
– proliferation, concentration &
diversification of companies today

Having looked at the evolution of the corporate concept and the nature of corporate governance, we consider now the different types of company that exist in Britain in some detail.

In particular we shall see: –
  .. a massive proliferation of companies on the register
  .. the commercial and economic scale of relatively few.

The Proliferation of Companies

In the nineteenth-century sole proprietorship and partnerships far exceeded the number of incorporated companies. In recent years there has been a massive growth in company registrations.

At the beginning of 1983 (the latest data available at the time of writing) there were 807,817 companies on the register of companies[1], incorporated in Britain.

Only 5,324 of these companies were registered as public companies, required to include "public limited company" (plc) in their name, and able to invite public subscription for shares.

at 31st December	Number of Companies on the Register in Great Britain						
	1911	1921	1931	1951	1961	1971	1982
Public companies	18,600	12,700	16,831	14,504	14,491	15,451	5,324*
Private companies	31,400	62,300	92,499	230,721	368,702	512,189	802,493
	50,000	75,000	109,330	245,225	383,193	527,640	807,817

Table 1   New company registrations, less removals

Source: Department of Trade reports: supplemented by Hadden (1972)
       *After 1981 Companies Act redefining the public company

The growth rate in registrations over the past decade is shown in table 1.

Of the 81,639 companies registered with a share capital in 1982, 52,127 were formed with a share capital of £100 or less as shown in table 2. In other words the total capital authorised for them all was under £4.5 million.

By contrast, only 458 companies were registered in the major league – with a capitalisation of £500,000 or more. But the total capital thus authorised was in excess of £175 million.

Companies Registered in Great Britain in (analysed by size of registered capital)	1971	1982
Not exceeding £100	26,295	52,127
Over £100 to £10,000	10,812	19,334
Over £10,000 to £500,000	1,928	9,720
Over £500,000	27	458
	39,062	81,639

Table 2   Companies registered in Great Britain during 1971 and 1982

Source: Department of Trade reports

Thus we see an explosion of private company registrations, most of them very small in terms of their equity capital. Evidence given to the Jenkins Committee[2] also referred to this phenomenon, commenting on "the irresponsible multiplication of companies", "the dangers of abuse through the incorporation with limited liability of very small under-capitalised businesses" and to consequential administrative problems[3].

Over the years there have been a number of proposals to reform the law relating to the incorporation of small firms. Each of them recognise that the existing requirement in company law to distinguish members and directors, in a business where they are the same, is artificial and can lead to farcical situations in which meetings are convened, prescribed notice waived and minutes taken of decisions not made.

The crucial issues, in formulating an alternative form of incorporation, are the form and registration of the entity; its size and the number of members; the limitation of liability; disclosure of information; and a requirement for a minimum paid-up share capital. It will be worth while comparing the proposals made to date, because these matters are fundamental to the conceptual framework to be proposed later in this book.

The Limited Partnership Act of 1907[4] permits the creation of a special form of partnership with one or more general partners who assume a personal liability for the business debts and one or more limited partners with liability limited to their initial capital subscription. Registration is required under the Act and there are no further requirements on disclosure or minimum capital. However, only 700[5] limited partnerships were registered in 1981. This relatively little use is hardly surprising given the need for the "sleeping partner" to stay asleep, even if his capital was being consumed, or to find himself liable, jointly and separately, for all partnership debts if he intervened to influence business affairs. Not surprisingly, the limited company, giving the limitation of liability to all "partners" was preferable.

Then, under S.202 and 203 of the 1948 Companies Act it is possible to introduce directors with unlimited liability whilst the other non-executive shareholders enjoy limited liability. This form is useful where the rules of a professional body only allow practice by its members as a company if they accept unlimited liability for the firm's debts. Otherwise it is seldom used – directors preferring the limited liability granted as members in a company.

The White Paper on Company Law Reform[6] in 1973 recognised the artificiality of companies which were owner-managed and proposed a new form of incorporation without limited liability for the members. A more detailed proposal was made by Lowe[7] in 1974. He suggested that the new form of entity should be incorporated, be capable of having a single member, with unlimited liability for managing members (the owner-managers) but limited liability for any "dormant" members who did not take part in management. He recognised that the unlimited liability for owner-managers would be less attractive than the protection granted in a small limited liability company: but proposed that all companies should be a statutory minimum paid-up share capital as the price for limiting liability. The Jenkins Committee[8] in 1962, incidentally decided that it would be undesirable to institute another type of corporate body.

The National Chamber of Trade, in a memorandum to the Department of Trade in 1981, recognised that limited liability in a small company can be illusory since "directors will be required to underwrite the company's overdraft at the bank; few landlords will let premises to such a company unless the directors act as guarantors, and the same conditions are likely to attach to other potential sources of credit"[9]. As the Green Paper on a New Form of Incorporation for Small Firms comments[10]: –

"In other words, on the failure of the company the members, or some of them, do not escape personal liability; the banks and other sources of formal credit facilities recover from them, if necessary making them bankrupt. The only result of limited liability is that the unfortunate trade creditors who have not been in a position to demand personal guarantees are left to whistle for their money."

The National Chamber of Trade propose a form of entity for owner-managed firms with a minimum of two and a maximum of twenty members, and that none of the members should be corporate bodies. Members should underwrite normal business debts up to an agreed and disclosed amount: beyond that their liability to contribute to firm debts should be limited.

An annex to the Green Paper "A New Form of Incorporation for Small Firms"[10] contains proposals by Professor Gower[11] for a new form of entity, which would be incorporated under a completely new act, have a minimum of two and a maximum of ten members, with liability of the members limited to their initial capital stake, but with safeguards such as the filing of charges on the firm's assets and requirements for disclosure of accounts and audit.

In commenting on the Gower proposals the Consultative Committee of Accountancy Bodies[12] made a counter-proposal to create a new class of limited liability company: the "proprietary company" in which the proprietors are also the managers. They wrote in explanation: –

"We consider that there is a strong case for exempting those small firms, where there is a complete identity of management and ownership, from all those provisions of company law which presume a separation of management and ownership..... In view of the complex nature of existing company legislation we believe that it may be desirable to remove proprietary companies from the ambit of company law and enact separate legislation."

These various proposals have been summarised in table 3.

The Significance of the Largest Quoted Companies

As the number of small companies has grown dramatically,

Source of Proposal	Form of Entity	Number of Members	Limitation of Liability
Limited Partnership Act (1907)	Special partnership with registration	1 or more general partners 1 or more limited partners	– with personal liability for firm's debts – with liability limited to initial capital
Companies Act (1948) – S.202 and 203	Incorporated limited company	2 or more	Liability of directors unlimited Liability of other members limited
Company Law Reform (1973)	New form of incorporation	2 or more	None
Lowe (1974)	New form of incorporation	1 or more	Unlimited for owner-managers Limited for "dormant" members
National Chamber of Trade (1981)	New form of incorporation "Incorporated Limited Partnership"	2-20 (natural persons)	Members underwrite debts up to a defined amount
Gower (1981)	New form of incorporation "Incorporated Limited Firm" or (PTY) Ltd.	2-10 (natural persons)	Limited but with safeguards including filing changes and publishing audited accounts
CCAB (1981)	The Proprietary Company	1-10 all owner-managers (natural persons)	Not stated but detailed financial disclosure proposed

Table 3   Comparison of proposals for alternative forms of small firm incorporation

the significance of the few really large corporations has increased.

Growth in *corporate size* is not a new phenomenon. Success in the market place generates internal growth with increased market standing and shares. Mergers and acquisitions add further scale to corporate activities.

Though there had been earlier company mergers, particularly in railway companies, during the nineteenth-century, some significant mergers developed towards the end, as we saw in chapter 3.

In the early years of the twentieth-century, in the United States, market domination by groups of companies under common financial ownership led to the anti-trust laws to reduce abuses of monopoly power.

Sargent Florence[13] showed that by 1916 some 20% of all

profits in British business were earned by the 100 largest quoted companies and, in the manufacturing sector, that the 93 largest companies owned 65% of all net assets in manufacturing. Since then nationalisation of sectors such as steel and the wave of company mergers during the 1960's and early 70's has further concentrated companies into fewer, larger groups. Ulton[14] in more recent work has shown that concentration is greater in Britain than in the USA.

The Report of the Committee on Industrial Democracy (Chairman, Lord Bullock)[15], published in 1977, commented that

"The last twenty years have seen the growth of the giant industrial enterprise, and the concentration of economic power in the hands of fewer and fewer such companies. For example, in 1953 the 100 largest manufacturing enterprises in the UK accounted for 25% of the total net output; in 1971 the corresponding figure was 40%."

Bringing the data up to date, the top 100 quoted companies account for well over half of the turnover, profit and capital employed of the entire top 1000 quoted companies. Table 4 develops these data further, and shows rather dramatically that the top 10 on their own account for 28% of turnover, 47% of profit and 25% of capital employed of the entire top 1000.

	Top 10 UK Quoted Companies	Top 50 UK Quoted Companies	Top 100 UK Quoted Companies
Turnover	28%	51%	65%
Capital employed	25%	45%	60%
Profit before	47%	63%	75%

Table 4   Percentages of turnover, capital employed and profit before tax and interest of top 1000 UK industrial companies (ranked by turnover)

Source: derived from Times 1000: 1982/83

Table 5 gives the detailed information for the top 10 quoted companies, and table 5A puts the global picture. DuPont's successful merger with Conoco in 1981, bringing together America's ninth largest oil company with the largest chemical company, for £4.2 bn., demonstrates the potential scale of corporate mergers.

In terms of international comparisons table 6 shows the increasing number of companies, world wide, with sales over

Rank by Turnover	Company	Turnover £'000,000	Capital Employed £'000,000	Net Profit before tax & interest £'000,000	Number of Employees
1	British Petroleum	30,624	6,614	6,586	153,250
2	Shell Transport	18,782	9,198	2,915	–
3	BAT Industries	9,091	3,524	808	169,500
4	ICI	6,581	5,294	736	132,400
5	Esso Petroleum	5,324	3,044	983	8,186
6	Shell UK	5,182	3,520	843	20,033
7	Unilever	4,935	2,156	412	73,252
8	Imperial Group	4,526	1,085	168	122,400
9	GEC	3,462	1,796	513	193,000
10	Grand Metropolitan	3,221	2,264	283	131,757
	TOTAL	91,728	38,495	14,247	1,003,778
Percentage of top 1000 UK industrial companies		27.6%	24.9%	47.3%	

Table 5   The significance of the 10 largest UK industrial quoted companies, ranked by turnover

Source: The Times 1000, 1982/83

Ranked by Turnover	Company	Corporate Base	Sales £Billion
1	Exxon	US	66.7
2	Royal Dutch Shell	Netherlands/UK	54.8
3	AT&T	US	42.5
4	Mobil	US	41.3
5	Mitsubishi	Japan	40.2
6	General Motors	US	39.2
7	Mitsui	Japan	36.2
8	BP	UK	34.6
9	C Itoh	Japan	33.8
10	Marubeni	Japan	31.6

Table 5A   The World's Top 10 Companies

Source: Times 1000 1983/84

	1962	1967	1972	1977
USA	9	25	35	98
UK	–	2	7	13
Germany	–	–	8	17
France	–	–	4	13
Japan	–	–	8	20
Other European Countries	2	2	9	17
Other Countries	–	–	–	11
TOTAL	11	29	71	189

Table 6   Number of companies with sales over £2.5 billion

Source: Dunning, John H. & Robert D. Pearce:
            The World's Largest Industrial Enterprises: 1981 (Based on data from Fortune)

£2,500 billion. Even taking the effects of inflation into account the increasing scale and operation of the major international companies is apparent.

If instead of sales turnover, companies are ranked by stock market capitalisation, the 10 largest UK industrial companies account for 29.5% of the market value of the entire top 500 such companies (table 7). Three British companies – BP, GEC, and Shell Transport – stand out, showing their appeal to the investor.

Rank by Capitalisation	Company	Market Capitalisation £'000,000
1	British Petroleum	5,909
2	GEC	5,163
3	Shell Transport	4,533
4	Marks & Spencer	2,127
5	ICI	1,896
6	Beecham Group	1,743
7	BAT Industries	1,623
8	Grand Metropolitan	1,337
9	Barclays Bank	1,307
10	Great Universal Stores	1,233
	TOTAL	26,871
Percentage of top 500 UK companies		29.5%

Table 7   The Significance of the 10 largest UK industrial companies ranked by market capitalisation

Source: The Financial Times UK 500: 21st October 1982

As a proportion of all UK registered companies quoted on The Stock Exchange, the top 10 account for some 16% of the total market valuation. At 30th June 1983 there were 2,234 such companies with a total market valuation of £159,823.8 million[16].

The Significance of the Largest Private Companies

It should not be concluded, of course, that large companies are necessarily public and quoted. There are some significant private companies; larger than most public companies in fact.

But the significance of the few, by contrast with the many, is dramatic in the case of private companies. The significance of the top 10, 50 and 100 respectively, compared with the top 1000 is as follows: –

	Top 10 UK Private Companies	Top 50 UK Private Companies	Top 100 UK Private Companies
Turnover	28.9%	42.9%	51.9%
Capital Employed	25.3%	41.6%	51.4%
Profit before	27.9%	44.1%	55.6%

Table 8   Percentage of turnover, capital employed and profit before tax and interest of the top 1000 UK private companies (ranked by turnover) 1981/82

Source: Derived from Jordans "Britain's Top Private Companies" 1983

The data for the top 10 UK private companies are given in detail in table 9. As with the public quoted companies we see how a few large corporations account for a major proportion of the top 1000 such companies.

Rank by Turnover	Company	Turnover £'000,000	Capital Employed £'000,000	Net Profit before tax & interest £'000,000	Number of Employees
1	Czarnikow Group Ltd.	3,123[1]	22	3.6	688
2	Western United Investments Co. Ltd.	1,120	5	0.2[2]	14,131
3	Littlewoods Organisation Ltd. (The)	951	471	12.5	30,407
4	Wellcome Foundation Ltd.	500	403	50.1	6,688
5	C & J Clark Ltd.	473	160	18.7	17,426
6	Palmer & Harvey Ltd.	349	20	6.6	3,160
7	Heron International Ltd.	303	236	13.2	3,418
8	John Swire & Sons Ltd.	292	322	51.1	614
9	Socomex Ltd.	285	1	−0.9	NA
10	Geest Holdings Ltd.	269	55	7.1	4,828
		7,665	1,695	162.2	81,360

Table 9   The significance of the 10 largest UK private companies, ranked by turnover

Source: Jordans "Britain's Top Private Companies" 1983

(1) Turnover in trading activities
(2) Parent company only: consolidated accounts not published

Corporate Concentration

The concentration of firms within industries is often cited as another mark of the power of the relatively few large companies. However, care has to be exercised before concluding that industries are becoming increasingly concentrated and determining whether competition is increasing or decreasing.

Dunning & Pearce[17] have developed a concentration index by relating the proportion of sales of the three largest companies worldwide in an industry with the sales of the largest 20 (or smaller number if that is the only data available). Their results are given in table 10.

	1962	1967	1972	1977	x
Aerospace	42.7	40.7	37.3	41.6	15
Office equipment (incl. computers)	65.4	70.8	70.2	70.3	8
Petroleum	46.8	43.2	41.4	36.9	20
Electronics and electrical appliances	39.4	36.2	33.5	33.7	20
Chemicals and pharmaceuticals	29.8	27.3	25.5	25.2	20
Industrial and farm equipment	33.6	31.9	32.9	34.8	20
Shipbuilding, railroad and transportation equipment	74.0	65.1	52.8	53.8	7
Rubber	52.3	55.8	57.9	55.9	8
Motor vehicles	67.5	64.6	58.1	54.3	20
Metal manufacturing and products	31.7	29.1	27.2	26.7	20
Building materials	44.1	46.3	50.3	52.9	11
Tobacco	61.1	59.8	58.0	61.8	8
Beverages	53.9	52.8	56.2	57.1	8
Food	38.8	36.3	34.6	34.9	20
Paper and wood products	29.5	26.8	26.6	28.4	19
Textiles, apparel, leather goods	28.6	28.5	30.0	28.7	20

Table 10   Concentration ratios of largest firms by industry – sales of the largest 3 firms as a percentage of the sales of the largest x

Source: Dunning & Pearce, The World's Largest Industrial Enterprises: Gower 1981

The trends shown in table 11 suggest that in the decade up to 1972 the predominant tendency was towards a decline in concentration in the industrial muscle of the top few companies. However, a reversal of this decline is shown in subsequent years and table 11, which shows the sales of the largest firms as a percentage of the sales of the top 483 in the Dunning & Pearce sample, confirms this trend.

	1962	1967	1972	1977
x = 25	31.0	28.7	27.6	30.5
x = 50	42.8	40.4	38.8	42.8
x = 100	57.5	54.9	54.0	57.3
x = 150	67.4	65.5	64.9	67.6
x = 200	75.3	73.9	73.5	75.4
x = 250	81.5	80.6	80.2	81.6
x = 300	86.7	86.1	85.7	86.6
x = 350	91.2	90.7	90.4	90.9
x = 400	95.0	94.6	94.4	94.7
x = 483	100.0	100.0	100.0	100.0

Table 11   Sales of the x largest firm as a percentage of sales in a sample of 483 largest firms

Source: Dunning & Pearce 1981

Interviews with directors of large British companies, undertaken in The Corporate Policy Group studies, particularly with those in the more mature industries such as volume car manufacture, commercial vehicles, shipbuilding, computers and aircraft, frequently expressed the view that concentration in such sectors would inevitably increase.

"We may well reach the stage at which there is room for only one company in each industry in each major country. Perhaps not that in the longer term."

Inevitably when a company is at the top of the market curve it becomes increasingly difficult to maintain its market position against substitute products and competition with declining unit costs.

The high cost of product development and launch, the capital intensity and investment required for production, the need for government support by direct subsidy or contract, and the trend towards joint ventures between otherwise competing manufacturers were all cited in evidence[18].

Corporate Diversification

By contrast, diversification within groups of companies into production processes, markets, products and services outside the scope of the original industry sector, has also been marked. Acquisition strategies since the 1960's have taken many large companies into fields quite different from their main and original activity. More recently, though companies have shown a preponderance to divest subsidiaries and rationalise their product/market strategies, the extent of diversification remains high.

Such diversification may have been horizontally into new product lines, vertically by engaging in upstream or downstream processes, or towards conglomerate diversification employing a new business sector with little, if any, direct link to either existing manufacturing or marketing sectors.

Whether or not such diversifications are in the long term interests of the shareholders is a matter for conjecture. The additional diversity of their investment and the, presumably, spread risk may or may not be what they want. Certainly such diversifications can be presumed to be in the directors' interests.

Stopford, Dunning and Haverick[19] in their 1980 study took

431 multinational enterprises with sales in excess of £1 billion and showed that 22% of their sales were in products outside of the company's principal category. This proportion varied from 49% for companies in aerospace to 15% for those in motor vehicles and 16% for those in the oil industry. Many multinational companies were diversified into two industries, some indeed many: of the 431 companies in the study, 1,168 diversifications into 13 different industrial sectors were noted – an average of 2.7 per firm.

International acquisitions have been a feature of recent corporate growth, particularly European companies acquiring United States companies. Dunning & Pearce suggest that, outside their home countries, the horizontal extension of domestic activities tends to be the main form of foreign direct investment. In 1968 they estimate (quoting Stopford, Dunning and Haverick) that 48.9% of US controlled assets abroad were of this type. Forward vertical diversification accounted for 21.9% and backward vertical diversification of 6.9%. The balance of 22.3% comprised fundamental (conglomerate) diversification. It is their belief that the conglomerate proportion has continued to grow subsequently.

The proposals of the European Commission for the creation of a new form of joint enterprise across the frontiers of member states – the European Economic Interest Group – would further facilitate such joint ventures[20].

Summary

In this chapter we have looked at some of the facts behind companies. We have seen a proliferation of relatively small company incorporations, and reviewed various proposals for distinguishing the small owner-managed firm. Then, on the other hand, we saw a growing scale of operation, concentration, diversification and internationalisation of large companies.

Any conceptual framework for companies must differentiate such corporate entities if it is to be useful for corporate governance.

Chapter 5

The Complexity of Corporate Groups
– the number and levels of subsidiaries and a mismatch with management structures

The activities of practically all large companies today are carried out through the operations of a group of companies. In this chapter we explore the extent and complexity of such corporate groups; and also see how the legal corporate structure may not reflect the business organisation.

Corporate Complexity

Little has been published on the structure and size of corporate groups. Although organisational theorists often prefix their studies of management organisations by emphasising the complexity, there is no readily available measure of corporate complexity.

Accordingly a project was undertaken in The Corporate Policy Group to develop some data on the situation in larger UK quoted companies. The sample included some 144 companies, drawn from The Times 1000 UK industrial, quoted companies, and lying in the 1-100 and 401-500 size bands.

The data was drawn from "Who Owns Whom – UK and the Republic of Ireland", Vols. 1 & 2, Dunn & Bradstreet, 1983 cross checked by direct reference to a sample of companies and from published directors' reports and accounts.

Relevant definitions were:–

Parent – a company which has subsidiaries and is not itself controlled by any other company.

Subsidiary – a company with a parent, which either controls the composition of the board of directors or holds more than half the equity share capital.

Associate – a company in which another holds a significant equity interest but less than or equal to half (10%–50% in the sample); and thus likely to play an important role in governance.

In the study the number of subsidiary companies (excluding those not trading) and associate companies were counted. Also the number of levels at which subsidiaries were controlled was calculated.

The level of subsidiary was defined as the number of layers below the parent. Thus a subsidiary of a subsidiary of the parent would be at level two, as figure 1. It is necessary to add the level of the parent company itself to obtain the overall height of the corporate pyramid.

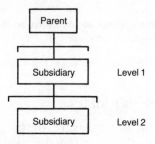

Fig. 1 Levels of subsidiary company

The Number of Subsidiaries

In the sample 12 companies from the Times 1000 proved themselves to be the subsidiaries of other companies, typically resident in the US or continental Europe, such as Esso, Ford, Gallaher and Philips Electrical, and were omitted from the study.

The top 50 UK companies have over 10,000 subsidiaries, as shown in table 1. The arithmetic average is 230 each, with a range from 5 (Sainsburys) to 858 (British Petroleum). Even companies in the 451-500 ranking have an average of 25 subsidiaries each, with a range from 2 to 74. (Dormant companies were excluded.)

The complexity introduced by the sheer number of subsidiaries in a group becomes apparent from these data. Of course, the number itself gives no indication of the scale of operation of each subsidiary: some will themselves be vast with complex trading and managerial structures, some will be relatively small formed, perhaps, to govern a specific contract, a site or a ship. However table 1 does highlight the governance issue in groups with such substantial numbers of entities, each of which is an autonomous company, incorporated under the Companies Acts, with a board and the responsibility to be properly governed.

Number of companies in the sample	Rank in Times 1000	Total Number of Subsidiaries	Average Number of Subsidiaries	Range
44	1 – 50	10,127	230.16	5 – 858
39	51 – 100	4,083	104.69	2 – 259
35	400 – 450	1,252	35.77	1 – 211
26	451 – 500	665	25.57	2 – 74
144		16,127	111.99	

Table 1   Total and average number of subsidiaries in large groups, ranked by company size

Source: Corporate Policy Group Study based on 1981/82 data

The Levels of Subsidiaries

To obtain a further measure of corporate complexity we analysed the sample groups by the levels at which subsidiaries are held. Table 2 shows the number of subsidiaries held by the sample companies at each level; and table 3 gives the same data expressed as arithmetic averages.

Number of Companies in the sample	Rank Order	Level of subsidiary										
		1	2	3	4	5	6	7	8	9	10	11
44	1 – 50	2291	3381	2085	1255	721	254	127	8	2	2	1
39	51 – 100	1099	1521	1025	292	80	26	37	3	–	–	–
35	400 – 450	991	185	60	16	–	–	–	–	–	–	–
26	451 – 500	421	167	64	13	–	–	–	–	–	–	–
144		4802	5254	3234	1576	801	280	164	11	2	2	1

Table 2   Total number of subsidiaries at each level, ranked by company size

Source: Corporate Policy Group Study

One company (BP) actually has subsidiaries recorded at the eleventh level, giving a corporate structure with twelve levels; but this is abnormal. Nevertheless in the top 50 companies the average of 230 subsidiaries is significantly ranged down to the fourth and fifth levels. On average the parent has 52 subsidiaries at the first level, which themselves have 77 subsidiaries at the second, which have 47 at the third, with 28 at the fourth and 16 at the fifth.

Number of Companies in the sample	Rank Order	Level of subsidiary										
		1	2	3	4	5	6	7	8	9	10	11
44	1 – 50	52.1	76.8	47.4	28.5	16.4	5.8	2.9	0.1	0.1	0.1	–
39	51 – 100	28.2	39.1	26.3	7.4	2.0	0.7	1.0	–	–	–	–
35	400 – 450	28.3	5.3	1.7	0.5	–	–	–	–	–	–	–
26	451 – 500	16.2	6.4	2.5	0.5	–	–	–	–	–	–	–
144		33.4	36.5	22.4	10.9	5.6	1.9	1.1	0.1	–	–	–

Table 3 Average number of subsidiaries at each level, ranked by company size

Source: Corporate Policy Group Study

In an attempt to depict the structural complexity across the sample of companies, the number of companies having subsidiaries only down to first, second and subsequent levels was calculated. Table 4 shows these data. For example, in the top 50 companies only three have but one level of subsidiary, and the median is at the fourth level; in the 451-500 ranking no company goes further than the fourth level and the median is at the second. The table clearly depicts the structural complexity in large groups of companies and shows how it varies by absolute size.

Number of Companies in the sample	Rank Order	Level of subsidiary										
		1	2	3	4	5	6	7	8	9	10	11
44	1 – 50	3	7	9	10	6	5	1	2	–	–	1
39	51 – 100	2	5	14	7	6	3	1	1	–	–	–
35	400 – 450	18	12	3	2	–	–	–	–	–	–	–
26	451 – 500	8	10	4	4	–	–	–	–	–	–	–
144		31	34	30	23	12	8	2	3	–	–	1

Table 4 Structural complexity in groups of companies, ranked by company size: showing the number of companies at the maximum extent of subsidiary level

Source: Corporate Policy Group Study

Further complexities may arise where subsidiaries are not wholly-owned, giving rights and responsibilities to minority shareholders; also where companies are incorporated under the jurisdiction, and thus under the regulation, of other nation's company law. Although our researches did not attempt to trace such instances in detail for the sample companies, there were ample examples of both situations.

Confirming the Corporate Complexity

We followed up the desk research from published sources by approaching a sample of 92 companies (drawn from the same populations) for confirmation and additional information. 57 companies co-operated, a gratifying 62% response rate, and particularly significant given the amount of work some companies had to undertake to establish the actual number and levels of their own subsidiaries, using our measures.

The individual results from the companies tallied closely with the published material. Differences arose from changes since the date of the original study and the classification of dormant companies and overseas groups.

However, the original conclusions on the extent of corporate complexity, both in terms of the number of subsidiaries and the levels at which they were held, were confirmed. The number of subsidiaries in the second sample were: –

Number of companies in the sample	Rank in Times 1000	Total Number of Subsidiaries	Average Number of Subsidiaries	Range
20	1 – 50	4,613	230.6	12 – 800
17	51 – 100	1,758	103.4	10 – 315
10	400 – 450	268	26.8	3 – 51
6	451 – 500	216	36.0	1 – 48

Table 5   Structural complexity in groups of companies

Source: Corporate Policy Group – (direct contact research)

From the individual contacts we were also able to obtain additional material on the way companies coped with such complexity.

● *Case example: company 201*

"This group comprises some 580 subsidiary companies, of which 380 are non-trading companies, and approximately 38 associated companies. The group is divided into three divisions which are responsible for commercial activities. Each divisional company and the companies within each division are separate profit centres, operating with a high degree of autonomy and individuality.

The parent company retains responsibility for overall planning and development, financial control and the provision of the necessary finance and management resources. The subsidiary companies within the group are typically held at levels 2 to 3."

- *Case example: company 202*
  "The complexity of levels at which these are all held has been something of a surprise even to us. Some of the chains are, I have to confess, somewhat artificial and have been dictated by taxation or other fiscal reasons. They also reflect, in some cases, the residue of historical operations since discontinued which, for one reason or another, we have not yet completely cleared up."
- *Case example: company 203*
  (12 subsidiaries held at two levels)
  "The board of all subsidiaries includes at least one member of the ultimate parent company board. All subsidiary management is local, although there is some involvement from London in the operation of trading companies based in continental Europe."
- *Case example: company 204*
  "1) Within the group there are some 220 subsidiary and associated companies, excluding dormant companies.
  2) These can be held up to eight levels if one includes intervening holding companies that are essential for financial/taxation reasons, but otherwise no more than four levels normally exist if such companies are excluded and one deals solely with trading companies.
  Indeed when submitting the group's entry for the 1983 edition of "Who Owns Whom" I deliberately omitted the financial/taxation holding companies so as to minimise confusion."

We were given information on trends:–

- *Case example: company 206*
  "However the group is actively reducing the number of subsidiary companies by making businesses trading divisions of large companies rather than separate subsidiaries. As part of this rationalisation 6 companies at level 1, 3 companies at level 2 and 1 at level 3 will become dormant, their businesses becoming divisions of level 1 companies."

We also discovered reasons for certain companies' results which did not conform to the pattern: –

- *Case example: company 207*
  "We notice that when compared with the average figures we have a disproportionate number of subsidiaries in level 3 as opposed to levels 1 and 2. This reflects the

divisional structure adopted by the group and the fact that we have acquired a number of companies which already had subsidiaries at the time of acquisition which therefore fall into level 3."

● *Case example: company 208*
"These figures could be misleading since many of the companies are not significant in trading terms or in some cases have only the role of holding company with or without an inter-company financing function. We include in our annual report each year a summary of the principal subsidiaries and associates. This excludes the smallest companies, intermediate holding companies, and companies which are for practical purposes branches or divisions of another company."

Two other aspects were noted by another respondent:—

● *Case example: company 103*
"The first of these is that one finds in some cases that at the third or fourth level of subsidiary there are outside shareholdings which bring into the relationship considerations which may weaken the total dependence of the subsidiary (say 60-70% owned) on the parent. Secondly, even where subsidiaries are wholly owned in countries outside the UK they may have external directors who are themselves men of considerable substance in the local community, who will be anxious to see that interests other than the parents' are fully taken account of in local board decisions."

Associations, Consortia and Joint Ventures

In addition to the corporate complexity within groups of companies linked by ownership control, we also wanted to explore interdependencies between companies linked by associations not dependent on ownership domination, because such groupings also raise governance issues.

Using the same sample of companies from the 1-100 and 401-500 bands of UK industrial companies we counted those reporting associate companies and the number of them. Table 6 shows the results. Some companies in each ranking have no associate companies at all. In the top 50, the 39 companies with associates report 1,329, an average of 34 each. The range is from none in companies like Marks & Spencer, to 280 in British Petroleum, 243 in Shell Transport and 102 in Inchcape.

Number of Companies in the sample	Rank Order	Number of Companies with Associates	Number of Associates	Average Number of Associates	Range
44	5 – 50	39	1329	34.1	0 – 280
39	51 – 100	34	564	16.6	0 – 60
35	400 – 450	18	180	10.0	0 – 39
26	451 – 500	12	49	4.1	0 – 12
144		103	2122	20.6	

Table 6   Associate companies of top UK corporations

Source: Corporate Policy Group Study

Considerably fewer of the smaller companies in the 451-500 ranking band have associates and those that do have an average of 4 each.

A study of directors' reports and other published material provided evidence of considerable activity in joint ventures of various types between companies, which are separately owned and often in competition in some market places.

Recent examples include: –

British Homes Stores and J. Sainsbury Ltd.

BL and Honda

British Telecom and various equipment manufacturers

Fiat and Alfa Romeo

ICL and Fujitsu

Lucas Industries and Smiths Industries

Philips and Sony

Rolls-Royce and Pratt & Whitney

The European Air Bus Consortia

The European Space Satellite Programme

Such joint activities may be motivated by a commercial advantage to share development and launch costs, to transfer, extend and exploit technology, to tender as a consortium for a major project or to combine scarce resources in a specifically designated segment of a market.

The creation of corporate interdependencies, other than by the traditional route of acquisition and merger, when power is rooted in ownership, raises important questions about the governance of the resultant network.

It seems that there are various vehicles by which companies pursue interdependent activities – associations, consortia and joint ventures.

An association recognises a common project, of potential commercial benefit to the partners, and the joint activities are planned, coordinated and managed by the partners, under contract law. The separate organisational, technical, physical and financial resources to be committed to the project are identified and the managerial objectives, performance measures and accountability agreed.

In *a joint venture* the partners typically incorporate a separate corporate entity, in which they each hold a stake, to handle the joint activity. Again the coordination and the project and its management must be determined by the partners, but they do operate within the legal framework and liability limitation of a corporate entity.

A consortium is a grouping of otherwise independent, indeed often competing, companies to pursue a specific business opportunity jointly. The members may organise their joint activity as an association or a joint venture.

Research by Mak[1] has confirmed the growing significance of such joint activities. The absence of a codified body of knowledge is also emphasised. Companies rarely train their managers to operate in the collaborative environment of a joint activity and much trial and error is involved.

> Mueller[2], in an unpublished doctoral thesis, writes on the use of consortia in the European Communication Satellite Programme. There is a core of relatively prominent consortia members, but "little emphasis is put on joint decision-making, profit sharing and long term planning, with company relations being characterised by a prime contractor/subcontractor relationship". The consortia arrangements are highly flexible, being put together from the consortia members for each major contract. But though the core members have "built up joint working arrangements", the consortium itself is highly unstable.

Federations of Companies

A further type of interdependency, with implications for governance, can arise from part ownership and cross-holdings between companies.

Take, as an example, a company with $100 million to invest in capital acquisitions. At one end of the scale it could make wholly-owned acquisitions, putting the entire funds into one or two subsidiaries, which it would manage. This has been the pattern in most UK and US groups in recent years.

At the other end of the scale, it could make, say, 50 investments of $2 million in different companies, when it would be in the position of an investment trust or other financial institution.

But, between these two polarities, it could invest twenty or thirty million pounds into, say, three or four companies, to obtain a stake of between ten to thirty percent. Such arrangements are found in some South African mining groups.

In such circumstances the investing management can exercise considerable influence over the member companies, but not sufficient for them to become associates. Consequently the balance sheet of the owning company does not consolidate fixed assets and working capital, but shows investments in other companies. Obviously if holdings are greater than 50%, or de facto the investing company wields dominant power a group will exist.

There may be tax disadvantages in the inability of a federation to set off losses, but in international operations this may be inconsequential.

If companies in which an investment has been made now acquire a parcel of shares in the investing company we have the basis for a federation. Power can now be exercised not along the ownership and financial channels, but by the informal relationships between the directors and top management.

In other words a federation is not a group, with whole or dominant ownership as the basis of its power; nor is it a set of arms length holdings relying on the annual meetings of members to exert influence: it is a network of interests bound by limited cross-ownerships, and the interpersonal links between cross-directorships.

In a federation each member company is responsible under the company law of its country of incorporation. There is, however, no "meta" legal entity for the regulation of the behaviour of the federation. Consequently benefits might accrue to members from the relationship.

For example, the disclosure and liability creating effects of the 9th directive on groups might not apply, although the existence of a "control contract" under the directive might be limiting. Nor would disclosure and participation requirements of the Vredeling draft directive, or United Nations codes of practice necessarily apply. Filing of accounts, as appropriate, would be needed for the individual members; but not for the federation.

Federations could be potentially valuable vehicles for world-wide corporate development: or they could provide the means for circumventing legitimate corporate regulation. Where companies have a substantial stake in other companies with whom they trade, and perhaps share directors, more attention may be paid to anti—trust policies.

Structural Mismatch

Another vital aspect of governance in complex groups arises where the organisation structure adopted for running the business, taking management decisions and exercising management control, does not reflect the corporate structure of the member subsidiaries. In other words, where there is a mismatch between the legal structure and the underlying business reality.

The individual studies provided ample confirmation:

● *Case example: company 209*

"Companies can be grouped together for management purposes on an apparently random basis, for example, one which is based on product groups, and these can have no logical connection with the way the shares are held. The share organisation in a company may be like it is for various reasons, for example, historical reasons arising from previous organisations or acquisitions, particularly where overseas companies are concerned. Taxation also plays a part."

● *Case example: company 210*

"I am sure you appreciate that the legal structure of a group of wholly-owned subsidiary companies is not necessarily the same as the group's management structure; lines of communication in the management structure are normally much shorter than is apparent from a study of the corporate legal structure."

● *Case example: company 211*

"If I have a general comment it is that, in my experience, legal structure lags — sometimes for years — behind management structure; that the time lag arises mainly from constraints on the transfer of businesses arising from tax, company and employment law; and that, other things being equal, benefits flow from aligning legal and management structures."

● *Case example: company 010*

This London based international business has manufacturing plants and sales operations in all major European countries. For management purposes Western Europe is treated as the home market. Cash and funds flow are managed centrally.

Subsidiary companies are created to cover the business operations in each separate country, primarily for taxation, legal and regulatory purposes.

There is a need to govern each subsidiary and to produce accounts, which must then be consolidated. However, as explained by a head office director:

"The really useful accounts are by product and product line across the various business units. The legal entity accounts are only meaningful when combined by product across the reality of the business."

The implication of such cases is that, whilst the boards of directors of the subsidiary companies carry out a de jure accountability function and are the focus of regulatory activity, the reality of the business decision stream and the exercise of executive power flows through different channels.

Two questions seem pertinent:

1. If the product accounts across the European markets are really the ones with the valuable information, and the legal entity accounts an artificial reflection of the business reality, would not most users of accounts find them more useful?
2. Why have such subsidiary companies at all?

The principal arguments advanced for the creation and sustaining of subsidiary companies on a state by state basis are, typically,

1. For taxation reasons, recognising that each state has its independent tax structure, and thereby legitimately planning affairs to maximise taxation advantages of, for example, capital allowances, the treatment of losses, the allowance of specific expenditures, the timing of payments, and so on.
2. For contractual and business reasons, being able to contract through a legal entity, rather than through an agency or branch of a foreign based company.
3. To limit financial exposure on the group as a whole by limiting liability within the boundaries of a particular entity. This raises questions of the protection of credi-

tors' interests, which are addressed by the 9th directive.

4. For regulatory reasons, it being easier to do business in a particular state by means of a corporation registered in that state, fulfilling the requirements for regulation, registration, filing, disclosure as necessary.

The Agency Company

Another way in which a mismatch between the corporate entities and the business reality arises is in the *agency company*.

● *Case example: company 005*

This medium sized public company is a conglomerate, with interests in engineering, steel manufacture and stockholding and consumer products, based in the UK Midlands.

An agency company has been formed, bearing a well recognised trade or brand name as the basis for commercial activities including the purchase of goods and services and the sale and distribution of manufactured and factored products. But the company only acts as an agent on behalf of the holding company. It does not trade in its own right.

The accounts of the agency company show neither profit nor loss; nor does it own any assets. All actions are taken on behalf of the principal company.

The reason given by the chairman of the holding company for the use of the agency subsidiary is to use the name and goodwill inherent in the trade reputation of a business which was previously acquired.

"The commercial benefit lies in using the name and business standing of the company."

● *Case example: company 212*

"We are, of course, dealing with legal structures and in a number of cases these are different from the management structure within our operating groups. In management terms, we tend to have the four or five main operating divisions represented at parent board level. Each director has reporting to him 3 or 4 (and no more than 5) divisional managing directors of principal product groups. Within these groups, our objective is to concentrate the assets employed and the personnel at the top of the group pyramid, preferring to keep the trading companies on an agency basis where they can operate under their locally established trade names. We find this the best working method for a large group as diverse as ours."

● *Case example: company 213*

"Most of our UK subsidiaries carry on business as agents for the parent company, but for the purpose of your survey these have been counted as operating rather than dormant companies."

The danger inherent in such a situation is the risk of exposure of a creditor to a corporate shell, with no right of recourse to the dominant partner. This could happen where contracts were expressly with the subsidiary company and there was no express or implied agency contract involving the parent company.

Strategic Business Units

The final example of a structural mismatch between the business reality and the corporate entities in the group is found, typically, in very large groups which have formed strategic business units which map across a number of subsidiaries.

In relatively simple groups, with little inter-group trading or interdependence, each subsidiary might indeed map directly onto an autonomous trading entity. Where there are product, market or geographical commonalities between subsidiaries, they might be grouped into divisions. But in larger, and more complex groups the underlying business process may cut across the responsibilities of a number of subsidiary companies. Then, if a fundamental regrouping of activities is to be avoided, some form of strategic business units becomes necessary, relating the different business activities across the companies.

● *Case example: company 001*

A major international oil company has subsidiaries, both wholly and partially owned, and associate companies in many countries around the world. For many years these companies have been grouped regionally: reporting through regional directors to the main board.

In 1981 an additional dimension was added to the corporate organisational matrix by creating strategic business units responsible for product related businesses globally.

The head of each strategic business unit reports to the

main board. Consequently the chief executive and the directors of each subsidiary company have responsibilities both to their regional director and to the heads of the appropriate business units (see fig. 2).

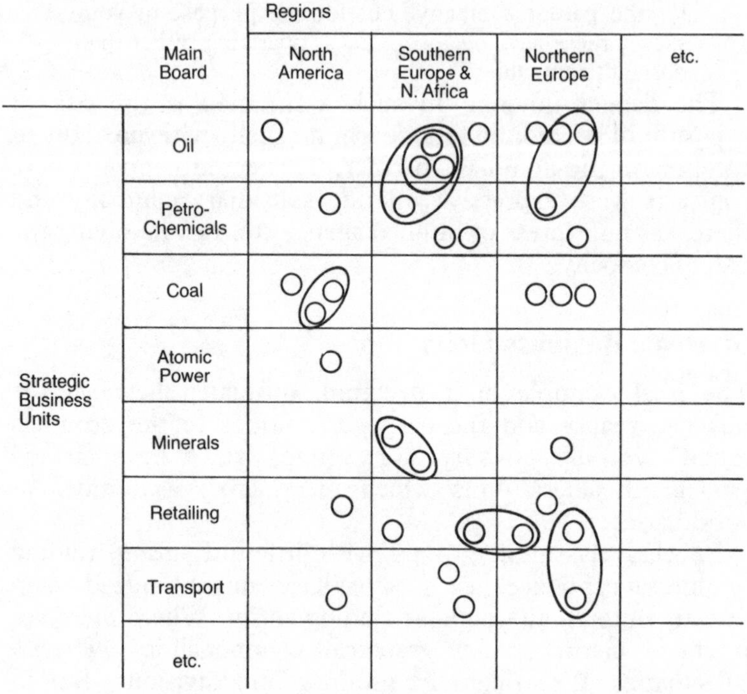

	Main Board	Regions			
		North America	Southern Europe & N. Africa	Northern Europe	etc.
Strategic Business Units	Oil				
	Petro-Chemicals				
	Coal				
	Atomic Power				
	Minerals				
	Retailing				
	Transport				
	etc.				

Fig 2.   A typical example of subsidiary companies in a Group, with Strategic Business Units and Regional co-ordination

Subsidiary companies are shown thus: ◯

Nested groups of subsidiaries are shown thus:

The existence of such dualities in the decision-making structure – caused by a mismatch between the corporate entities and the business processes – adds a further dimension to the study of corporate governance. It is another aspect that needs to be reflected in a conceptual framework for corporate governance in the modern corporation.

Summary

We have seen, in this chapter, the complexity of large

corporate groups, both in terms of the absolute number of subsidiaries and the levels at which they can be held. Joint activities between companies based on associations, joint ventures, consortia and federations (rather than equity participation) were also reviewed.

Another cause of complexity arises where there is a mismatch between the corporate structure of the subsidiaries in a group and the way the business is structured for operational and management purposes. If the corporate structure does not mirror the decision-making reality should the legal framework be adopted as the basis for governance?

A conceptual framework to provide a basis for improving corporate performance and corporate governance must recognise the nature of such corporate complexity. In the next chapter we can move towards an alternative conceptual framework based on these facts.

Chapter 6
Rethinking the Corporation
– towards an alternative conceptual framework

We have seen how the original conception of the joint-stock limited liability company stems from an elegant and simple nineteenth-century idea, which facilitated the raising of capital from non-executive investors. Their interests were protected against unscrupulous and over-ambitious company promoters by giving them the power to appoint the directors, demand accountability and overall to control the company, the investors meeting together as the members of the company.

We also saw the subsequent development of private companies, with proprietors incorporating their own business to obtain the protection of limited liability. Here the basis of power was, clearly, with the owners.

Successive companies Acts, throughout the twentieth-century to date, and the increasing self-regulatory demands of The Stock Exchange, have increased the demands on companies for the disclosure of information and the regulation of behaviour, to protect the interests of creditors, potential investors, employees and others. But, though challenged by the original draft 5th directive[1] and the Bullock Committee Report[2], both of which advocated employee directors, the basis of power in British company law remains with ownership, as it does in most other legal systems.

By any standards the blossoming of the corporate concept has been impressive. But we saw that its very success has led to a massive proliferation of companies being incorporated, the bulk of them small. At the other end of the scale we also saw the considerable size, concentration, diversity and international nature of the large companies, operating through groups of companies with a significant number of subsidiaries at many levels. Moreover, we found evidence of a mismatch between the legal structure adopted in groups and the organisational structure used as the basis for business operations and management decisions.

The original, simple and successful concept no longer

mirrors the totality of corporate activities. The conceptual foundations need rethinking: an alternative typology or framework has to be developed so that the different corporate types can be properly compared and contrasted.

Such a schema is proposed in this chapter. Whereas the traditional approach emphasises structure, the alternative proposed focuses on the reality of corporate power.

Sources of Corporate Power

By power is meant the ability to directly affect corporate direction and control. Such powers may not be exercised regularly, but the potential must be there. In our explorations of corporate power we have used seven basic business decisions as an indicator of the source of power; viz:–

1. Membership of the board
2. Remuneration of directors
3. Raising of capital
4. Allocation of resources (finance, labour, management, products and markets, research, etc.)
5. Acquisition of other companies
6. Appointment and remuneration of top executives
7. Oversight and control of management performance.

By reviewing such decisions across the various types of company, four primary sources of power have been identified: –

Ownership Power
Corporate directors' power
Managerial power
Institutional shareholders' power

We shall review each in detail, but figure 1 attempts to differentiate the different sources. Of course, the balance of power will depend on the specific corporate situation: the recognition of the potential sources, however, is directly relevant to the conceptual framework to be proposed.

Ownership Power

Under British company law the primary duty of the directors is to the company[3]. Since the company is made up of the members, this duty lies to the body of members as a whole. The members nominate and elect the board, which is

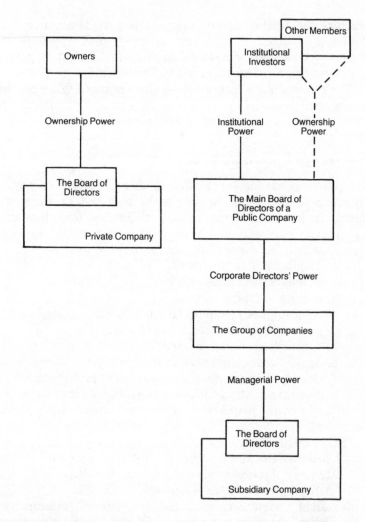

Fig. 1 Sources of corporate power

accountable to them. Such are the tenets of company law, as we have seen.

In a private company, in which the owners are also the directors and play a large part in the management of the enterprise, the dogma is not difficult to accept. There is no separation of interest. Power lies with the owner-managers who can legitimately claim the company as their own.

Problems can begin to arise when an incumbent chairman

or managing director perceives the company as "mine", a personal fiefdom[4], when the reality of the ownership structure shows other member interests. If some members are remote, not involved in executive activities, and the board becomes dominated by those who do manage the business, questions have to be asked about the true locus of power over company affairs.

It is not a new problem. Long before the Companies Acts of the mid-nineteenth-century, Adam Smith[5] was worried about investors in unincorporated companies who knew nothing of the business, leaving it in the hands of directors.

> "The trade of a joint-stock company is always managed by a court of directors. This court..... is frequently subject to a general court of proprietors. But the greater part of those proprietors seldom pretend to understand anything of the business of the company..... contentedly receiving such..... dividend as the directors think proper to give them. This total exemption..... encourages many to become adventurers in joint-stock companies..... The directors of such companies, however, being managers rather of other people's money than of their own, it cannot be well expected, that they should watch over it with the same anxious vigilence with which the partners in a private copartnery frequently watch over their own."

We have also seen how the Companies Acts in the nineteenth-century were designed to protect investors from unscrupulous or speculative company promoters. Although Payne[6] reports that there is little evidence of significant divorce of control from ownership before the end of the nineteenth-century, the issue of power lying with the incumbent directors, rather than the owners, was a matter of concern long before.

At the beginning of the nineteenth-century risk capital was provided by relatively few people – thus further concentrating wealth in their hands. By the twentieth-century the Stock Exchanges had become vital for financing large scale enterprise and spreading ownership more widely[7]; large sums were attracted from an increasing number of investors. The Balfour Committee, reporting in 1927, showed that the average holding then was only about £300, although, of course, this cloaks the large number of small shareholders balanced against fewer wealthy investors with considerable, large holdings.

In one of the classic, and original, works in the field of

corporate governance, first published in 1932, Berle & Means[8] traced the evolution of companies in the United States of America, from small and relatively insignificant origins in the nineteenth-century to the enormous concentration of power that a few had achieved by the early twentieth. They showed, for example, that by growth, merger and acquisition, the combined assets of the two hundred largest, non-banking corporations had climbed to £81 billion by 1930, representing nearly half of all corporate wealth in the United States.

They also showed that stock ownership had grown and become widely dispersed. Large holdings accounted for small proportions of the capital and often amounted to no more than 2 or 3% each. Management's holdings in many large companies were negligible.

Thus, Berle & Means argued, as companies grew and increased their share capital, and as national prosperity increased and more people invested in shares, so the proportion of voting stock held by the largest shareholders decreased. Consequently the power of the shareholders to control large corporations had diminished. Directors, who were originally the agents for the owners, would develop policies of their own and assume a self-perpetuating power. The interests of ownership and control had diverged: power had shifted from members to managers. Four years before Berle & Means wrote, the Liberal Industrial Inquiry in Britain was recognising similar issues[9].

In Britain by 1930 seven companies had reached a similar 'giant' size: J. & P. Coats, Courtalds, Distillers, ICI, Imperial Tobacco, Guinness and Unilever[10].

The limitations of ownership power in the public company and the difficulties of very large, diverse and geographically spread groups of shareholders influencing company affairs, have been well chronicled.

Rubner[11], in his book "The Ensnared Shareholder" and Midgley[12], in a research study "Companies and Their Shareholders − the Uneasy Relationship" demonstrate the limitations of ownership power in the public company. The annual meeting is an inadequate forum for exercising governance where there is a wide spread of shareholders, most of whom do not attend. Boards are required to submit relatively few resolutions for the company as a whole to decide − restructuring the capital or entering fundamentally different business areas, for example. Only in extremis does an incumbent board, typically, find itself under any pressure from the body of members as a whole to bring about changes in the direction or executive management of the business.

The advent of "ginger groups" of dissatisfied shareholders (other than institutional shareholders) seeking to change board policies – and usually board membership – are newsworthy by their rarity in Britain; and even in the United States where members, or their nominated representatives, are more active in public company members' meetings, boards are still criticised[13] for their failure to respond to members' perceived needs. Similarly the inability of interest groups, wishing to influence a company's policy on, for example, activities in certain parts of the world or involvement in military markets, to have an impact through the members' meetings reinforces the view that, in the large and diffusely held public company, membership power is seldom convincing.

Corporate Directors' Power

The significance of power lying with the directors has been discussed by a number of authorities, although they disagree on the implications.

Berle[14] argued that, freed from direct shareholder control, managers would act with a perceived responsibility to a range of interest groups. This notion was certainly supported by the Watkinson Committee[15] of the Confederation of British Industry, who reported in 1973 that "for long term profitability, directors must recognise responsibilities to employees, creditors, customers, the local community and society in general as well as their clear commitment to shareholders; and emphasises particularly the importance of satisfactory working relationships with employees".

Burnham[16], writing in 1962, took the theme of management power further and suggested an entire society dominated by management. He foresaw a managerial meritocracy and was particularly interested in state enterprise. Burnham's views were influential in the British Labour Party in the late '50s and early '60s. Managerialism still has many advocates today.

However, Crosland[17] interpreted the situation differently. He argued that ownership had not, in fact, been dissipated, but was increasingly concentrated in institutional holdings.

Such concentration ensures control, he argued. Moreover, owner control can be reinforced through interlocking directorships and, even where control does vest in management, it will be exercised in the interests of the property owning class. In other words, he believed that there had not been a real divorce of ownership and control, but rather a "managerial reorganisation of the propertied classes". Pahl & Winkler[18] have also claimed that, through mergers and reorganisations, "shareholders are no longer weak relative to managers"; "capitalists..... buying up scattered holders and agglomerating them until they were able to agree or force a takeover". Though they were mainly writing about conglomerates and asset stripping cases.

Dahrendorf[19] took another line. He agreed that ownership had been superseded by management, as the spread of shareholdings had reduced the power of property; like Berle, he believed that the joint-stock company had broken with earlier capitalist traditions ("separating ownership and control..... gives rise to a new group of managers who are utterly different from their predecessors"). But he also believed that the absence of owner-managers was virtually irrelevant. Authority, he argued, determined class boundaries and created class conflict. Property ownership was not a prerequisite for class membership, rather it was the ability to exercise authority. Consequently he advanced the view that modern industrial nations are "pluralistic societies with power being exercised between a plurality of the ruling classes, that is between those with authority".

The actual balance of power between the members of a public company and the directors on the main board, and in particular the chairman of that board, can be tested, in any particular case, by the seven basic business decisions adopted in this study.

1. *Membership of the Board.* Contested elections in public companies are rare[20]. Indeed nominations to fill places typically come from the incumbent chairman supported by his board colleagues; attendances at annual members' meetings are small and proxies preprinted.

   In the United States, the Securities & Exchange Commission has endeavoured to increase members' involvement[21], but in the UK the choice of directors lies more with the existing board, than with the owners.

2. *Remuneration of directors*. The Companies Acts lay down requirements for directors' remuneration to be reported in the accounts laid before the members[22]. Otherwise it is typically the board which determines the remuneration package of directors, not the members of the company. In some cases a remuneration committee, composed of non-executive directors, is formed to provide some objectivity and independence.

3. *Raising of capital*. Members, in general meeting, do have to approve significant changes in capital structure, borrowings and other fundamental matters in the holding company. Such actions, required by the Companies Acts, are intended to protect the financial interests of the investors — not to provide a mechanism for supervising the directors' management of the specific business interests.

   The main board, and, in so far as they delegate authority, the directors of subsidiary companies and various echelons of management, have a wide managerial prerogative to take business decisions out of view of and without prior permission of the owners. (Subject to the company's Articles).

   The directors may not change the nature of the business fundamentally, nor go outside the objects of the company as laid down in the company's Memorandum of Association; but since such objects clauses are, typically, drawn very wide for modern companies this is unlikely to be much of a constraint.

4. *Allocation of resources*. The directors of public companies, interviewed in our studies, expect to be able to allocate resources between the subsidiary companies and business activities in their group, moving funds, people, and other resources between them as they see fit. In some cases the overall corporate strategy for the group included the treatment of some companies in the group as "cash cows", to be run without reinvestment to provide a cash flow for investment in the growth businesses in the group. Members' approval was only sought in rare cases when required by the Articles of Association or where the change would result in a fundamental restructuring of the company.

5. *Acquisition of other companies*. Subject to any constraints

in the Articles of Association, and provided a fundamental change in the basic nature or financing of the company was not involved, directors tended to assume a prerogative to undertake acquisitions and to divest of subsidiaries. Where members' approval was necessary they, typically, felt that this was a formality. Only if the acquisition was controversial, for example in the Lonrho bid for Harrods, would the corporate directors' power be under the spotlight.

6. *Appointment and remuneration of top executives.* All directors agreed that a primary duty of the main board was to ensure the effectiveness of subsidiary company management, to lay down appropriate management policies and to be concerned with management succession.

7. *Oversight and control of management performance.* Again board members accept the responsibility for executive management performance. In the large public company the members' knowledge of the corporation is probably limited to some familiarity, or at least awareness, of some of its products and services, and the periodic Directors' Report and Accounts. The independent auditors provide a legitimising role when they report that the accounts show a true and fair view[23]. But the annual members meeting is not generally recognised as an appropriate vehicle for exercising supervision of executive management.

In the early days of company incorporations it was usual for the business to be relatively local and clearly identifiable as a unique business enterprise. Moreover, the investors would be drawn from the same geographical area as the business. The investors invited to subscribe for shares in, say, a gas works in a Lancashire town could be expected to see the results of their investment and to be directly aware of the company's activities. Subsequent wider flotation tended to change that situation. In today's large corporate groups, with many business units, the activities of the parts may be largely invisible to the owners.

Consequently we have to recognise that, though members retain certain powers (which they exercise when necessary), significant power in public companies tends to lie with the board and its chairman.

A Department of Trade Inspectors report[24] into the Cornhill Consolidated Group Ltd. raised some interesting issues that are relevant to the appreciation of directors' powers and responsibilities.

The Cornhill group was owned by its directors. Within the group, however, were companies in which a significant proportion of the shares were owned by members of the public. Moreover, since the group's directors had invested little by way of capital in the Cornhill group, almost the entire risk of the undertaking was shouldered by its creditors, though this was not apparent at the time. Where conflicting interests arose in the Cornhill group, it was the interests of minority shareholders or creditors which went unprotected.

The Cornhill group was managed by a small number of individuals, all of whom held a number, and some of them many, directorships within the Cornhill group. The financial affairs of the principal companies in this group were controlled from the centre. Demands for funds, whether in the form of cash loans or the proceeds from discounting bills, were satisfied by Cornhill Consolidated Company Limited and surplus funds were deposited with CCC.

As the Inspectors observe here is a case of significant conflicts of interest[25]: –

"Where companies which are members of a group share common directors and are financially inter-dependent, it appears to us that those directors need to be especially alert to the need to consider the separate interests of each company.

Those of the Cornhill group's directors who were, in effect, nominees of Cornhill Consolidated Group Ltd. ("CCG") – the ultimate holding company of the group – appear to have proceeded on the assumption that what in their view was good for the Cornhill group as a whole was ipso facto good for its component parts. As a result the interests of individual companies often went unrecognised or were ignored."

Managerial Power

The theories of corporate power developed by Berle & Means, Burnham and Crosland focused on two parties – the owners and the managers. Dahrendorf recognised that power was exercised by a plurality of interests.

But none have explored, at length, the dispersion of power in complex groups. In a large public company, with many subsidiaries and divisions, operating in various businesses, in different parts of the world, power is likely to be exercised in various roles and at various levels[18]. Understanding corporate governance is not just a matter of determining whether the main board or the members exercise power. It involves appreciating the roles and responsibilities of directors of subsidiary companies, managers of divisional businesses, and head office staff.

One of the great strengths of the corporate concept − the ability to buy and sell shares in the company − also held the seeds of a fundamental flaw. Having created an artificial, legal persona able to contract and buy and sell, the law had enabled companies to buy and sell shares in each other.

We saw, in chapter 3, how many existing businesses were forged together, in the mass mergers of the turn of the century, losing their individual identities in the process. Then there were rationalisation and restructuring mergers in the inter-war period (1919-1939) in which subsidiary companies retained their business and management identity. In the spate of post-war mergers, led for example by the IRDC and Salter-Walker, the management of the acquiring company used its financial purchasing power to acquire shares (and thus votes and decision taking authority). Companies had become commodities.

Hayek[26], in an interesting paper written in 1960, about corporate power raised an important point about companies owning and controlling other companies: −

> "I must admit that I have never quite understood the rationale or justification of allowing corporations to have voting rights in other corporations of which they own shares. So far as I can discover, this was never deliberately decided upon in full awareness of all its implications, but came about simply as a result of the conception that, if legal personality was conferred upon the corporation, it was natural to confer upon it all powers which natural persons possessed. But this seems to me by no means a natural or obvious consequence. On the contrary, it turns the institution of property into something quite different from what it is normally supposed to be. The corporation thereby becomes, instead of an association of partners with a common interest, an association of groups whose

> interests may be in strong conflict; and the possibility
> appears of a group who directly own assets amounting
> only to a small fraction of those of the corporation,
> through a pyramiding of holdings, acquiring control of
> assets amounting to a multiple of what they own
> themselves."

Galbraith[27] described the shift of power, from stand-alone, competitive and visible entities, towards a less visible corporate centre, as the development of the "technostructure" in modern corporations. But his image of grey business bureaucrats in head office wielding corporate power may be an over-simplification, given the evidence of corporate direction and control obtained during our studies.

Directors on the main board, not unreasonably, expect to set the overall business direction – its mission and objectives, and to see that appropriate strategies are developed for products and markets, research and product development, labour, investment, finance, acquisition and divestment. They are under no compulsion to make such strategies explicit, indeed, they might well argue that to do so would give away valuable competitive information. The chairman's or the directors' report may be used to report on recent strategic changes, or to indicate longer term aspirations; but, in many companies, such reports hardly enable the members to supervise the board's activities[28].

> Nor may this hidden strategic agenda be unwise. In the
> words of the highly successful Chinese general of the 5th
> century BC, Sun Tze[29] "All men can see the tactics
> whereby I conquer: but what none can see is the strategy
> out of which victory is evolved."

Directors on the boards of wholly owned subsidiary companies are in a special position. As directors, under British law, they bear all the responsibilities of any directors to their company, irrespective of the fact that it has a single shareholder – the parent company: but as managers they are in the managerial command structure within the group, dependent upon their bosses for the allocation of resources, approval of their plans and oversight of their performance. They are also likely to be constrained by group policies and dependent on top management for their remuneration and career prospects.

This special circumstance will have to be recognised in the conceptual framework to be proposed. It is even more significant where the subsidiary company has external, minority shareholders or is an associate company, under managerial control from the group.

Institutional Shareholders' Power

A fourth source of power in matters of corporate governance has recently emerged in some public companies. The classical discussion, that we have already rehearsed, argues that the separation of ownership from management, and the increasing spread and diversity of shareholders, leads to the dilution of ownership power.

As we saw when discussing ownership power, only in cases of extremis, for example when the company seems on the verge of collapse or a contested take-over bid appears, do views tend to polarise, alternative courses of action become apparent, and members' votes begin to count. Otherwise, it appears that members are more passive investors than active participants in the governance process.

Previously this was thought to apply to institutional shareholders as well as individuals. The argument was that the financial institutions – unit trusts, investment funds, pension funds and so on – would rather cut their losses, "voting with their feet", than become involved in attempts to influence corporate governance.

But exceptions have been occurring. Institutional shareholders, even though individually holding only a small proportion of the total equity – 3 to 5% perhaps – have been taking action rather than selling their shares.

In 1978 the Clerical, Medical and General Assurance Society led the fight for S. Pearson Ltd. to take over the remaining 37% of the holding in Pearson Longman, the publishers of Penguin, Ladybird Books, the Financial Times and the Westminster Press.

> The Post Office Staff Superannuation Fund managers, in 1982, raised questions about a series of property deals arranged by Marks & Spencer for the benefit of their directors. Following criticism by the Fund on the lack of disclosure, the Chairman of Marks & Spencer admitted an "omission" to shareholders and sought approval for the transactions, which was duly given[30].
>
> Pension funds, with the backing of the National Association of Pension Funds, challenged the £40m. involvement

of Globe Investment Trust in Mercantile House's take-over of Oppenheimer Holdings, a US stockbroker. The National Coal Board's Pension Fund managers led a committee to examine the basis of the investment policy[31].

The National Association of Pension Funds, led by the Post Office Pension Fund, launched a court action to prevent the payment of a £560,000 golden handshake to Associated Communications Corporation Deputy Chairman, Jack Gill, following his dismissal[32].

More recently, in 1983, a group of institutional investors, coordinated by Prudential Assurance, Robert Fleming (the merchant bank and investment group) and the Post Office Superannuation Fund, pressed for senior management changes at the Rank Organisation, which led to significant changes at board level[33].

In retrospect this latest case may prove to be a turning point in the exercise of oversight and supervision by some institutional investors in public company affairs. When such investors accounted for a relatively small proportion of the total equity in a company, a "hands-off" policy, it can be argued, was appropriate. Like the other shareholders, the institutions had limited knowledge and were able to sell shares when concerned about company prospects.

As the scale of institutional ownership mounted so the ability to exercise informal influence − the "nods and winks" approach − grew. Now, in the larger public companies the institutional shareholder may well dominate. Moreover they have far more information, through better research and closer contacts with the company. They may, thus, be less able to unload shares if company affairs look dubious, because the other institutional investors know too. Consequently the institutions may, increasingly, be forced to take action.

The increase of institutional investment in public companies, at the expense of the private investor has been chronicled in the Wilson Report[34]. An analysis by the Stock Exchange in 1980[35] questioned the rate of change: but the latest data[36] shows that the financial institutions now account for 58% of holdings in large public companies. Of course the number of individual private shareholders is likely to be much higher. (See figures in the next chapter).

What is less clear is how, when, and to what purpose such power is to be exercised? Are the actions taken by institutions over the affairs of a company automatically in the interests of *all* shareholders? By circumventing the meeting of members and taking direct action do the institutions disenfranchise the legitimate rights of other members? Might two institutional investors disagree on the appropriate action to take? What triggers an institutional investor to take action: or more to the point, what prevents them from acting? Furthermore, we have to remember that there is potential competition between the institutions: and not all institutional investors will want to adopt a proactive stance.

Sir Arthur Knight[37] has suggested that institutional investors might set up qualified professional teams to appraise the performance of large companies. In particular they would review the longer term business strategies and report on the financing implications to existing and potential investors. He further argues that many institutions are not equipped at present to undertake such essential monitoring and appraisal.

Here are further issues about the exercise of corporate governance. If institutions are to act, how and to whom are *they* held accountable? It is quite likely that the Pension Funds, in particular, will face growing pressures for performance, in the future.

From this review of the basis of power in the modern company, some essential differences between the private company, the public company and the subsidiary company became apparent. These differences directly affect the exercise of corporate governance, and need to be differentiated in the proposed conceptual framework.

First let us remember the existing categorisation of companies in British law.

The Existing Typology

Over the years company law has recognised few differences between types of company, preferring to treat all alike in their regulation.

For the first fifty years, as we saw in chapter 3, there were no distinctions at all. At the turn of the century, private companies, which were prohibited from inviting public subscription, were distinguished and the legal demands for filing documents, publishing financial information and appointing auditors were reduced[38]. This differentiation was maintained in the 1929 and 1948 Acts but dropped in 1967.

Recent developments in company law have again catego-rised companies, but on two other dimensions.

Firstly, the Companies Act 1980 introduced the Public Limited Company, registered as such and with the words in the name, enabled to invite public subscription for shares[39]. Private companies were distinguished as all those other than public companies. Notice that no distinction was drawn between those run by individual owner-managers, and those run by corporate groups.

Secondly, the Companies Act 1981, reflecting the 4th European Community directive, introduced a size categorisa-tion, principally for limiting the requirements for smaller companies to file detailed accounts. The details of the steps between the small, medium and large company, on turnover, net worth and number of employees were given in reference 16 to chapter 2.

A Green Paper (Cmnd. 7654, September 1979), seeking consultation prior to the 1981 Act made more radical proposals for the classification of companies. These are discussed in Appendix 3.

Thus, the present legal typology for British companies distinguishes public ownership and size, viz:

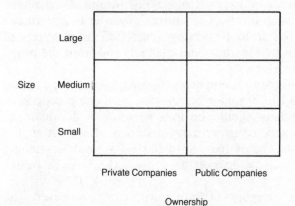

Fig.2 Existing Typology of Companies

A further distinction was introduced by the Companies Act 1980 in new rules on companies and their directors in respect of loans and related transactions. The law distinguished between so-called "relevant companies" — that is every public company and any company in a group where there is a public company — and "non-relevant companies" which are all other companies[40].

It is also worth pointing out that EEC directives are all directed to governance in public companies. Consequently whenever a directive is incorporated into UK law a decision has to be made — are *all* companies to be covered by the legislation uniformly or is the duality between types of company to be increased?

An Alternative Typology

We are now in a position to propose an alternative basis for categorising companies. The typology is founded on the proposition that the underlying sources of power to govern — that is the ability to affect corporate direction and to exercise power over executive actions — should be made explicit for the purposes of governance.

The classical model of the company is essentially a public company; that is one in which outside, non-executive investors are invited to subscribe for shares. In the public company (PLC) today, however, such investors may be private individuals, corporate bodies or financial institutions, such as unit trusts and pension funds. The sources of power to govern can thus be derived from ownership (exercised in meetings of members), through institutional channels and from the board members themselves.

The first category of company proposed mirrors the existing definition of a PLC[39] under British law, with one exception — no other company should be in a position to dominate its affairs. *The public company* may invite investment from the public, and its shares may be listed on a stock exchange, traded on an unlisted market or, outside the UK, be bearer bonds.

Under this category of public company, however, the methods of governance must recognise the reality and diversity of source from which power can be derived. Although many PLC's will be vast corporations, it should be remembered that others can be relatively small, with only a few investors.

Under British company law, all companies that are not

public companies are private companies. But this is too broad a classification for our purposes.

The next category to be proposed is *the proprietary company* – a definition not known to UK law at present. In the proprietary company investors, directors and top management would be synonymous. It is the owner(s) who runs and controls the business. This is the owner-managed entrepreneurial enterprise; and there are some hundreds of thousands of them incorporated in Britain.

The definition of a proprietary company, suggested here, has three elements: –

1. the ownership, governance and top management are, effectively, in the same hands; a single person could form such a company;
2. members should be limited (to, say, 8 or 10) – beyond that number the company acquires wider dimensions which raises other implications for governance;
3. no corporate body may be a member. The shares must be in the hands of individuals – and they must exercise governance.

If venture capital was injected into a proprietary company it would become a private company in the definition adopted here.

There are, of course, parallels with the close company definition adopted for tax purposes in Britain: any company that is owner-directed might find the Inland Revenue reserving the right to direct that distributions be made, if the company is retaining profits (and paying lower corporation taxes) solely for the purposes of reducing the owner's income tax liabilities, although the close company rules were relaxed in the 1980 Finance Act.

In chapter 4 we discussed similar proposals for distinguishing owner-managed firms. In proposing a new form of incorporation for small firms, the consultative Green Paper[41] suggested four reasons why governance under the existing company law might be regarded as inappropriate: –

1. The law requires a formal distinction between members and directors. In the owner-managed firm this is asking people to be schizophrenic.
2. Members and directors are required to hold meetings in each capacity. When they are the same people this is farcical.

3. Resolutions have to be formally passed, minuted and, where necessary, registered. The proceedings are to protect members' interests against dominating executive directors. In the owner-managed firm it is tantamount to protecting the owner from himself.
4. Ordinary special and extraordinary resolutions have to be adopted at meetings for which the prescribed period of notice is given or waived. Where the owners are also the managers they may be presumed to be aware of company affairs and not need such statutory protection.

There are various proposals for alternative forms of incorporation described in chapter 4. The classification suggested here is close to that of the CCAB[42] in 1981. In chapter 14 further proposals will be made for the related limitation of liability, disclosure requirements, audit and other regulatory matters for the proprietary company.

The third proposed category is that of *the subordinate company*. This is any company in which direction and control can be exercised by another company. All companies in a group whose accounts are required to be consolidated into those of a holding company[43], would, de facto, be subordinate companies.

Such a categorisation of companies into those able to dominate the affair of dependent companies is not, currently, recognised in UK law, but is the underlying concept of the European Community's 9th directive. Under this directive[44] one undertaking is presumed to be dominated by another where that concern directly or indirectly:

a) holds the major part of the undertaking's subscribed capital,

or b) controls a majority of the voting rights attaching to the shares in the undertaking,

or c) is in a position to appoint at least half of the members of the administrative, management or supervisory body of the undertaking, provided that those members have the majority of the voting rights.

"Where two or more undertakings are in a position to jointly exercise, directly or indirectly, a dominant influence over another undertaking, each of the first mentioned shall be considered to be a dominant undertaking and the latter to be a dependent undertaking."[45]

The basis of power in the subordinate company is managerial power, backed by the whole ownership of a subsidiary company, partial ownership with outside minority shareholders or an associate holding which enables the company to determine governance.

A subordinate company could have considerable autonomy. The directors might have authority, delegated to them by the dominant company, for the formulation of strategy, acquisition of subsidiaries, and raising of funds. But if a member company has the power to appoint and remove the directors, or to set policies for the determination of direction and supervision, then it has the power base to dominate. In such cases, even though delegated considerable authority, the company dominated would be a subordinate company.

A subordinate company may be dominated by a public company, a proprietary company or a private company – which is the final category to be defined. See figure 3.

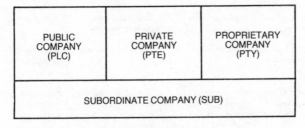

PUBLIC COMPANY (PLC)	PRIVATE COMPANY (PTE)	PROPRIETARY COMPANY (PTY)
SUBORDINATE COMPANY (SUB)		

Fig. 3   Proposed typology of companies – by basis of power

Private companies for the purposes of our definition, are those which do not (and by law cannot) invite public subscription for shares, are not dominated by another company, and yet are not proprietary companies. In other words they are those companies owned by individuals and/or corporate bodies, which are not themselves subordinate to another company, and where some separation of ownership from management and direction has occurred.

The basis of power in a private company will be ownership power and the power of the corporate directors. Although institutional investors may acquire shares in private companies (and indeed are increasingly so doing as venture capital is invested in high technology ventures) the vehicle for exercising power is through the members' meeting or membership of the board rather than institutional power.

For convenience in the remainder of this book each type of company will be designated: —

Public company	–	PLC
Private company	–	PTE
Proprietary company	–	PTY
Subordinate company	–	SUB

Table 1 attempts to summarise the distinguishing features. Later we will consider how each is to be governed.

PLC	PTY	SUB	PTE
Public invitation to invest	Owner-managed	Wholly or partly owned subsidiary or associate company	Public invitation forbidden
Inside and outside investors – individuals – corporate bodies – financial institutions	Inside executive investors only – individuals No corporate bodies No financial institutions		Inside and outside investors – individuals – corporate bodies – financial institutions
No domination by another company	No domination	Dominated by another company	No domination
Minimum of 2 members, probably many	1 – 10 members	1 or more members	Minimum of 2 members
Separation of owners from management	No separation between owners, directors and managers	Dominant company executives exercise management oversight with executive board members	Some separation of owners from management

Table 1   Principal features in the different types of proposed corporate entity

Summary

The existing conceptual framework for the corporation is rooted in nineteenth-century thinking and treats ownership as the basis of power. We saw, however, that in the modern company power could derive from ownership, the incumbent members of a corporate board, management in a group of companies and financial institutions.

An alternative conceptual framework for the corporation was proposed, derived from the reality of the power base existing in each case.

This framework differentiated the public company (PLC) with external non-executive investors and no domination by another company; the subordinate company (SUB) which was in a position to be dominated by another holding or associated company; the private company (PTE) in which there was no public investment, no subordination to other companies, but some separation between owners and managers; and the proprietary company (PTY) in which the owners were the managers and no limited company was a member.

The fundamental differences in ownership patterns, sources of power, and, thus, processes of governance are emphasised by this four part classification.

The typology is not an attempt to regiment the means by which companies are governed. On the contrary, it facilitates the different, flexible and adaptable solutions to corporate organisation that typifies UK practice, within a framework that would enable legitimate and proper governance.

Part 2 –
Alternative Ideas on Governance

Chapter 7

The Reality of Corporate Power
– understanding the constraints

Having developed a simple typology for differentiating companies, we use it, in this chapter to explore the limits of corporate power in the different types of company. We consider the extent to which those directing company affairs are free to make things happen; and how countervailing checks and balances operate in practice.

The legitimacy of the modern corporation and the use of power by those who control its activities are issues at the heart of our studies.

On the one hand people like Nader and Green[1] believe:

"We must redesign the law to keep up with the economic and political evolution of giant corporations, which are tantamount to private governments. One definition of "government" would be an entity that can tax, coerce or even take life.....

They (giant corporations) can spend decisive amounts in elections to determine which towns thrive and which gather cobwebs, corrupt or help overthrow foreign governments, develop technology that takes lives or saves lives.....

.....The economic government (giant corporations) is largely unaccountable to its constituencies – shareholders, workers, consumers, local communities, taxpayers, small businesses, future generations."

On the other there are those who argue that market forces will see fair play, as Millstein & Katsch[2] point out.

"This strident and partisan concept of substantially unrestrained corporate power and discretion is, in a more moderate form, among the most important fundamental public concerns with large corporations. However expressed, there appears to be widespread fear that corporate managers have significant unrestrained discretion to make critical choices regarding a myriad of economic, social and political issues touching the lives of every citizen — including, to name but a few: what products and services to offer; what prices to charge; whether to invest in existing lines of business, to build new lines or buy out existing companies; where to locate corporate headquarters and new facilities; what plants to open and close; whether to adopt measures to protect the environment and conserve energy; whether to adopt worker benefit, safety and health programs; which philanthropic endeavours to favour; and so on.

At issue ultimately is whether the nation, in responding to these concerns, will essentially continue its traditional preference for pluralism. Will it accept larger private corporate size as it does larger governments and seek only to adjust the corporation's relationship to society where absolutely necessary? Or will it, instead, accelerate the decline of pluralism either by relegating, or by greater responsibility in all areas to government, or by requiring fundamental changes in the internal government structure of our major corporations? Or will the nation adopt some combination of the above courses of action?"

We have to recognise that there are many perspectives on companies; and no universally accepted view from which to understand their activities. Consequently we begin this chapter with an examination of some of the alternatives. For convenience these have been grouped into five different insights, or bodies of knowledge: though there are few clear cut boundaries.

These viewpoints are:

- Legal
- Normative and descriptive
- Rational and economic
- Organisational
- Socio/political

Just as different spotlights can cast moving and overlapping circles of light on a stage, so there are many contributions to understanding board level activities. Yet none completely illuminate the action. Obviously in this book we can only hint at the breadth of the literature in these fields.

After exploring the five bodies of knowledge briefly we develop a framework for considering the checks and balances on corporate power and contrast control in the different types of company.

The Legal Perspective

A joint-stock, limited liability company is first and foremost a legal entity. Not surprisingly the literature of corporate jurisprudence is voluminous. But, principally, its orientation is explanatory – describing content and application of statute and case[3].

The classical ideas of the company – an autonomous legal entity, shareholders with liability limited, ownership the basis of power, authority with the board elected by the members, and regulation under the Companies Acts – which lie at the heart of the legal concept, are seldom made explicit. Moreover, they owe more to nineteenth-century notions of entrepreneurial capitalism than to modern business reality.

As Hadden[4] puts it

"British company law is not unworkable, but it is tied to a conception of capitalism which has been discarded by all but the most ardent free market economists. It has also ceased to reflect the realities of the commercial and industrial world."

But rigorous attempts to explain, question or reformulate the underlying philosophical assumptions about the corporate concept have been few, although the divergence of the reality of board level activity from the legal image has been rehearsed by Harvard Business School, Professor Mace[5]: –

".....boards do provide a source of advice and counsel to the president. Those interviewed – company presidents as well as outside directors – perceived the role of outside directors to be largely advisory and not decision-making."

"Also it was found that in most companies the boards of directors serve as some sort of discipline for the management – the president as well as those in subordinate positions. Company presidents and their associates know that periodically they are required to appear before the board of directors and to account for their stewardship of the company's operations since the last reporting date."

"Almost all the executives interviewed stated that the concept of accountability to a board, even boards composed of the most understanding and sympathetic friends, provided an important discipline for the organisation."

"It was found also that most boards of directors exercise a decision-making power only in the event of a crisis such as the sudden death or disability of the president."

"The other crisis situation where boards of directors fulfil a decision-making role is where the profitability of the enterprise declines steadily, and mounting and persuasive evidence suggests to the board that the president must be replaced as chief executive officer."

"It was found that boards of directors of most companies do not do an effective job in evaluating, appraising, and measuring the company president until the financial and other results are so dismal that some remedial action is forced upon the board."

We must, of course, exercise care in relating American research experience to UK situations. But Pahl & Winkler[6] support this thesis, and also draw a useful distinction between the board as an executive functioning organ and as a legitimising, proforma one.

Constitutionally a company is incorporated to carry out the objectives in its Memorandum of Association for the economic benefit of its members. The primary focus of the Companies Acts is the regulation of the relationships between the company and its members. For example, the major sections of the Companies Act 1948 cover incorporation, share capital, registration of charges, meetings and procedures, accounts audit and annual return, the duties of directors and winding up.

Company law does not attempt to regulate the means by which business decisions are taken. The enterprise has a duality being both a corporation under company law and a business, a means of organising production and markets under contract, labour, monopoly and other laws.

The overriding purpose of the company, under company law, is the longer term, profitable growth of the enterprise for the benefit of the shareholders. Apart from the affirmation that directors have a duty to take the interests of employees in general into account on their decisions (section 46 Companies Act 1980), company law does not deliberate on the rights of other parties whose interests might be affected, for good or bad, by corporate decisions.

The Bullock Committee[7] confirmed that

"..... interests of other groups, like employees, creditors and customers (are relevant) only insofar as they coincide with those of the shareholder."

John Fidler[8], in his important work on the British business elite and their attitudes to class, status and power, commented

"Many top directors now attempt to conceptualise the

objectives that they have for the firm in a way which reconciles the long term interests of all principal groups associated with it. Although..... I found no deviation from the traditional goals of capitalism."

Constitutionally the company, that is the members voting together, exercise the ultimate powers of the company. It has been widely recognised in the literature that it is a "cumbersome piece of machinery to run day to day administration"[9].

Consequently most Articles of Association provide for a board to direct the company. A proforma set of Articles is provided in Table A of the Companies Act 1948; and states that "the business of the company shall be managed by the directors". However Gower[9] confirms the legal perspective

"The shift of power from the general meeting to the board has received a considerable measure of legal recognition, but this is hardly true of the further shift from the board to the management. The latter is regarded by law as fully answerable to, and controlled by, the board."

The legal viewpoint sees the nature of the company and the role and responsibilities of its directors in terms of current interpretation of company law. Such law, however, has derived from classical ideas of the company in society: it often fails to reflect the complexity of modern business and ignores many of the issues that face directors as they undertake their task.

A Normative and Descriptive View

Contrasting with the legal angle, those who write from a normative and descriptive perspective set out to explain the directors' task, basing their opinions on experience drawn from practice. Their orientation is often exhortatory and advisory, with suggestions for improving performance and normative, with recommendations about the way directors should behave under given circumstances.

Some of these works, being written by those with significant experience in the boardroom or in advising directors, have added important case material and commentary to the, relatively sparse, stock of knowledge on board matters[10].

Serious corporate history, written by the social and economic historian, can also throw light on the development of corporations and their changing strategies, top level structures and styles of direction[11]. The knowledge base has also been widened by contributions from those personally responsible for direction in specific companies. Obviously, being written by those involved in and, often responsible for, the developments described, such works lack the objectivity of independence: the compensatory benefit is the personal knowledge, insights and perceptions of a participation in the action.

A classical example would be Sloan's[12] book in which he describes the creation of the General Motors Group from separate, entrepreneurially led, companies and the development of a divisional structure with a specific management style. Drucker[13] provides relevant commentary on Sloan's experience whilst Wright[14] paints a much less eulogistic picture of General Motors with divisional executives dissatisfied with head office domination.

The Rational and Economic Schools of Thought

Much of the literature discussed thus far and the conventional wisdom in the field of corporate governance tend to assume rationality in business behaviour. The prerogative to direct the enterprise, whether as an entrepreneur or as a member of the top management peer group is unquestioned. Activities can be planned, actions monitored and controlled, people organised, motivated and managed and the parts of the enterprise coordinated by those directing the company.

The Watkinson Committee of the CBI, writing on the responsibilities of the British public company[15] typified this perspective

> "The main spring of the enterprise system is striving for profit. Profit is a surplus fund that remains after all proper commitments have been met. It is neither a magic word nor a dirty one, it should be regarded as the principal yardstick by which to judge the success or failure of a company. In the long run only a profitable company can obtain funds from the capital market and provide a reliable source for the supply of goods and services for its customers, stable employment, and profitable business for its suppliers."

Those who write from the normative and descriptive viewpoint usually assume rationality in corporate decision making and a unitary chain of command and authority through which they are implemented.

Similar assumptions are made in the prescriptive theories of economics. The freedom and ability of those directing the firm to exercise rational choices in the allocation of scarce resources is treated as self-evident; rational means applying economic criteria. Echoes of Adam Smith[16] are found underpinning modern economic thinking.

"The corporation's raison d'etre is the efficient provision of useful needed goods and services — spurred by the profits essential to produce and provide them". Millstein & Katsch[17].

Critics of economic rationality, such as Simon[18] point out the lack of empiricism and that the development of such "deductive theories require little contact with empirical data once the underlying assumptions are accepted". Furthermore Simon observes that the rational perspective "makes strong assumptions about human behaviour without performing the hard task of observing people".

The assumption of rationality also presupposes that the decision-maker's authority is unassailed. As Fox[19] argues — only insofar as the behaviour of other organisational participants is congruent with the goals of the decision maker is the situation rational. Critics of rationality in economic theory such as March & Simon[20] and Cyert & March[21] have argued that reality of business decision-making involves decision-making under uncertainty and recognising specific constraints. As a result the objectives and a driving force is not a single profit goal to be optimised in the long term but a process of satisfying a range of, potentially conflicting, interests, including a comfortable life for the decision-maker.

An Organisational View

Studies of bureaucracy stemming from Weber[22] have drawn attention to the administrative situation in large organisations. Selznick[23] suggests that the classical minded pursuit of profit may become subordinated to the attainment of efficiency in the bureaucratic organisation. The controlling of people and the creation of an efficient structure become ends in themselves. This reflects Bagehot's[24] reflection on the English constitution that "bureaucrats will care more for the routine than for results". Consequently the focus of board attention can readily turn to running and supervising internal organisation than involvement with longer term strategy and coping with external issues, opportunities and threats[25].

Writers on strategy formulation however – Ansoff[26], Argenti[27] and Andrews[28] – tend to assume a rational attitude for the directors who attempt to maximise the long term return on resources employed in the business.

The importance of the board accepting a responsibility in strategy formulation has been recognised by many writers, Peters & Waterman[29], Grinyer & Spender[30] and others. Andrews[31] argues that directors should play an active part in determining the future direction and character of their companies. The stimulation of fresh thinking, prevention of inertia and generation of a climate where real alternatives are articulated and business values shaped, is a leadership role for the board.

The literature on organisation theory has many pertinent insights into the tasks of direction. Chandler[32] points to the link between formulation of strategy and the development of structure, and illustrates how, if the structure does not match the strategic positions, boards can be drawn into operational matters at the expense of policy issues. Burns & Stalker[33] show the significance of management style and the rate of change in the organisation's evolution. Mintzberg[34] challenges the concept of the organisation chart arguing that "while most organisations continue to find it indispensable many organisational theorists reject it as an inadequate description of what really takes place inside the organisation (with) important power and communication relationships that are not put down on paper". His attempts to describe organisations do recognise a group of people able to exercise power around the apex of an organisation, rather than a single person at the top of a pyramid.

In the complex organisation the interdependencies between strategy formulation, organisation structure and management style are reinforced by the corporate systems and procedures. For example, Solomons[35] highlights divisional performance measures and the problems of cost allocation and transfer pricing, showing the direct relationship between organisation structure and the information needed at top management level for its operation.

The Socio/Political School of Thought

The fundamental challenges to the rationalised ideology is

made by those who see the corporation in a pluralistic world — interest groups, with power to influence corporate direction, exist both inside the company and in its external environment. Consequently the strategic direction of the company is not solely in the directors' hands. Moreover the boundaries of the corporation are no longer simple, moving transiently, between those interest groups able to bring influence to bear and exercise power.

The role of directors in monitoring and responding to the external environment has been emphasised — Aguilar[36] — whilst Pfeffer[37] and Selznick[38] go further and emphasise a need to take action to influence that environment positively. As Pfeffer[39] says "the power (of the public company) is not a managing body but exists to control management as well as being 'an instrument to deal with the organisation's external environment'".

In 1975 a discussion paper was published for comment by the Accounting Standards Steering Committee (of the main professional accounting bodies in the UK). It argued that all economic entities should recognise their pluralistic situation and respond by accepting a responsibility to disclose information to interests affected by its decisions[41].

The call for companies to accept a wider "social responsibility" to stakeholders, beyond the members, has been widely pursued in the literature, in Europe mainly in relation to participation by employees[41], and in the United States by stakeholder groups such as consumers[42] or various minority interest groups.

Mitroff[43] discusses how complex interrelationships between internal and external stakeholders affect managerial decision-making and planning. His stakeholder list includes internal managers, stockholders, trade unions, holding companies and saboteurs.

Elsewhere in the literature the legitimacy of corporate direction has come under question. Useem[44] talks of a corporate élite and the concentration of power, and attention has been drawn elsewhere to possible dominations of companies by financial interests and of interlocking directorships[45].

However to ascribe beliefs and expectations about corporate behaviour to society may be questionable. The existence of vocal interest groups does not automatically mirror the views of society as a whole. The difficulty is in providing objective criteria for determining what is important for the responsibility of corporations and what is not.

Also, some socio/political thinkers assume that the organisation reality is the outcome of a conflict resulting in consensus between the individuals and groups involved. This is only feasible if sufficient power can be mobilised and committed to the respective demands. The existence of social order does not in itself guarantee that legitimate social interests have not been ignored and indeed could reflect a world of inequality and injustice.

> "By focusing on the influence of business in particular policy disputes, pluralists have tended to pay insufficient attention both to the boundaries of corporate political influence and to the processes by which political agendas themselves are formed[46]."

Then there are those who adopt, so called, agency theory, seeing the interactions between people *within* an organisation as a set of contractual relationships between agents and principals. Governance involves a negotiated agreement with all those who can exercise power, internal and external. Therefore, let us identify, in broad terms, who they might be.

Constraints and Balances in Corporate Power

The efficient market and rational decision theories argue from the premise that, in the longer term at least, the invisible hands of the market lead to efficient use of resources and the satisfaction of people's needs; with knowledgeable and informed decision-takers making logical, rational choices.

But even those who take such an arms-length, economic and rational view recognise that checks and balances are necessary, in the shorter term, to mitigate hardship, reduce turbulence and respond to human greed and fallibility. Consequently societies create rules and laws to regulate corporate behaviour; and institutional mechanisms are developed to apply self-regulation in lieu of state regulation.

In capitalist society the legitimacy of corporate business enterprise is the efficient provision of goods and services needed by the society, fuelled by the creation of surpluses to reward the investor and provide for reinvestment and growth.

But, as the socio/political viewpoint recognises, at the heart of every enterprise are people. People with their own drives, ambitions and needs. It is such people who create businesses and give companies their stimulus. People, not markets, make companies. Companies are the vehicles by which *their* needs are met.

With this background we can create a very simple model of the constraints and balances in corporate power.

Fig. 1 Constraints and balances in corporate power

NB: In all the diagrams of corporate power, the respective size of the slice of power is not intended to indicate its potential weight or significance.

The external factors that influence the enterprise stem from the market place, self-regulatory mechanisms and demands of society. Then we recognise the essential driving force at the centre of the business, whether this be a single entrepreneur, a dominant leader in a management team, a chief executive, a chairman, a group of executives, a board of directors or even a cabal.

We can now apply this basic model to the different types of company, to see the potential for power in practice.

Control of the Company – 1. The PTY

In the proprietary company the owner-manager is at the heart of the enterprise (see figure 2). The company is his, and his decisions dominate. Of course, in some proprietary companies there may be more than one owner-manager; but in such cases the relationship between them is absolutely crucial. The self-regulatory factors are very much a matter of self-control.

It is the market factors, the business reality, which are likely to provide the greatest constraints to uninhibited exploitation of the company. In essence the business must buy goods and services, add value, and sell them at an overall profit. It is a world in which suppliers, with the terms they can demand, customers with their choices, and competitors with their activities in pricing and product, can place highly challenging constraints on the company.

Bankers, and other sources of finance, can also be part of the mechanism of constraints and balances on the PTY, from a business and market standpoint.

In the sector of societal factors, the PTY is, of course, subject to company law like every other incorporated entity.

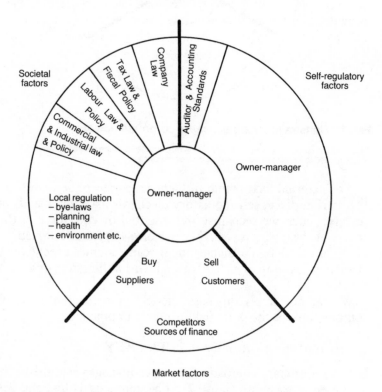

Fig.2   Constraints and balances to power in the PTY

But, apart from the publishing requirements[47] which have been reduced by the 1981 Companies Act, company law is unlikely to place significant constraints on company behaviour. Because the owner wields voting power he is responsible predominantly to himself.

The important exception is the legal requirement to appoint an approved auditor and to file accounts on which the auditor has reported. Such accounts also fall into the net of accounting standards, having to comply with the standards set by the Accounting Standards Committee of the Consultative Committee of Accountancy Bodies. Because the influence of auditor and accounting standards is principally an exhortatory matter, rather than a requirement of company law, it is shown in the self-regulatory sector. We shall discuss the necessity for such controls in the proprietary company further. Obviously the rights of creditors must be recognised and protected.

Tax laws, including VAT as well as Corporation Tax, provide another legal constraint; as do labour laws and the entire range of commercial and industrial legislation. Local regulations, too, affect the degrees of freedom over matters such as planning consents, health and safety, environmental controls and so on.

Control of the Company – 2. The PTE

The private company may not invite public subscription, may be of any size, sometimes very large with its own group of companies; able to have other companies as shareholders, provided that they are not able to dominate its governance; and with shareholdings spread beyond the people who are directing the company. The dominance of the owner-manager over corporate governance has been diluted.

In the PTE, power at the heart of the company may, of course, still be wielded by a single, dominant individual. But leadership over corporate affairs could be more widely exercised by a board of directors, some of whom may have minimal or no shareholdings; senior managers, too, may have considerable authority. This shift from the dominance of the owner-manager is shown in figure 3.

Shareholders, in the PTE, no longer automatically run the business as in the PTY. Their power is exercised through the annual general meeting and the other processes of the law giving rights to members. They have the opportunity to vote on the appointment of directors and the auditors, and to receive director's reports and accounts on the state of the company's affairs.

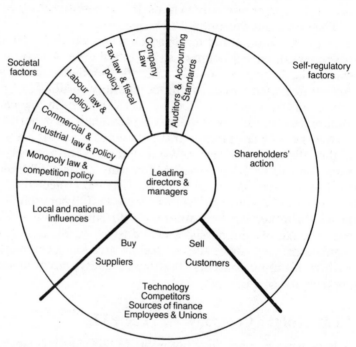

Fig. 3   Constraints and balances to power in the PTE

In the case of the owners of large shareholdings in a private company, personal contact with members of the board may exercise considerable influence over corporate affairs.

In the market place the PTE may have a large influence. Consequently, unlike the PTY, constraints on its power may come from monopoly control and anti-trust legislation enacted around the world from which it generates its revenues. Where its impact is significant in other fields, for example environmental pollution or ecology, product safety, selling or pricing methods and so on, the company could also find itself constrained by lobbying forces, using pressures beyond those available directly from the law.

As the company becomes larger and more diverse, the potential role of employees and their union representatives in governance may emerge. This can take many forms. On the one hand management may take the initiative to disclose information to employees and encourage commitment and identification with the company and its business. Formal channels of representation, through works councils and similar vehicles may be created, to supplement the more informal links through the management chain. The collective bargaining process with the employees' unions may also have an effect on corporate governance, if issues of corporate strategy and direction, such as relocation or the closure of factories, become significant.

In the German model of the larger company, codetermination of decisions affecting the future of the company leads to employee representatives on the supervisory board, as proposed in the original draft 5th directive. A similar attempt to depict the company as a joint venture between labour and capital is seen in the Bullock Report[48] proposal for worker representatives on the unitary board.

Control of the Company – 3. The PLC

The public company is the most heavily constrained in the exercise of corporate power: not unreasonably, since members of the public and institutions external to the company are being invited to invest.

The checks and balances of business and market place, and other external societal factors, that feature in the areas around the world in which the company operates, affect the PLC very much as the larger PTE. The details are, therefore, not further elaborated here. Figure 4 shows these areas in general terms. For further discussion on the government and the negotiated environment in Britain see Thomas[49] and Crouch[50].

It is in the area of stock market regulation and the protection of investor interests that the predominant difference with the PTE lies. In the UK considerable emphasis is placed on the self-regulation of the financial institutions. Consequently the stock exchange, rather than the law, exerts control over the regulation of issuing, buying and selling shares in companies.

PLC's traded on the stock exchange in London and the

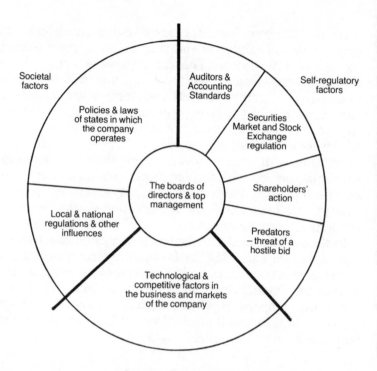

Business & Market factors

Fig. 4 Constraints and balances to power in the PLC

provinces must comply with the requirements of the listing agreement, and the Yellow Book of regulations; and be subject to the rules of the Takeover Panel and the oversight of the Council for the Securities Industry[51].

In the stock exchanges of Europe there is tighter regulation imposed by statute, whilst in the United States a middle road is steered between self and state regulation by a Federal Agency, the Securities and Exchange Commission.

The ability of external shareholders to influence corporate governance is the conceptual soul of the corporate idea; but is, in practice, an unpredictable element.

On the one hand shareholders in public companies can act as relatively remote investors, exercising few, if any, rights as members, and "voting with their feet" if dissatisfied. This tendency, with the effective power it bestows de facto on the incumbent board, has been widely discussed.

On the other hand the potential power, if the forces of the

membership are mustered by a contentious issue or a ginger group, to influence policy and to change direction and directors lies with the members acting together.

The size and structure of the membership in PLC's are also quite varied. In the smaller PLC, particularly those floated on the Unlisted Securities Market, the outside shareholding may be in a minority, with the founder or incumbent directors holding the voting power. In other cases one or a few shareholders may hold large blocks of shares and, in effect, influence or control the voting in members' meetings. Such members are able to exercise power over governance should they wish.

In the top 1000 quoted companies in the UK the number of members is quite varied. ICI has most shareholders and the holdings of the top 10 UK PLC's is shown in table 1. The top 50 UK companies have 4.6 million shareholders and ICI, thus, has nearly 10% of the total.

	Ordinary Shareholders
ICI	421,146
Shell Transport	362,000
BP	268,150
Marks & Spencer	237,303
Imperial Group	154,837
GEC	150,000
European Ferries	135,472
BAT	130,000
Barclays Bank	119,036
Distillers	114,000

Table 1   Number of shareholders, top 10 quoted companies (UK)

Source: Stock Exchange Fact Book, 1983.

A minor trend in recent years to encourage employee shareholdings and to give price and service incentives to shareholders who use company services, (as in European Ferries), has tended to increase the number of small holdings in such companies.

But a most significant development in recent years has been the growing proportion of shares held by financial institutions. Table 2 summarises research by the Stock Exchange and others. Notice that the proportion of shares held by individuals has fallen from 54% to 28% in less than twenty years, whilst that by the institutions has grown from 30% to 58%. The pension funds now hold over a quarter of all shares by value.

The implications of this trend for governance are important if the financial institutions continue the tendency, discussed in chapter 6, to take unilateral action to influence board actions, supplementing and supplanting the power of the members' meetings.

If this development continues, with the institutions acquiring ever increasing proportions of holdings, their power base by the end of the century will be dominant and potentially narrow. As The Times has commented[52] a continuation of present trends would mean the end of private direct investors by 2000[53].

	1963	1969	1975	1981
Persons	54.0	47.4	37.5	28.2
Financial Institutions				
Banks	1.3	1.7	0.7	0.3
Insurance Companies	10.0	12.2	15.9	20.5
Pension Funds	6.4	9.0	16.8	26.7
Unit Trusts	1.3	2.9	4.1	3.6
Investment Trusts	11.3	10.1	10.5	6.8
	30.3	35.9	48.0	57.9
Others				
Charities	2.1	2.1	2.3	2.2
Other Companies	5.1	5.4	3.0	5.1
Public Sector	1.5	2.6	3.6	3.0
Overseas Sector	7.0	6.6	5.6	3.6
	15.7	16.7	14.5	13.9
	%	%	%	%
	100.0	100.0	100.0	100.0

Table 2   Distribution of shareholdings between beneficial owners (%)
Sample size: 222 UK quoted companies

Sources: The Stock Exchange Survey of Share Ownership: 1983 The Department of Applied Economics, Cambridge: from 1957 Department of Industry & Central Statistical Office: 1975

N.B.   Despite the fall in the percentage of ordinary shares held by individuals the money value of such holdings in 1981 is estimated at £28.0bn compared with £14.9bn in 1963.

Finally it should be observed that in the PLC, in which the incumbent board cannot rely on or dominate a majority of votes of the members, the threat of a predator making an unwelcome take-over bid is a motivating factor in corporate governance. Of course, the potential loss of power or even loss of office is likely to be unwelcome to the existing individual directors: the bid may not be unwelcome to the shareholders. This challenge has been one of the most significant aspects of exercising power in recent years over corporate governance.

Control of the Company – 4. The SUB

Finally we come to the company in a group, dominated by another company – the subordinate company. Governance in SUB's is the least well chronicled aspect of corporate control. In law the SUB is simply a private company or, rarely, a public company which happens to have another company with a majority holding or able to exercise effective control. A SUB, by our definition, has another company able to dominate its processes of governance.

Top management in the SUB are dependent on the managerial chain of command (fig. 5) for their own appraisal,

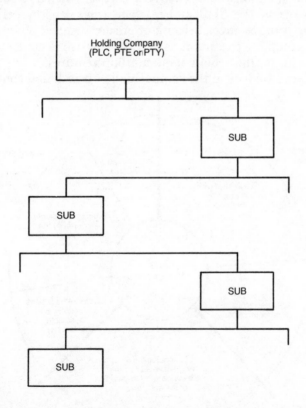

Fig. 5 The SUB in the group's organisation hierarchy

rewards and promotion, and consequently their decisions are influenced by the organisational hierarchy. A SUB may be dominated by a PLC, a PTE or, more rarely, a PTY.

In a wholly-owned subsidiary the principal strategic decisions, the allocation of group resources and the supervision
and control functions may, effectively, be carried out higher in
the organisational charge. Despite their de jure responsibility
for governance of the SUB, its board are, de facto, subject to
the decisions of higher management, who have the ultimate
sanction of hiring and firing.

When there are minority interests in the ownership of a
SUB, or the SUB is jointly owned by two or more companies,
the board of the SUB has to find a compromise solution to
governance that satisfies the various partners. This can lead to
difficult situations, particularly where a holding company
want to treat the SUB at less than arm's length, perhaps
starving it of resources because of greater demands elsewhere
in the group, or treating it as a "cash cow" to generate short
term funds for the benefit of other group ventures.

In Part 3 we look at the composition of boards and consider

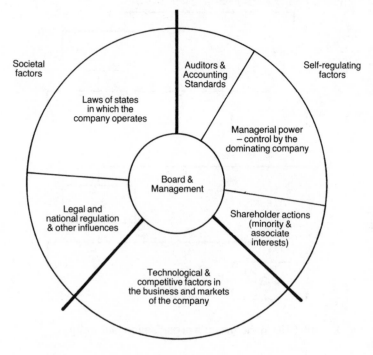

Business & Market factors

Fig. 6 Constraints and balances to power in the SUB

the role of the non-executive and the independent director on the boards of SUB's. The importance of protecting the rights of minority and associate interests in the SUB are shown in figure 6, with their legitimate shareholder power attempting to balance the managerial power of the dominant company. In chapter 9 we shall also be looking at the position of the SUB in terms of the draft 9th directive.

Conclusions

In this chapter we have looked at different perspectives on the governance of the corporation in society and identified five predominant viewpoints: –
- The legal view
- The normative and descriptive views
- The rational and economic views
- The organisational views
and ● The socio/political perspective

Constraints and balances to the exercise of corporate power were then considered and differentiated for the four major types of company, proprietary, private, public and subordinate.

Chapter 8

Accountability, Liability and Regulation
– reappraising some basic concepts

In the last chapter we saw how each different type of company existed in an environment of countervailing power and identified the various checks and balances. A key element in any schema of governance is the idea of accountability, which we consider in this chapter. It will be argued that there is confusion, both in the minds of executives and the academic literature, between the notions of accountability, disclosure and social responsibility. A precise view is taken of the duty to be accountable, based on the power to demand accountability[1].

Corporate Accountability – Its Significance

In the private sector, since the nineteenth-century, companies have replaced all other forms of business organisation as the predominant vehicle for investment, product innovation, employment and the satisfaction of needs through the market place. The way in which companies are directed, run, controlled and held accountable is an important element in social and economic policy. Yet the means by which that accountability is exercised has been brought, increasingly, into doubt.

The traditional idea of the company, of course, saw it as a self-regulating entity. Directors, appointed by (and often from) the shareholding members, were accountable to those members. Limited liability was granted for relatively few demands for accountability except the recognition of the principle. The prerogative to manage and the legitimacy of the enterprise were unassailed.

But we have already rehearsed various reasons for challenging the traditional perspectives, viz:

- The *profusion* of different types of company now incorporated raises different questions about their regulation, oversight and control[2].

- The Gladstonian idea of the corporation did not envisage one company owning another. Today the *complexity* of corporate groups can be immense[3]. Not only can groups be multi-product, multi-plant and multi-national, with many levels of wholly owned subsidiaries, there can be partially owned subsidiaries and associates with outside, equity interests, interrelated networks of cross-holdings, joint ventures bridging otherwise competing companies, and federations of companies, sometimes in complex coalitions with governments.
- The *separation* between ownership and management in the public company has been amplified by the significance of institutional investors[4].
- A stream of *critical reports*, from Department of Trade Inspectors, which are concerned about the interests of shareholders (occasionally depositors), basing their conclusions on the classical model of the company[5].
- The validity of *shareholder democracy* in the public company with diverse holdings has also been questioned[6], with shareholders' apparent lack of interest in anything other than investment performance and the potential for their shares. Annual meetings, attended by a minute proportion of the members, are not, it is argued, an appropriate mechanism for exercising accountability.
- In more general terms, the unitary board reflected a unitary world: some believe this has been replaced by one of *increasing pluralism*[7].
- *Changing social expectations* have also been cited as a reason for rethinking accountability. Bullock[8] expressed the view thus:

"There has been a growing recognition of the influence of (large) companies on many aspects of people's lives at home as well as at work. As companies have grown in size and complexity, they have also tended to become remote from the communities in which they operate and from the people whom they employ. Major decisions about the nature of a company's or plant's organisation, affecting closely the future of the local community or the jobs of the employees, may often be taken far away from the site by the directors of a parent or holding company, sometimes by the management of a parent company overseas."

> "The power and complexity of the industrial enterprise and the remoteness of decision-making have led to demands for large companies to be more responsible to the needs of society in general and of their employees in particular."

The 1977 Green Paper[9] on the conduct of directors spoke of "an increasing public interest" in corporate affairs. Other commentators have written as though the large corporation was a public domain: for example, Professor Flint[10] writing in response to a Corporate Policy Group working paper commented

> "In my thinking about the evolving social function of the audit, I have canvassed the idea that the prospect is for all organisations, including unincorporated bodies, above a certain size judged either by number of employees or economic resources, to be required to have an audit to demonstrate their accountability and social legitimacy".

● The European Commission has also been concerned about the apparent power of transnational firms to affect the interests of employees far removed from the locus of executive power. In a proposal, associated with a former Commissioner, Mr. Vredeling, employees in undertakings "with a complex structure" – typically groups of companies, whether or not they operated across international boundaries – would have a responsibility for informing and consulting with their employees. Management, in such groups, would be obliged to provide information at least every six months to employees' representatives about the activities of the concern as a whole. Prior consultation would also be required, "with a view to reaching agreement" about major decisions liable to affect employee interests directly, such as plant closures, major organisational changes or long-term strategic changes. Where local managements fail to fulfil such obligations, employee representatives would have the right to apply directly to the "dominant" undertaking[11].

The original Vredeling proposals were diluted by the Commission following strong lobbying from business interests, particularly US multinationals and adverse reaction from the European parliament.

Vredeling, Bullock and the draft 5th directive all raise questions about the basic concept of the company, its accountability and processes of governance.

● The report of the CBI's Company Affairs Committee (Chairman; Lord Watkinson 1973) "Responsibilities of the British Public Company[12]" argued that, for long term profitability, directors must recognise responsibilities to employees, creditors, customers, the local community and society in general as well as their clear commitment to shareholders; and emphasised particularly the importance of satisfactory working relationships with employees. A similar point was made in the Green Paper (Cmnd. 7654)[13] which suggested the addition of substantial amounts of additional information in the annual reports of large companies. The Corporate Report of the Accounting Standards Committee[14] in Britain argued that all economic institutions should be held publicly accountable for their activities where they could affect other interest groups.

● In the United States some spectacular company collapses, the highlighting of questionable payments by companies[15], and evidence of non-compliance with environmental and other laws has focused attention[16].

● Public interest groups, as well as shareholder litigation, have reinforced the call for a widespread review of corporate accountability. The SEC, in their Staff Report on Corporate Accountability expressed the view that "there is a breakdown in the corporate accountability process. The corporate accountability system as a whole needs strengthening"[17]. The decision of the Supreme Court in the Bellotti case[18], concerning the political activities of companies and the disclosure of "socially significant information", also raised the question of a corporation's duty to be accountable.

These eleven issues do not represent a comprehensive survey, but they do indicate concerns about the effectiveness of present day corporate accountability. Nevertheless the thought that the processes are in need of review does not find ready acceptance among some British directors, who, perhaps, fear an erosion of their prerogative to act decisively.

Attitudes Towards Reformulating Accountability

Discussants to a Corporate Policy Group seminar on

accountability[19] expressed their concern about rethinking corporate governance: —

> "I want to question the concept that has been mentioned that, because companies are so important to the economy of the country, this gives a lot of people the right to interfere with them.
>
> If control of business activities is to be based on the good of the State then that is a different way of running the economy seen from the other side of the Iron Curtain. It seems to me that if you believe in a free enterprise system, which amazingly seems to work, then you have to be very careful how far you interfere with the way it operates."

> "At best this could be a waste of management time and lead to an information providing bureaucracy; and at worst management's power to take risks and act entrepreneurially could be lost."

Another interpretation of such comments is that far deeper issues may be involved.

Could it be that the British executive has underlying philosophical perceptions, about the relationships between the individual, the enterprise and the state, that differentiate him from his continental European counterpart? His education, religious and political orientations, business training and experience, commercial and professional practices, indeed his entire cultural conditioning may have led him to have business expectations that are threatened by some of the proposals he hears for reformulating corporate governance; and that are significantly different from those of a continental European executive.

Moreover, the adverse response of many North American executives to the draft 9th directive and, particularly, the Vredeling draft on disclosure and participation in multinationals, suggests more homogeneity with the Anglo-Saxon perspectives in the UK than the continental views.

From case notes and discussions between directors it seems that the underlying assumptions about the company in society, held by British directors, might be typified as: —

> "The company is a vehicle for capital with necessary controls imposed by society (planning law, environmental law, health and safety at work, labour law, monopoly regulation, consumer protection and so on). Shareholders risk their capital and thus wealth is created, market needs satisfied, innovation pursued and (with less conviction these days) employment provided.

Labour is engaged and the contractual relationship negotiated through collective bargaining. A climate of participation and involvement is desirable at the level of the work place and, ex gratia, disclosure of information and briefing by management is desirable.

Authority to manage the resources has been delegated to the board and thus to management by the shareholders and there are accountability mechanisms through the annual reports and members' annual meeting. Checks and balances can be provided by a minority of non-executive directors, 'of the right sort', on the main board (see Fidler, Gower and Spencer)[20].

Self-regulation is the more desirable form of oversight and control of corporate activities with a minimum of State involvement and intervention."

By contrast a more prevalent perspective of the larger, public company held in continental European countries might be typified as:—

"The company is a partnership or coalition of interests between capital and labour. Capital acquires rights by providing funds: employees obtain rights by providing labour. The right to participate in decisions, a de jure right to information and the opportunity to be involved in the co-determination of corporate governance is recognised, although significant power must remain with management if it is to be accountable for performance.

Although there are inevitably difficulties with works councils and two tier boards, these can be overcome in most cases, thus providing a vehicle for satisfactory governance of the enterprise. Although some top managers wonder if we have gone too far."

Moving the focus to the other side of the Atlantic, a clash between the legal and the business viewpoints has arisen in the United States. In 1982 the American Law Institute, an organisation of law professors, judges and lawyers, issued a restatement on principles of corporate governance and structure[21]. Though lacking the force of law such restatements of principle by the ALI have considerable influence and authority in court judgements.

The Institute's proposal outlines the desirable top structure for large, public corporations, in which a majority of the directors would have no significant relationship with the company's management. There should also be audit, nominating and compensation committees of the board, with specified duties, to preserve independence of supervision of executive activities.

Then the proposals attempt to define the director's duties and set out procedures for handling shareholder derivative suits, that is those in which shareholders derive their grievance from harm the corporation has suffered, not direct injury to them as shareholders. The Institute suggests that the courts should review a board's decision to terminate a derivative action.

Business critics of the Institute's proposals, reported by The New York Times[22], said that they would "make every board adopt monitoring methods that cannot work". "Ill conceived", "based on false premises in areas where (they) have little or no expertise", "presumptions for the legal community to tell the business community what the methods of corporate governance should be", were comments made.

The underlying concerns were whether the law should attempt to codify corporate governance ("a board needs flexibility") and the dangers of encouraging derivative actions and further use of the courts in business matters. But the most heated opposition, according to The New York Times, was reserved for the section on director's liability, in which it suggested that a director shall not be liable for the consequences of a business decision if he has informed himself about the decision, acted in good faith and had a "rational basis" for his judgement.

The concept of "rational basis" for judgement, the business community fear, would open director's decisions to review by the courts acting on the basis of hindsight. The ALI replied that, in effect, this was a restatement of the existing law and argued that a director's judgement would be protected "as long as it is not ludicrous".

Thus we have examples from both sides of the Atlantic, of the importance of underlying, philosophical attitudes as we review aspects of corporate governance. We need to be sensitive to such fundamental convictions. Technical, procedural solutions alone may fail to meet deeply rooted cultural and political ideologies.

The Concept of Accountability

A study of the literature suggests that, whilst it is strong on exhortation, it is rather weak on conceptual analysis. In proposals for reforming aspects of accountability insufficient thought is sometimes given to the underlying assumptions[23].

Different ideas about corporate accountability, information disclosure and communication, and corporate social responsibility become synonymous. Unless such ambiguities are clarified, it is now argued, the study of corporate accountability cannot proceed.

Initially, therefore, let us consider the underlying concept.

The Idea of Accountability — Accountability involves a requirement to give an account of actions taken. It represents a feedback mechanism by those held responsible for activities. Two parties are involved — the one with the right to demand accountability: the other with the duty to be held accountable.

Accountability involves more than a reporting of what has been done: it includes a requirement to say why and face the consequences. Accountability implies some degree of participation: it recognises the existence of power to demand compliance.

Accountability is not discretionary. It involves rights and duties; not interests and options. To be able to demand accountability presupposes the potential to exercise power — whether it is based on legitimate authority or the wielding of some other sanction.

By contrast *the disclosure of information* involves an ex gratia act, by those with knowledge, to convey information to others. The intention may be to orientate, or to motivate, to create a climate of understanding, acceptance, involvement and participation, or to reach a consensus between otherwise conflicting views: but it is not an act of accountability.

Similarly the processes of *socially responsible behaviour*, however desirable these may be, involve choices based on ethical and moral principles: these again are not processes of accountability.

The Context of Accountability — It is possible to distinguish various bases for the right to demand, and the duty to provide, accountability.

In the *constitutional context*, elected representatives have a responsibility to be accountable to their electorate. Examples are found in the relationship between professional bodies and their members; trade unions and their membership; and building societies and their members. The authority of the decision-makers derives from the appropriate constitutional context — a statute, charter, rule book or other constitutional mechanism on which the enterprise is founded. The power of the electorate lies in the ultimate sanction of the electoral process. The accountability mechanisms adopted need to reflect the time-scales and the political nature of the electoral process.

In the *proprietorial context*, the responsibility to manage assets and obtain performance from such resources has been delegated by owners to managers or agents. Authority, which derives from ownership, is delegated to those who are required to exercise stewardship over the assets ensuring their safe keeping and adequate performance. Accountability is required for the performance of this stewardship role. Sanctions will depend on the stewardship contract supported by the relevant law which might be company law, agency law or trust law.

Then there are a number of examples which might be described as the *situational context*. Here one finds examples of a right to expect accountability, for some specific matter, founded in the context of some specific relationship.

> In the employer/employee relationship, the employer may legitimately hold the employee accountable for actions taken under the employment contract within the protection of labour law. In the creditor/debtor relationship, the debtor is accountable to the creditor insofar as the contract requires satisfaction of the debt. Similarly in the supplier/consumer context, the supplier is responsible, and thus accountable, to the consumer under various Acts for the proper performance of that product or service.

In these examples the authority of the party requiring accountability derives from the specific relationship between the two parties. It may or may not be protected by the law. The sanction to back the available power may also reside in the law or involve some sanction — such as reward or punishment, the refusal to give further credit, purchase goods or provide labour.

Redefining Corporate Accountability

The above discussion concerned the general idea of accountability. How does that relate to corporate accountability?

We propose an empirical definition based on the reality of accountability relationships between the company and others. Corporate accountability, we suggest, is the duty a company owes to be accountable to those parties which can exercise the right to demand that accountability, and to none other.

In other words the accountability that a company gives must be based on a clear accountability relationship, involving the right to demand accountability on the one hand and the duty to be held accountable on the other. Corporate accountability should be specific and bounded. It should not be confused with the shibboleths and exhortations of general or public accountability.

It follows that, if corporate accountability is to be precise and meaningful, we have to clarify the accountability relationships. We have to answer the questions:

- Accountable to whom and when? This means identifying the legitimate power relationships and their dynamics.
- Accountable for what? This means recognising the performance objectives of the company or its component parts.
- How is such accountability to be satisfied? Who will act as the company's representative in fulfilling the accountability duty?
- What sanctions are appropriate and available if the position is unsatisfactory?

Corporate Accountability – To Whom?

The duty of a company, in the capitalist world, to be accountable to its *members* has not been seriously challenged in the literature. Rather the issue is how to make the accountability mechanisms more effective.

In the private and proprietary companies, with a close identification between owner, director and manager, few problems arise. In the subordinate company accountability can be exercised through the management stream. The duties of directors in PTE's, PTY's and SUB's, to ensure accountability, will be discussed in subsequent chapters.

But it is in the public company (and the PTE with widespread holdings and the SUB with minority or associated interests) that the issue of accountability is fundamental.

The Securities & Exchange Commission, in the United

States, describes corporate governance[24] as "the process by which the corporation reaches decisions and takes action". Their view is that the activity is mainly internal to the corporation by "the election of shareholders to the board, which oversees the management". The SEC, being primarily interested in investor protection, sees accountability as:

".....the means by which those who manage and oversee the affairs of the company are held to account for their stewardship of corporate assets."

This is essentially the proprietorial context. The mechanisms to fulfil accountability to the members include shareholder communications, shareholder participation in the electoral process, and shareholder meetings; support by State and Federal company laws and enforced through derivative legal actions against companies and their directors.

The SEC has sought to improve accountability to shareholders commenting, "the purchase of corporate securities creates an ownership relationship, which gives the shareholder an opportunity to participate in the corporation's electoral and decision making processes, as well as the right to share the company's profits".

The SEC further observes that "shareholders have little interest in participating in corporate governance: their interest lying primarily in the economic performance of companies". As a result the SEC has called for more information on board structure, composition and functioning. They have encouraged member nominations, allowing the inclusion of shareholder resolutions in a company's proxy material. Other ideas include alternative locations for meetings, shareholder surveys and publishing questions and answers from shareholder meetings.

A duty to be accountable to *employees* is a contentious issue in the UK.

Following continental European attitudes, the various drafts of the 5th directive[25] have called for some form of employee participation through a supervisory board. Employees at all levels, including middle management, would be represented. The Bullock Report[26] in its $2x+y$ formula recommended an equal representation of labour and capital on a unitary board.

The 1980 Companies Act[27] introduced the requirement for a company to have regard to the interests of employees in general, as well as shareholders, when taking business decisions. But this is a far cry from accountability to employees.

The focus of interest of employees is likely to be on that area of decision-making which is seen to affect their interests, either individually or in a collective agreement. The consolidated accounts of their diverse corporate group may contain less valuable information for, say, a truck driver or junior clerk in one of the subsidiary companies than information about the order book, the development of new products and the general market potential for their specific part of the organisation. Information acquires its value, and its potential to motivate and gain commitment, by being relevant to the perceived needs and interests of the recipient. This is a vital task for management: it is not part of the accountability responsibilities unless it is enforceable by company or labour law (as in the requirement for worker directors in Germany or directors sympathetic to labour interests as in Dutch two tier boards); or where the accountability relationship is enforceable by some other agreement or sanction (such as the inclusion of a trade union member on the board of Chrysler USA, following a labour agreement with the Union of Automobile Workers (UAW)).

Rethinking corporate accountability, however, might lead one to argue in the UK for accountability to employees for matters which directly affect their interests – and at the organisational level appropriate to those interests. For example, by providing feedback on commercial and economic performance and expectations, manpower policy and plans, investment and plant intentions, and so on where labour interests are involved. This is quite different, of course, from the publication of "employee accounts"; and is closer to the rationale already adopted by many companies as the basis for collective bargaining, supported by the ACAS Code[28]. It is also consistent with advice from institutions such as The Industrial Society which advise on management communication.

More widely, it has been suggested that a company owes a responsibility to interest groups other than the members and employees. The so-called "stakeholder theories" of accountability argue that the company owes responsibility to customers and consumers, suppliers, creditors, local and other interests, and the public generally. Literature in this field is well surveyed in Child[29], which shows the extent of the interest in the subject.

When the question of specific corporate accountability to *other interest groups* is examined it is found that, in many cases, their interests are already recognised and protected by law. For example, creditors and non-equity financial sources are interested in the financial viability of the business and the security of the assets. Contract law protects their position and the publication of accounts and their filing in the Registry provides the information.

Consumers, present and potential, are concerned with product quality, continuity of service, and so on, which is the subject for consumer protection law. It is apparent therefore that a wide array of law − planning law, environmental law, labour law, health and safety law, consumer protection etc. already exists to protect various external interests and provide the degree of accountability felt necessary by the legislature.

Nevertheless, advocates of stakeholder concepts argue for a wider recognition of a duty to be accountable and make various proposals for providing the power and legitimacy they demand for such accountability. Writing in response to a Corporate Policy Group working paper, Michael Shanks[30] wrote: −

> "The current view of the National Consumer Council, with which I certainly concur, is that there is a strong case for consumer representation on the boards of nationalised industries and other monopolistic organisations. As regards private sector companies, there may well be other ways in which consumer views can be expressed, e.g. by consultative panels or the like. We would feel that if other stakeholder interests were explicitly represented on boards − worker directors being the most obvious example: then consumer interests should also be so represented. But we, and I, do not feel it is necessarily the right thing given the present structure of boards of directors in this country to press explicitly for consumer representatives."

The Myth of Public Corporate Accountability

The authors of "The Corporate Report"[31] argue from the position that "there is an implicit responsibililty to report publicly (whether or not required by law or regulation) incumbent on every economic entity whose size or format renders it significant. The philosophical underpinning of their recommendations was based on the view that the responsibility to report publicly (referred to as public accountability) is separate from and broader than the legal obligation to report on and arises from the custodial role played in the community by economic entities".

Whilst there is an intuitive appeal in this argument, it is contrary to the stand adopted in this book. Accountability involves a precise accountability relationship. Whilst it is true to say, as do the authors of "The Corporate Report", that in addition to the exercise of a stewardship accountability to shareholders, so many other relationships exist of both a financial and non-financial nature, that does not render all these other interest groups with an inalienable right to demand accountability about the performance of the business as a whole; nor does it require the board, acting on behalf of the company to be exposed to demands for public accountability.

Rather the rights of any interest groups to seek accountability, and the duties of the board to fulfil them, need to be pursued in terms of the specific relationship between that group and the company and not in terms of general interests of all parties external to a company.

Much has been written on the idea of stakeholders. Essentially stakeholder theory perceives the modern (particularly the large and public) company as being surrounded by a circle of interest groups which have a legitimate interest in the activities of the company because, by its actions, the company can affect their interests. Although authorities do not agree precisely on the composition of such interest groups they typically embrace some or all of the shareholders, employees, managers, customers and end consumers, suppliers and creditors communities − at the local, State and Federal levels − and the public generally. We discussed the reality of such power groupings in the last chapter.

From such a perception the stakeholder theorists argue for an acceptance of responsibility, whether based on legal, ethical or moral grounds for the activities of the company to recognise responsibilities to their stakeholders[32].

There are serious limitations in the stakeholder model.

Firstly, the view of a company surrounded by a set of

discrete interest groups is naive. In practice these interest groups themselves may interact: some will be found to have members in common. The network of interacting interests can be highly dynamic; the sets are constantly being redefined. Moreover the active membership of any group is likely to be but a small part of that entire class and the interests of the vocal minority may not be representative of the interests of the class as a whole.

Secondly, groups are not homogeneous. In some cases, suppliers for example, there are precise and legally pursuable contracts between the company and the stakeholder. In other cases, the general public for example, only the most peripheral and general case may be advanced. In other cirumstances, for example with employees, whilst the legal case for accountability by the company may be limited there is a considerable compatibility of interest between the company and its employees which can be seen — not least because many of them are committing their working life to the enterprise. Some authorities argue that thereby they acquire a property which should become a basis for de jure power.

The modern enterprise, in reality, is itself loosely bounded and involves complex and interacting networks of relationships. It is better perceived as a set of dynamic open systems — coalitions of interests between various parties[33].

A modern public company, operating internationally, may well involve groups of wholly and partially owned subsidiaries and be, itself, enmeshed in joint ventures with other public companies and governments. In these cirumstances the concept of "the company" surrounded by a precisely bounded set of stakeholders is an abstraction at a very high level and probably unhelpful in practice in thinking through corporate responsibilities.

The good intentions of the commentators on corporate social responsibility, the contributors to stakeholder theory and the authors of "The Corporate Report" are not in question. But the belief that companies should account broadly to a wide group of interests, including the public at large, could lead to a discretionary response from management — a public relations exercise to demonstrate corporate good behaviour in social and economic terms.

Examples of this type of behaviour can already be found in the stereotype response that some companies make in their statutory declarations on the employment of the disabled, and are likely in the future on employee involvement.

Stakeholder theories of general public ("social") responsibility and accountability presuppose the existence of a duty on the part of a company to be accountable irrespective of the right of the other party to demand such an account. We assert that a duty only exists when based on another's right to demand.

There are intermediate cases, such as the OECD guidelines on multinational companies and their trading in South Africa, or the Sullivan "rules" for American companies. But the existence of a true accountability relationship, as against an exhortatory guideline, depends on the reality of power – the ability to do something as a sanction to require performance.

Whether there should be further legal demands on British companies to be accountable to further sets of interests is a matter for political debate. In the final chapter we will speculate about some possible directions. Expectations change and rights and duties are reformulated as companies and societies evolve. The essential point being made here is that accountability is not an ex gratia activity on the part of those governing a company, but a precisely bounded duty based on the reality of power, and with appropriate and effective sanctions if it is not properly performed.

Corporate Accountability – For What?

By what criteria are directors to be judged? How is the quality of their actions to be measured? The classical cliches, when such questions are asked of businessmen tend to be in terms of "the bottom line", short term profit and being in business to make money.

Such responses are as automatic as they are myopic. Profit is potentially a useful measure of short term corporate performance. Without funds generated by profit, and in the absence of capital transfusions, a company will inevitably bleed to death. But profit is a measure, not a purpose.

Moreover concentration on short term profit, it can be argued, has been a major failing of British company directors. Consider the following comments from a report to the House of Commons by the Boston Consulting Group[34]: –

> "The disastrous commercial performance of the British motor cycle industry in this decade has basically resulted

from failure to understand the strategic implications of the relationship between manufacturing volumes and the relative cost position vis à vis the Japanese."

Commenting on this Spurrell[35] observes:—

"Japanese business policy is growth minded and aggressive. The primary objective of Japanese sales companies are set in terms of sales volume rather than short term profitability. The essence of this strategy is to increase sales volume at least as fast or faster than any of your competitors. A number of more specific policies follow. Products are updated or redesigned whenever a market threat or opportunity is perceived; prices are set at levels designed to achieve market share targets, and will be cut if necessary: effective marketing systems are set up in all markets where serious competition is intended, regardless of short term cost; plans and objectives look to long term pay-off. The result of these policies has been spectacularly successful.

The contrast between this summary of Japanese policy and that of the British (and American for that matter) is stark and dramatic. Volume in place of short term profit; long term strategy rather than pursuing short term profit; heavy investment in R&D, and in sales and distribution systems, rather than making profit out of existing organisations."

It must be recognised, in fairness, that the typical large Japanese company is highly geared and not under pressure for short term performance from the stock market; although, of course, interest payments on the debt must be paid. A close relationship between the finance house and the trading company also facilitates the process.

Corporate accountability in fact is a function of a specific accountability relationship. What is the appropriate measure, and over what business element, will depend on that relationship. In addition to corporate accountability to relevant interest groups, the directors themselves are also accountable. In the British company, the entire board of directors, being elected by the members, is accountable to them. In addition they must ensure that statutory provisions designed to facilitate accountability are met in full.

We shall explore the work of directors in different types of company in the third part of the book, and be making specific proposals for sharpening the accountability focus in PLC's whilst reducing the exposure in PTY's[36].

Corporate Accountability – The Mechanisms

Having identified corporate accountability in specific terms and recognised that the criteria of accountability are dependent on the nature of the accountability relationship, it remains to consider the mechanisms by which accountability can be demonstrated.

There are more options available than most discussions of corporate accountability admit; these being typically confined to matters of financial reporting.

For example:
.. The formal publication of data – such as a prospectus, the director's annual report, filed reports, such as the 10K of the SEC or the annual return under the British Companies Acts
.. A formal presentation to a meeting
.. The opportunity to ask questions and receive replies – both verbal and written
.. The opportunity to have face to face verbal exchanges – discussions
.. The right to call for ad hoc special reports
.. The opportunity to have access to corporate files
.. The opportunity to have discussions with company officials
.. The opportunity to call for an independent study, for example by an auditor, a government appointed inspector or an independent director.

Which method of fulfilling the accountability contract will clearly be dependent on the nature and interests of the party concerned.

The Importance of Accounting Standards

Where information is to be published it is clearly important that ambiguities and inconsistencies in accounting conventions be kept to a minimum.

There was little call for published accounts which would enable comparisons to be made between the financial state and value of different companies, prior to the boom in take-overs of the 60's. Inadequacies in conventional accounting were revealed when such comparisons and valuations, based on the annual accounts of major companies, became necessary during merger negotiations. A demand arose for more informative accounts, based on consistent and higher accounting standards. This demand was fuelled by critical reports from Department of Trade inspectors following various company investigations.

In 1970 the Institute of Chartered Accountants in England and Wales[37] issued a statement of intent on accounting standards. Among the proposals were:

1. Narrowing the areas of difference and variety in accounting practice.
2. Disclosure of accounting bases.
3. Disclosure of departures from established definitive accounting standards.
4. Wider experience of major new proposals on accounting standards.

As Zeff[38] remarks, "the exposure process stands in stark contrast to the total secrecy that had characterised the deliberations of the English Institute's Council and technical committees". The Economist[39] commented that "mounting criticism of the accountancy profession's approach to accounting practices .... has obviously hit home".

But in the process the professional accountancy bodies had, inevitably, become interventionist both in the activities of their members and in the regulation of the activities of the preparers of company accounts.

Subsequently the Consultative Committee of Accountancy Bodies[40] was formed, together with the Accounting Standards Committee[41] and the Auditing Practices Committee.

However establishing standards, obtaining acceptance by accountants and requiring conformance by companies has raised political problems in the accountancy profession. For example, SSAP16 the standard requiring large companies to publish current cost accounting reports was introduced with the understanding that it would be reviewed after three years. Yet even during that period, members of the Institute of Chartered Accountants in England and Wales called for a special meeting to debate the matter, and very nearly carried the vote on a motion "deploring" the standard and calling for its immediate withdrawal.

Continuing calls for further disclosure, from various interests, and greater visibility of decisions in the large corporation, include proposals for greater disaggregation of published information by plant, by product and by location[42].

Where a legitimate accountability relationship exists at a business or local level, clearly consolidated accounts for a group as a whole fail to provide data relevant to the party with the right to be informed.

In France, following the Sudreau Report, companies are required to undertake a 'social audit', disclosing their plans and activities in areas such as manpower, energy conservation, and long range plans.

In the United States the SEC lays down the requirements for accounting standards of public companies, usually in close agreement with the Financial Accounting Standards Board of the American accounting bodies.

Corporate Regulation and Harmonisation of European Company Law

The European Commission is dedicated to a process of harmonisation in company law. Robert Coleman, speaking to a Corporate Policy Group conference in 1981[43] explained the Commission's view that "harmonisation was primarily intended to resolve substantial obstacles to cross-frontier activity and, the other side of the coin, (to fill) important gaps in the protection offered to interests affected by corporation operations".

In seeking to facilitate trade between the Member States the Commission is responding directly to the original Treaty of Rome: in developing social legislation they are introducing political policies.

Although Coleman was at pains to argue that the "view from Brussels" was *not* of harmonisation with a shared concept of corporate accountability he subsequently argued to the desire for a common conception as the goal, viz:

> "The view is sometimes put forward that the pursuit of harmonisation 'presupposes a shared concept of corporate accountability', or some other general conception concerning the nature and purpose of the enterprise. Frankly, this is not how we see the process from Brussels. On the contrary, harmonisation seems to us often to be of particular importance precisely when underlying conceptions diverge. After all, if everyone agrees on a given conception, harmonisation in that area will normally mean in reality the ratification of existing rules, subject perhaps to a certain amount of systemisation or tidying up. This

may not be totally without significance, for example, as regards the apparent completeness and coherence of the Community framework, and also the future liberty of action of the Member States. But of much greater importance is harmonisation that reduces the divergences in rules resulting from differences in the underlying conceptions prevailing in the Member States."

"Are group accounts prepared, exclusively in the interest of shareholders of the parent company or do they serve other interests? Should employee information and consultation systems deal exclusively with matters decided or implemented in particular establishments or should they in addition relate to issues concerning the enterprise as a whole or other establishments, and if so, to what extent? From this kind of difference in conception a large number of divergent rules tend to flow which affect the behaviour and interests of both enterprises and other actors on the economic scene, for example, investors, creditors, employees and their representative organisations.

At the same time, of course, this kind of harmonisation is much more difficult and takes longer to achieve. The political character of the process is important and should not be under-estimated. To change ways of thinking about the purposes of company, labour and similar laws takes time: time for concerned opinion to accept that the familiar may not be the whole solution and that the strange may have something worthwhile to offer. A long period of public discussion and negotiation may be required before the conditions are achieved in which an agreement is possible. Even then, the agreement may not be complete and definitive in the sense that a uniform set of rules based on a common conception will be universally applied. Rather the extent to which national rules diverge may be reduced; certain alternative approaches to a common conception may be admitted, together with rules designed to achieve as much equivalence as practicable; and sometimes a commitment may be made to re-examine the issue at a later date to see whether, in the light of experience, greater convergence can be achieved subsequently.

In brief then, harmonisation and similar forms of international rule making fulfil their most important function when they succeed in reducing important regulatory differences deriving from divergent underlying conceptions. Divergence is the point of departure; a common conception is the goal; and harmonisation is the political process, sometimes painful, by which we seek to move from the former towards the latter."

Corporate Regulation in the United States

In the United States of America each company is incorporated under the laws and jurisdiction of one of the States. Expectations and requirements of companies vary from State to State. There has been a call for "federal chartering" to enable country-wide company regulation, but this has been resisted by the autonomous States.

However, following the stock market collapse of 1929, federal securities laws were enacted in 1933 and 1934 to protect investors. The Securities and Exchange Commission, a federal agency, was created with considerable power to require disclosure and conformity. The form 10K, for example, which every public company must file, for use by the public and scrutiny by the SEC, contains not only the typical annual accounts and reports filed in Britain but very extensive supplementary and additional material on company background, performance, position and plans that might be relevant to present and potential investors.

Harold Williams, then the Chairman of the SEC, outlined the role of the SEC to a Corporate Policy Group Conference in 1980[44]:–

"Various Acts of Congress clearly state the authority of the Commission to prescribe the methods to be followed in the preparation of accounts and the form and content of financial statements filed under the federal securities laws. More generally, these statutes charge the Commission with responsibility to ensure that investors receive information necessary for informed investment decisions. In meeting this statutory responsibility, and in recognition of the expertise, energy, and resources of the accounting profession, the Commission has historically looked to the standard setting bodies designated by the private accounting profession, to provide leadership in establishing and improving accounting principles, subject to Commission oversight. With minor exceptions, the Commission has regarded the determinations of such bodies as responsive to the needs of investors."

"The Financial Accounting Standards Board (FASB) was established in 1972. The FASB is a seven member, full-time board composed of individuals from both within and without the accounting profession."

"In recent years, the respective roles of the FASB and the Commission have received an increasing amount of attention from both government and the business community. The result has been a broad re-examination of the nature and structure of the accounting standard setting process in particular, and of the accounting profession in general. That inquiry began in 1976 with the Report of the Subcommittee on Oversight and Investigations of the House Committee on Interstate ad Foreign Commerce, chaired by Congressman John Moss. It continued, a little over a year later, with the work of the Subcommittee on Reports, Accounting and Management of the Senate Committee on Governmental Affairs (Senate Subcommittee), chaired by the late Senator Metcalf, which held a series of public hearings concerning the accounting profession. Those hearings were preceded by a staff report of the Senate Subcommittee and were followed by the Senate Subcommittee's own report issued in November 1977."

"The primary question underlying these inquiries was where the initiative should rest for establishing and improving accounting standards — in the private sector or the public sector. The Commission, as reflected in its first two annual reports to the Congress on the accounting profession, continues to believe that the initiative for establishing and improving accounting standards should remain in the private sector — subject to Commission oversight. There are several reasons for this approach: the private sector has greater resources; its standards can be applicable to all companies, whether or not publicly owned; professionals are more likely than is government to respond in a sensitive and timely manner when new or modified standards are necessary to meet changing conditions and concerns in their areas of expertise; and professions are also more inclined to act effectively when enforcing their own standards, rather than when complying with rules imposed externally. In the aggregate, these factors make a compelling case for private sector primacy in routine standard setting."

Commenting further on the present position, Mr. Williams said that

"Today although economic and social conditions are radically different than they were in 1933, public confidence in our economic institutions, including the corporate community, has again eroded. For example, the incidence of significant unexpected failures by major corporations, as well as revelations, incident to the Watergate investigation, of corporate political and other dubious payments, both in America and abroad, have caused questions to arise concerning the auditor's role in detecting improper corporate financial transactions and bringing them to light. The result has been the intense Congressional scrutiny which the profession in the United States has experienced in the past several years."

Conclusions

The chapter began with the proposition that the corporate sector was important in social and economic terms and corporate accountability a vital element in policy making. Some issues giving rise to current concerns about corporate accountability, and the limitations of the classical concept of accountability were outlined.

It was argued that there is confusion in the literature between ideas about corporate accountability, the disclosure of information and corporate social responsibility. A precise view of corporate accountability was offered — based on the premise that accountability exists only where there is an accountability relationship between two parties: the one owing a duty to be accountable, based on the other party's power to require that accountability. Accountability, thus, involves a right and duty; it is not to be confused with disclosure or socially responsible behaviour which involves discretion and ex gratia action on the part of management.

Some of the implications of this rigorous definition of corporate accountability were suggested.

1. The notion of public accountability owed by a company to a wide range of stakeholders including the general public, was not a viable concept.
2. Corporate accountability needs to be defined in terms of specific rights owed to specified parties and identifiable duties to be held accountable on the part of the company.

We identified the need for companies, particularly PLC's to recognise their duty to be accountable in terms relevant to the interest group with the right to require accountability.

Corporate regulation involves the processes by which a State seeks to regulate the behaviour of companies operating under its jurisdiction, either by law or institutional practices, and seeks to protect the interests of those groups affected by a company's actions who cannot exercise specific corporate accountability.

Consequently the role of accounting standards should be seen as contributing to the satisfaction of corporate accountability where there is a precise accountability relationship; and facilitating corporate regulation as required by a given State.

We also saw how divergent philosophical attitudes could fundamentally influence expectations on corporate accountability. Differences between Anglo-Saxon and continental European ideas on the governance of companies may explain some of the difficulties in harmonising European company law.

Chapter 9

Liability and Business Reality
– on business boundaries and strategic units as accountable entities

The typology of chapter 6 distinguished proprietary, private, public and subordinate companies on the basis of owners', institutional investors', directors' or group managements' ability to exercise power over company affairs.

This classification depends on the existence of specific and separate corporate, legal entities. To that extent it relies on classical concepts. In cases where the boundaries of a company exactly match the dimensions of the business being run by the company, the schema should provide an adequate basis for the exercise of corporate governance. Company and business are one and can be governed accordingly.

But, as we saw in chapter 5, there are other cases where the corporate entity does not reflect the business reality. There is a mismatch between the boundaries of the company, usually in a group, and the organisational, decision-taking structure chosen to run the business activities.

Where business decisions, and consequently business risks, are taken in structures that do not match the corporate structures it is plainly wrong to rely on the corporate entity as the basis for accountability and the limitation of liability.

In this chapter we address such issues and consider the implications for the basis of governance and the limitation of liability.

On Corporate or Business Boundaries

The classical notions of the limited liability company assume that the structure of the company, defined for the purposes of ownership, also meet the needs of other parties to its activities, such as creditors, customers, employees and the tax authorities.

Where corporate and business activities are synonymous, as in most PTY's, such an assumption will, clearly, be true. But complex groups of companies can have a duality in their direction and control, as we saw in chapter 5. On the one hand subsidiary and associate companies have directors with governance responsibilities; whilst, on the other hand, the internal business systems, performance reporting and management decision-making structure supersedes such corporate boundaries.

For example, a US company, with 8 subsidiaries in Europe may organise them as:–

1. separate entities, in which case, no governance problem arises if they are independent of each other and autonomous of the parent

1.1

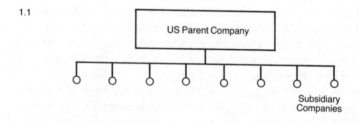

or 2. subsidiaries grouped under divisional headquarters, which might, or might not, themselves be companies

1.2

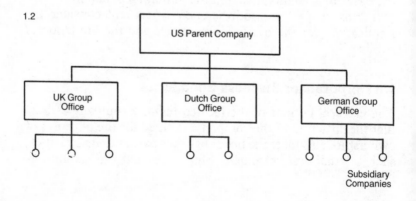

or 3. a hierarchy of divisions, perhaps with head office staff oversight

1.3

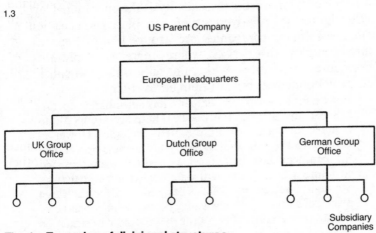

Fig. 1   Examples of divisional structures

Divisions may, of course, be grouped by products (the bus division, the tractor division, the spare parts division), by markets (wholesale division and retail division), by production or service technology (steel division, engineering division, exports) or by other suitable divisionalisation. The boundaries are drawn in an attempt to group relevant activities, in the light of group strategy, for the purposes of efficient and effective management.

A further complexity arises where the parent company, or a divisional company, itself trades in the business of the subsidiary companies; then management boundaries have to be drawn to include its activities.

In all such cases business decision-making is likely to transcend the corporate decisions at subsidiary company level. Strategies will be formulated at the divisional level and resources allocated, plans made to invest, divest, acquire or sell plants, create or reduce jobs, launch or drop products. Organisational responsibilities, plans, budgets and decision-making discretion will be determined at divisional level. The authority of directors in the subordinate companies are likely to be considerably limited.

Under such circumstances concentrating only on the

governance of the subsidiary companies will not address the governance of the essential business activities: whilst focusing on governance at the level of the parent company may be too far removed from the business reality at the operational levels.

But figure 1 is a relatively simple case of divisionalisation, in which subsidiary companies are grouped into divisions. A more complex case arises where there is a plurality of management structures, which not only transcend subsidiary company boundaries but cut right across them.

For example, a UK oil company has subsidiaries operating in many parts of the world. These are grouped into regional divisions, as in the first example. However, because of the scale and diversity of business operations, the company has introduced a product market related structure which is overlaid on the divisional structure. Strategic business units have been formed for the three principal activities − petroleum, petro-chemicals and coal − with the responsibility for the development of strategies and operations in each sector globally. The position is shown in figure 2.

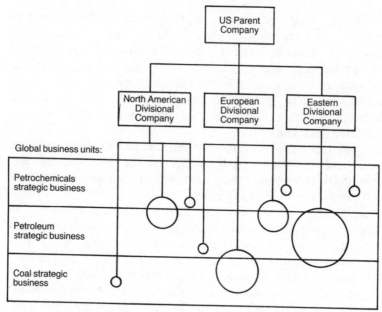

Fig. 2 Subsidiary companies, regional divisions and global business units structure

Subsidiary companies report to regional executives at the divisional level and also to the one, two or three chief executives of the business streams that operate in their company. Typical of matrix organisation structures such arrangements tend to need high levels of negotiating skills.

It is clear, in such circumstances, that governance confined by the de jure boundaries of each corporate entity will not reflect the reality of the decision-taking in the enterprise as a whole: neither will governance at the level of the parent company address issues of accountability and liability in the de facto business streams.

On Subsidiaries or Divisions

In recent years some authorities have advocated a move away from separate corporate subsidiaries towards divisions, which mirror the essential business activities, and have but one corporate entity. For example, Deloitte Haskins & Sells[1] explains the alternatives and evaluates them in favour of divisions:–

"Divisionalisation is the process by which the structure of a group of companies is changed from the traditional relationship of parent company and subsidiary company to one where all the operating functions of several, or possibly all of the wholly-owned subsidiaries are performed within one corporate entity, and the discrete functions are organised within separate divisions of that company. The previous structure, in which each function had a separate formal and legal corporate existence, is dispensed with.

Divisionalisation may take the form of a simple process whereby each previous corporate entity becomes a separate division of the new operating company. Or it may take the more complex form whereby those similar functions within the group that previously separate companies performed are merged into management reporting units with unified management and unified account systems.

Within any particular group of companies the choice between the simple or the more complex restructuring will depend on several factors, including:

– The similarity of the functions that existing operating units perform.

- Group management's wishes regarding the degree to which operating responsibility is to be devolved.
- The effect that the change will have on management morale.
- The consequences that the change may have on industrial relations.

Divisionalisation can produce several benefits, of which the main ones are:

- A reduction in external fees such as audit fees and registration fees.
- A streamlining of the accounting and secretarial functions, principally by reducing the amount of time that has to be spent on statutory requirements.
- The creation of a structure that is more tax efficient, in which all activities become part of either one tax entity or (at most) a very few.
- The creation of a corporate structure that mirrors the management structure of the business.

There are also possible disadvantages, including

- The loss by the directors and the managers of the companies that would be divisionalised of a feeling of responsibility and identity.
- The loss of flexibility, because businesses can be more easily disposed of if they are kept in separate legal entities.
- The loss of the "liability shield" that a group has when businesses operate as separate legal entities, which enables a group to put a subsidiary that has a massive liability into liquidation and so limits the impact on the group as a whole.
- The effect on trade union representation and industrial relations. This is especially relevant in the context of the Transfer of Undertakings (Protection of Employment) Regulations 1981.

We believe that the first two of these possible disadvantages can be overcome with adequate planning and consultation. The third possible disadvantage certainly needs careful consideration, but many groups feel that they would not, in any event, seek to avoid potential losses in this way. The final possible disadvantage is one that a group needs to consider carefully before embarking on divisionalisation."

On Joint Ventures and Federations

But there are yet more difficult situations in which to

determine the boundaries of governance.

Joint ventures between otherwise independent companies, as we have seen, are a significant and growing feature of modern, large-scale business activity. The need for large projects, drawing together different business activities and involving companies incorporated in different countries, was not apparent to the early makers of company law. Today consortium arrangements between companies, which may be competing in other fields, are commonplace. Examples abound in the automotive industry (British Leyland and Honda), defence (the Tornado aircraft), aeronautics (Concorde), oil (consortia of the major oil companies for exploration in the North Sea), construction (companies combining to tender for major projects), telecommunications and information technology (AT&T and Philips), aerospace (the contractors in the European satellite programme), and many other industries in which there are interdependent activities and massive costs of technological, product or market development.

The demands of the international business market place and the rate of change of technology have forced joint venture

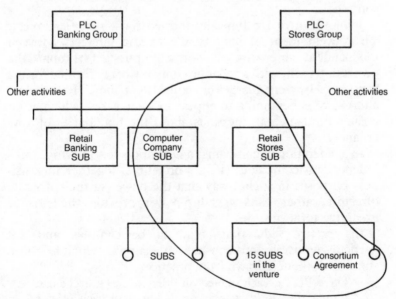

Fig. 3 Joint venture between two independent companies

endeavours for specific projects, which are not reflected by the perpetuity of the corporate model. Sometimes a joint venture company is formed: but the underlying basis of joint ventures is contract; with contract law, not company law.

> As an example, consider the joint venture agreement between a large banking group and a major stores company, to provide cash machines in retail outlets and direct debit facilities so that customers can charge their shopping directly from the point of sale check-out to their bank account.
>
> Various subsidiary companies and divisions of each of the partners are involved.
>
> Strategically, the bank directors have had to question whether they were going into retailing or the retailer into banking. This was not a trivial matter, when they realised that in-store banking and other financial services were feasible, without their help.

In such a joint venture where does responsibility for governance actually lie? Who sets direction? Who is accountable for performance? Should creditors or other affected parties, such as customers, have their rights limited by the limited liability of the subsidiary company with which they contract?

Joint ventures are typically formed for a specific project. The development of long term strategic interests between independent enterprises is normally pursued through the ownership path, with a separate company being formed for the venture or by some merger or acquisition policy. However, an alternative is beginning to appear in some cases, which again creates fundamental questions about the boundaries of governance.

In a federation of companies a network is forged which links independent companies (PLC's or PTE's) together for business purposes in such a way that the power of the corporate directors, rather than ownership power, provides the basis for executive authority.

In practice federations tend to be complex and not particularly visible; but consider an example, which has been simplified, though drawn from practice.

> Three PLC's, each quoted on different stock exchanges around the world, have cross holdings of each other's shares of between 27 and 30%. This is sufficient to provide interlocking directorships, but the companies are

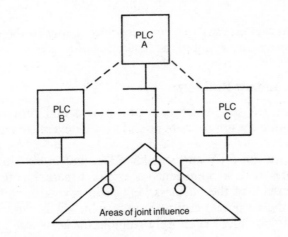

Fig. 4 A federation of companies

not subsidiaries or associates that would make any member a subordinate company.

The other equity interests are widely spread and shareholders look for capital growth and a dividend stream, rather than a close involvement in governance.

In this position the common directors and the chief executives of various SUB's on the three groups can exercise joint influence over areas of common interest, including bids, tenders, pricing and various aspects of market, product, research and financial strategy.

Under such circumstances there is no dominant legal entity, neither is there a joint venture contractual agreement; but decisions can be made and risks taken that can affect the interests of shareholders, creditors, customers and others.

However, benefits can accrue to the members of a federation from the synergy:

1. Corporate regulation, statutory disclosure and filing requirements apply to each PLC, according to the company laws of the country in which it is incorporated and trades. They do not apply to the federated area of interest.

2. Liability for debts is limited to each PLC, or SUB within each group: it is not related to the federated area of interest in which common decisions are being made.

3. Statutory requirements and codes of conduct, such as the draft Vredeling directive on transnationals, the OECD or Sullivan codes on business in South Africa, or

controls on cross-border data-flows apply to the corporate entities – not to the federation of interests.

The Boundary Problem

Thus we see that there can be fundamental problems in determining the appropriate boundaries for exercising governance.

True, in the PTY and smaller PTE, and indeed in larger companies with a homogeneous product-market enterprise, the boundary of the business being run is coterminous with that of the corporate entity through which it is run. Such a corporate boundary is entirely suitable for corporate governance.

But in other cases where
1. SUB's are grouped into divisions for strategic, managerial or operational decision-making that transcends the authority of the directors of the SUB,
2. business organisation structure and business streams cut right across the corporate boundaries of SUB's,
3. there are joint ventures between companies operating under a contractural arrangement, rather than a joint company,

or 4. there is a federation of independent companies to act together in an area of joint interest,

the way business decisions are taken, resources allocated, risks accepted and business directions determined no longer map onto the corporate entities. The corporate boundaries do not represent the structure through which the business is being run. Consequently legislation designed to provide relevant information about business affairs may, at best, be irrelevant and possibly misleading.

Such corporate boundaries may be suitable, indeed essential, for exercising accountability to the owners of that corporate entity. Obviously the boundary of the company is appropriate for demonstrating stewardship to those who own that company. But corporate boundaries may be quite inappropriate for creditors, customers, employees and others whose interests have been, or may be, affected by decisions taken outside the corporate entity. Such groups are interested in the business not in the company; it is the business decisions that affect them.

Hadden[2], in his recent work on the control of corporate groups recognises the dilemma:—

> "It will be clear.... that the primary problem in providing effective structures for the representation of both employees and investors in large groups of companies is the identification of accounting and decision-making units."

Later in this chapter we will make a proposal for overcoming this problem of governance. But before we do, let us review the issue of the limitation of liability of a company to its creditors, in cases where the decision-making structure is not coterminous with the corporate structure.

Piercing the Corporate Veil

Under British company law each company is treated as an autonomous legal entity, irrespective of its ownership or the locus of decision-making. Liability for debts incurred lies with the company, and, subject to any legal guarantees specifically given, only with that company.

Creditors must pursue their claims with the company with which they contracted. Their rights are limited to the wealth of that company alone: that is the net assets represented by the paid-up shareholder's capital and retained earnings. It is up to a person, before entering into a contract, to establish the financial standing of a company. Dissatisfied creditors cannot pursue unsatisfied claims onto the assets of a holding company, or other companies in a group (subject only to the holding of a guarantee or lien as part of the initial contract).

Each company is treated as a legal persona and stands alone in matters of liability for debts[3]. As a judge expressed the idea — a company is surrounded by "the corporate veil" which may only be pierced in rare circumstances.

By contrast the management in a group of companies may move funds between companies in the group, provide or withhold resources, treat a SUB as a "cash cow" milking it to provide funds for developments elsewhere and generally manage the affairs of the company as they see fit for the benefit of the group as a whole (subject to any minority interests involved in the SUB's).

In a British SUB, even though de facto power over management decisions lies with the holding company or a dominating divisional management in an insolvency, ceteris paribus, creditors are constrained by the corporate veil. Some specific issues have to be considered:—

1. Families of companies sometimes present themselves as a group entity and potential creditors may believe they are contracting with the group — which could have an impressive standing — whereas their action in pursuit of a debt lies with a subsidiary which may have little financial standing.

2. If a subsidiary company falls on adverse financial circumstances it may be supported by its parent company. However, in a subsequent liquidation outside creditors may find their position is worse than if the company had been forced to face its financial position earlier. They have no recourse to the holding company.

3. Sometimes intercompany loans are made under letters of subordination, which rank such indebtedness below that of ordinary creditors. There can be doubts about the legal validity of such contracts, permitting a liquidator to claim the loans and thus threatening the position of other creditors of the borrowing company.

4. A bank may offer credit facilities to a subsidiary company on the guarantee of the parent or other associated company. (The letter of comfort in US terminology). Such relationships may not be apparent to an ordinary creditor of the subsidiary company.

The position of minority shareholders in such a subsidiary company would be constrained by the concept of corporate autonomy. A dissatisfied minority may only use the power that lies in its votes in a meeting of the company; again it may not pursue its dissatisfaction beyond the corporate bounds to the parent company or any other member of the group (subject to rights in the case of fraud or misfeasance)[4].

The Draft Ninth Directive

However, the EEC's draft 9th directive specifically recognises the position of companies in groups. Moreover it would give rights to creditors, minority shareholders and employees of SUB's to know about the interests of other group companies and to bring actions against the dominant undertaking and its directors.

The directive emphasises that such groups are of major

importance to the functioning of the Common Market. Groups play a significant part in many sectors in industry, commerce and the provision of services. They employ a significant proportion of the working population and play a major role on the capital markets. Cross frontier groups which operate in different member states are also of particular importance to economic integration. The Commission therefore is striving to eliminate legal difficulties which hinder the economic grouping together of undertakings in order to give them the necessary freedom of action to achieve economic targets.

The European Commission explain the thinking behind the 9th directive: —

"Companies in a group often have links which make them interdependent on the other member enterprises, no longer carrying on their business as economically independent entities.

Incorporation into a group.... is characterised by the fact that the undertakings concerned retain their individual legal form but lose their economic independence. In a group the economic activities of the various members is focused on the objects and interests of the larger association, the group and the management of members of the group is coordinated at group level, at least as it concerns its most important aspects (planning, investment, finance etc.)[5]."

The draft directive suggests that: —

".... in the majority of member states legislators have not concerned themselves with the phenomenon of groups at all or have dealt with only certain aspects such as disclosure or the protection of employees. Reality and law have become divorced to such an extent that the law on limited liability companies covers only an exceptional situation, namely a company acting exclusively on its own responsibility[5]."

The draft 9th directive is not only concerned with the elimination of legal obstacles to trade, it is intended to provide a framework in which groups can be managed on a sound legal basis, whilst ensuring that interests affected by group operations are adequately protected.

The directive introduces two fundamental concepts in group relationships — domination and dependence.

Domination arises when one company has the possibility of

exercising a long lasting influence over the corporate affairs of another. Dependence is the opposite. Figure 5 endeavours to contrast the present UK position of the autonomous subsidiary with the proposals of the draft 9th directive for domination and dependent companies in a group.

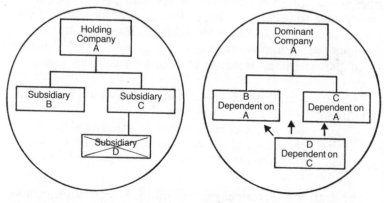

The autonomous subsidiary
– UK concept

If subsidiary D becomes insolvent its creditors, employees and any minority shareholders have no rights to "pierce the corporate veil", to pursue the assets or the directors of the holding company or any other group subsidiary.

The dominant and dependent company
– draft 9th directive concept

If D becomes insolvent its creditors, employees and any minority shareholders would have rights to pursue the dominant companies C and A, and their directors, for damages resulting from decisions taken which were at fault or not in the best interests of the dependent company D.

Fig. 5   The UK and the draft 9th directive concepts

The common form of dependence would arise from the holding of a majority of shares or voting rights in a subsidiary or an associated company. The directive does not offer a concrete, rigid definition or domination, leaving the courts to determine where necessary matters of substance and scope in the light of the circumstances. The point is that domination can be exercised over corporate decisions.

The draft 9th directive also introduces the concept of a "control contact for vertical groups". Principally these clauses are for the protection of minority shareholders in groups where management power is exercised by a dominant holding company. However, in such cases the management organisation and control structure in the group would have to be identified publicly. This has a close parallel with the accountable business activities we are about to propose.

German law recognises a right of creditors, under a domination contraction, to pursue any owner deemed to be in a dominant position. This includes the parent company of a wholly-owned subsidiary.

The directive would require fundamental changes to UK company law:−

> Firstly, interests that dominant companies have in their dependents must be disclosed and directors would be penalised for failure to do so.
>
> Secondly, creditors, employees and minority shareholders of a dependent company would be given rights to seek damanges from a dominant undertaking and its directors for losses resulting from the decision of the dominant company which had been at fault or not in the best interests of the dependent company. The liability for dominant undertakings and their directors for losses caused to a dependent company would be both joint and several.

The draft 9th directive, passing into UK legislation, would strike at the very heart of the concept of corporate autonomy and the present British right to treat every corporate autonomy and the present British right to treat every corporate company, irrespective of its ownership, as a totally separate entity[6,7].

It has to be said that the directive attempts to mirror the related corporate power within a group rather than permitting dominant companies to shelter behind the protection of the limited liability of its dependent companies. In discussing the implications of such thinking in Corporate Policy Group interviews it is apparent, on the one hand, that some British company directors cannot countenance their own group ever letting a subsidiary be would-up to the detriment of creditors; and, on the other hand, that a number of British groups, including some that are well respected, had already done exactly that.

As a matter of interest the EEC, in proposals for a statute for creating a European company, with rights across the jurisdiction of all members states[6], suggested that:−

1. The controlling undertaking of a group shall be liable for the debts and liabilities of dependent group companies.
2. Nevertheless, proceedings may be brought against the controlling undertaking of a group only where the creditor has first made a written demand for payment

from the dependent group company and failed to obtain satisfaction.

But it can be seen that neither the draft 9th directive or the proposal for a European company tackle the fundamental problem outlined at the beginning of this chapter. Both suggestions adopt the corporate model and focus on relationships between legal entities in a group. The dilemma remains where there is a separation between the corporate entities in a group or joint venture and the executive decision structure.

On Unitary Taxation

Another development threatens to override corporate boundaries in multinational companies. Under the principals of unitary taxation, which have been spreading through various states in the USA, the host country to a subsidiary of a group seeks to tax the global group profit instead of the profits of the resident subsidiary.

Broadly the idea is to tax that proportion of the total profits that the local subsidiaries' business bears to the whole business. Thus, it is argued, multinational companies cannot shift profits by transfer price mechanisms or the allocation of charges to tax havens or other tax beneficial locations.

Unfortunately unitary taxes may raise more than a "fair" share of taxes, which would mean that if such methods became widespread, the aggregate tax charge to the group would be excessive.

The net effect, in the longer term, might be to encourage companies to relocate or to find ways of reducing the effective size of the group for purposes of the tax calculation. Joint ventures or federations might achieve this result.

But let us return to the crucial aspect of governance in a group of companies.

An Idea – The Accountable Business Activity

We have identified a basic need – to find an appropriate way to exercise governance in groups in which a separation has occurred between the corporate structure and the structure used for making business decisions. In other words, there is a need to reflect the reality of managerial power, in a group enterprise, where it transcends or cuts across corporate boundaries and the duties of corporate directors to govern.

The intention would be to make explicit the business reality, and to use that as the basis for governance, rather than to shelter behind corporate convention. Where, in a group, a consortium or a federation of companies, there was a plurality of decision-making power, an attempt would be made to recognise the relevent basis of power.

The proposal is that every group, consortium and federation of companies, over a certain size[8], be expected to identify the boundaries, status, and performance of its business activities, irrespective of the corporate structure that it actually adopts, and to report on those business activities both financially, operationally and strategically. It would be management's responsibility to identify the boundaries of each accountable business activity (ABA).

Such an idea may seem highly radical and likely to present major problems for management. However, since the boundaries of each ABA are defined by management and reflect the actual way the business is run, all the necessary structure and systems must already be in place.

The company's management accounting systems will be reporting by ABA; the management information systems, data-bases, management controls and performance measures will relate to the ABA's and strategic planning, management control and operational actions will be undertaken at the level of the ABA, because it is the way the component business activities in the group are actually being run.

In some cases, of course, the boundaries of the SUB's in a group will be identical to the ABA's. In other cases a group of SUB's in a division will be designated an ABA. In a group with strategic business units that cut across the SUB boundaries in a matrix, the business units will be the ABA's.

It might be argued that a requirement for reporting by ABA's would emphasise the separation between business structure and corporate entities, and lead to a rationalisation of complex corporate structures. This might be beneficial. Others might expect a tendency to broaden the boundary of the ABA, consolidating businesses, until it covered the entire group with little, if any, segmentation into separate businesses. But remember that the management would have to stand behind their definition of business boundaries.

Responding to the problem of identifying accounting and decision-making units, to provide effective structures for the representation of both employees and investors in large groups, Hadden[9] makes two proposals: —

"The first is to ignore the formal corporate organisation of a complex group and to impose obligations on establishments or other units within the group which are identified in physical or operational rather than legal terms. The second is to require complex groups to adopt a corporate structure of holding and subsidiary companies which meets the objectives of the legislation.

The first of these approaches is initially attractive. It forms the basis both of the existing legislation for works councils in Germany and of the proposed Vredeling directive. (The legislation) identifies units within which a works council must be formed without reference of any kind to corporate status, and takes account of group structures only in so far as is necessary to identify units within groups as subsidiaries with separate corporate status, but provides in addition that establishments without such separate corporate status must be treated as if they were subsidiaries. In either case the objectives of the legislation can be achieved without interfering with the freedom of groups to create whatever corporate structure they please."

Hadden also recognises some drawbacks. Obligations to provide information for units without corporate status would not have a legal audit, nor be a legally identified body against which legal sanctions could be taken. He concludes that these drawbacks would be remedied by prescribing a corporate structure which must be adopted by large groups.

Here we take a different line. Since the structure of the ABA's will be determined by management, and will reflect the reality of the business organisational and decision-making structure, the information and control systems to provide the information will already be in existence. Independent verification, by external auditors, of the validity of the management's report on each ABA should be straightforward. Indeed in some cases, with inter-trading, transfer prices, and expense allocations between corporate entities, it may be more relevant than the audit of the SUB's.

The idea is that the ABA's should form the basis for governance in complex groups, consortia and federations of companies. The form that ABA reports should take, whether they should be public documents and filed, or available only to interest groups are matters for further discussion.

Likewise whether there should be a "governance meeting", open to interests affected by the activities of the ABA, at which the managers of the ABA would explain their activities, present their performance and outline their plans and expectations, is also a matter for conjecture.

The ABA's could also be used as the basis for limiting liability: although, then they would have to be given a precise statutory boundary – which might have the effect of incorporating ABA's as companies. Although, of course, companies have to be incorporated, and operate under the laws, of one and only one state, ABA's by their very nature, would cover whatever countries the business spanned.

The identification of ABA's would also facilitate a voluntary approach to employee information, consultation, participation and even codetermination (in some countries). Although in most cases, since the ABA reflects the real business structure, existing works councils and similar liaison committees will already relate to the ABA structure.

In other words, in defining the ABA for governance purposes, we are not proposing the creation of any business structure or entity that does not already exist. The ABA is a mirror to the decision-making and organisational structure that is there in practice. What it would do is to give credibility to the business reality, and provide mechanisms for realistic governance; rather than relying on archaic corporate structures which are relevant only to those with an interest in the company itself – that is the shareholders of that company.

Analysis of Information: "Disaggregation" and "Segment" Reporting

The idea that large and diversified companies should analyse corporate information between separate divisions or classes of business, which are individually of economic significance, is not original.

The Companies Act 1967[10] requires directors to report, where different classes of business are carried on, the turnover divided amongst those classes and "the extent (expressed in monetary terms) to which, in the opinion of the directors, the carrying on of business of that class contributed to or restricted the profit or loss of the company...." The Acts do not attempt to define the relevant classes of business or determine materiality in reporting.

A research study[11], published in 1977 by the Institute of Chartered Accountants in England and Wales, reviewed the experience in publishing analysed reporting. It concluded that a significant number of companies did not appear to comply with the statutory requirements. Some gave an analysis of turnover but not of profit and loss. There were also variations in the level of reporting profits – some using trading profits, others profit before tax; some allocating overheads to the lines of business, others showing the costs separately.

The 1967 Act[12] also requires holding companies to state in the company's accounts the names of subsidiaries and the country in which they are incorporated; also the proportion of the nominal value of the issued shares held, whilst the 1981 Companies Act[13] extends the disclosure requirement to include the aggregate amount of capital and reserves, and the profit or loss of such subsidiaries, where material. However it should be noted that such information follows the corporate structure and may not reflect the organisation structure of the economic entities in a group.

The Stock Exchange listing agreement requires listed companies to provide a geographical analysis of turnover and of contribution to trading results of those trading operations outside the UK. Such analysis need not be country by country, but by broad geographical areas.

The Corporate Report[14], published by the Accounting Bodies in 1975, discussed the reporting requirements for diversified companies, as follows: –

"6.49   The problem of disaggregation (i.e. the analysis of general corporate information between separate divisions or classes of business which are individually of economic significance, sometimes called segment or site reporting) arises in the context of the degree of disclosure appropriate in basic financial statements. The problem is found at its most extreme in organisations of vast size and spread such as nationalised industries and multinational companies.

6.50   While the 1967 Companies Act requires companies to disclose the profit and turnover of substantially different classes of business, the manner in which this provision has been interpreted and applied by individual companies varies and gives room for improvement. Stock Exchange disaggregation disclosure requirements relating to geographical divisions have proved less difficult to implement.

6.51 We approve of the concept of disaggregation while recognising the difficulties that any comprehensive system would impose on large organisations. We believe that an important step forward in this area would be improved implementation of the relevant provisions of the 1967 Companies Act, but that further research is needed to arrive at a generally applicable and practicable basis for disaggregation.

6.52 Our suggestion is that the basis of division of activities selected should be the one which in the opinion of the management will most fairly represent the range and significance of the entity's activities. The division could be based on groups of products or services, group companies, operating or geographic divisions, markets served or any combination of these items which would assist fair presentation. The basis of division used for internal management reporting operations and for external special purpose reports, for example to the Price Commission, will provide a useful guide to appropriate bases of division."

In the United States the SEC require companies to report[15] on analysis of turnover and profit or loss before taxation for each line of business or class of similar products or services which contributed 10% or more of the total turnover or profit or loss before tax. A limit of 10 lines of business is allowed. Material changes must be shown. The information is not audited. As with the 1967 Companies Act in Britain, the SEC regulations do not define what is to be regarded as a line of business or class of similar products or services for the purpose of their disclosure requirements, although they state that appropriate consideration should be given, inter alia, to the rates of profitability, degrees of risk and opportunity for growth of the different activities when deciding the basis of the analysis. In the release announcing the regulations, the SEC state that, in view of the numerous ways in which companies are organised to do business, the variety of products and services and the diversity of operating characteristics such as markets, raw materials, manufacturing processes and competitive conditions, it was not deemed feasible or desirable to be more specific in defining a line of business. The SEC stated that management, because of its familiarity with company into components on a reasonable basis for reporting purposes and accordingly have allowed management the discretion to determine the most appropriate basis for the provision of analysed information.

Welchman[16] comments that, "as in many fields of business report, the US has set the pace with it comes to disclosed semental information," but adding that, "the practice in other countries throughout the world has been slow to move in the same direction, despite convergent pressures from a number of international organisations". (Such as OECD, the United Nations and the International Accounting Standards Committee).

Given the requirements for segmental reporting that currently exist, and the proposals in this book to use ABA's as a basis of governance, it will be worth while mentioning the objections advanced against such analysed reporting.

The Coopers and Lybrand study[17] already mentioned marshalls the negative arguments under four headings:–
1. That it is irrelevant. Investors are only interested in the business as a whole. Diversifications is to spread the risks for the investor.
2. Analysed information can mislead. The impression may be given that the activities could be run as separate businesses – which may be untrue. Transfer prices and cost allocations could distort results. Comparisons between companies could be misleading. The accounts would be even more complex.
3. Publishing analysed information could reveal valuable commercial secrets.
4. The exercise would be expensive and not cost beneficial.
This study subsequently answers each of these criticisms.

Furthermore, in the context of our considerations here, the proposal to recognise Accountable Business Activities (ABA's) in complex groups goes far beyond the needs for information on the part of investors. We are proposing a mechanism for the exercise of governance – the setting of corporate direction, supervision of executive management as well as the exercise of necessary accountability.

Summary

We recognised the possible mismatch, in complex, diversified groups, between the corporate structure of subsidiary companies held at various levels, and the organisation and management decision-making structure adopted to reflect the reality of the economic entities.

The idea of the Accountable Business Activity (ABA) was proposed as a means of addressing governance processes to the reality of decision-taking power; and not to the fiction of legal entities.

Part 3 –

Rethinking the Work of Directors

Chapter 10
Governing Companies
– what boards really do

The focus of this chapter is on the work of the company director. Requirements of the law and ideas in the literature are contrasted with empirical evidence. Material derived from discussions with directors is used to develop a general model of corporate governance, covering processes that have to be carried out, to a greater or lesser extent, in all companies.

The Role of Directors in Law

British company law, up to now, has drawn no distinction between types of director. Executive and non-executive directors are not recognised. Such categories are unknown to the Companies Acts. Had the 1977 White Paper[1] on the conduct of directors, or Sir Brandon Rhys Williams' private members bills[2] led to legislation the role and nature of the non-executive would have been defined[3]. Similarly, if the proposals in the draft 5th directive, for two tier boards or unitary boards with non-executives, were to become the basis of British company law, fundamental changes would be necessary. Company law does not recognise functional directors, such as the finance director or the marketing director.

Neither does British statute law, at present, define the work that directors are expected to do with any precision. In this it gives more degrees of freedom and flexibility than company law gives to directors in most other European countries. Let us look at the position of directors in British law.

The Companies Acts are, of course, the statutory underpinning of the director's legal position, amplified and elaborated by case law and enhanced by the Memorandum and Articles of Association of the specific company.

As Jenkins (1972) wrote[4]:

> "While the Companies Acts expressly lay down certain duties of directors they are by no means exhaustive, since the larger part of director's duties have been determined by extensive and complex case law...."

167

Broadly the courts have determined three broad areas of duty for directors:

1. The fiduciary duty of loyalty and good faith

A director must act in what he believes to be the best interests of the company. His power must be exercised for the purposes for which the company was created and for the benefit of the company.

He must avoid conflicts between his duty to the company and any personal interests. For example, he must not have outside interests which prevent compliance with his duty to act in the best interests of the company. He must not make a secret profit by virtue of his dealings with the company: he is under a duty to disclose all such interests. A director is also under a duty not to reveal confidential information, obtained through board service, to outside parties.

The 1980 Companies Act concerned the fiduciary duty that the director owed to the company, emphasising that it was to the company (that is to the members) alone. However, the Act also stated "the matters to which the directors of a company are to have regard in the performance of their functions shall include the interests of the company's employees in general as well as the interests of its members". The full effect of this clause has still to be put to the test in the courts.

2. The duties of care and skill

Statute law, at present, does not recognise any distinction between the role, duties and powers of the executive and non-executive directors: all are equally responsible for the direction, executive action, supervision and accountability of the company[5].

A director is not required to give continuous attention to the company's affairs, as a director: of course he may additionally have a contractual relationship as an executive employee. A director may rely on properly delegated officers of the company or sub-committees of the board acting properly, in the absence of any evidence to the contrary.

A director is expected to bring to bear that degree of care and skill to the affairs of the company which might reasonably be expected of a person of his knowledge and experience. In other words a director's liability for negligence is a subjective measure of his behaviour and duty of care. There is no prescribed knowledge, experience or ability required of a director in a British company.

In the United States directors are expected to act prudently and to exercise business judgement[6].

When a company has failed the liquidator is able to bring misfeasance proceedings against any director for actual losses suffered by the company, if the director has misapplied or retained assets of the company or if he has been guilty of breaches of trust in relation to the company.

Fraudulent trading occurs if a business is carried on with intent to defraud creditors or for any other fraudulent purpose. Again a liquidator or other affected party can apply to the court to have any director who is knowingly a party to such fraud made personally liable for the debts of the company.

Finally, the legal position of the director is affected by the company's Memorandum and Articles of Association.

The Memorandum, under which the company is incorporated, lays down the objectives for which it has been formed, gives its name and registered office, defines its capital and confirms that the liability of its members is limited to their equity stake. The directors may not authorise activities outside the stated objects. In practice objects clauses tend to be drawn widely, giving boards much freedom: but contracts made outside the stated objects cannot be enforced.

The Articles of Association of a company lay down the rules by which it is to be governed, including the restrictions on directors' ability to exercise the company's powers. The Articles are likely to cover the calling and proceedings of shareholders' meetings, the number of directors and their share qualifications (if any), the rotation of directors, procedures at directors' meetings, the duties of the managing director, the appointment of chairman, and so on.

Thus the legal framework within which duties must operate provides certain constraints and lays down various duties; but it does not attempt to describe the nature of the director's work, nor define the knowledge, skills or abilities needed, nor identify the measures by which performance can be assessed.

The Role of Directors in the Literature

In the normative literature[7] on British boards an assumption is often made that the board is the ultimate vehicle for the management of the company – the top of the managerial pyramid. Such assumptions may well be valid in the PTY and PTE in which the board is, indeed, the top executive echelon, as we shall see in chapter 13. In such cases decisions of top management will be decisions of the board and vice versa; the only issue will be the extent of formality in bringing matters to minuted meetings of the board.

But what is the job of the board in a SUB, when strategy must be formulated in line with Group plans, where policy is laid down by Group head office staff, and control is exercised over corporate performance by Group systems and procedures? Or in the PTE or PLC with outside directors on the board, who are not part of the top management team, what is their role vis-à-vis the executive directors? In such cases the British literature is less clear.

The classical literature on strategic, long range planning tends to assume that those at the top of the enterprise have the prerogative and the power to make such decisions. Anthony's[8] definitive framework for planning and control, written in 1965, remains the underpinning model of much present thinking (fig.1).

Fig. 1   The framework for planning and control systems

Source: Anthony Harvard 1965

But the model does not differentiate the role of the board from that of management. The assumption that top management has the prerogative and the power to make such decisions is misleading. Today's company directors may not have such degrees of freedom. Their top level decision-making has to harmonise conflicts between many external forces as well as internal conflicts. Theirs is not solely a world of entrepreneurial creativity; it can involve political expediency.

Perhaps entrepreneurial small businessmen can still act under the old assumptions. But even for them the assumptions about the role and responsibilities of company directors in the modern corporation need further thought. Private company failures, such as Laker Skytrain is an example of the owner-dominated enterprise, which was highly successful at one stage, running into difficulties. Critical reports of Department of Trade Inspectors have drawn attention to the dilemma of the dominant chairman or chief executive in the public company.

Mace[9] whose researches in US companies have already been discussed, suggested that outside board members see themselves, firstly, in an advisory rather than a decision-making role. They provide "additional windows on the world"; and, being members of the President's (CEO's) peer group, widely experienced in business issues of real magnitude, are able to be a source of advice and counsel to him. Secondly, the board serves "as some sort of discipline for the management the president and those in subordinate positions.... a sort of corporate conscience".

Spencer[10], in the only empirical study by a sociologist of the role perceptions of British non-executive directors, concludes that:—

> "Non-executive directors are serious people going about serious business....(who) generally define themselves as influential rather than powerful (and) tend to perceive the role they play as more passive than active.... The most usual view is that the non-executive director, since he is respected for his wisdom and independence, will be influential and listened to, although it may not be his function to actually institute policy."

Focusing on the process, rather than the content, of the role she comments that, though boards are unique and thus demand different responses from individual directors, the process invites socialisation — a negotiated activity to determine the acceptable role with one's fellow directors. Competence is expected; both socially, to be able to relate to the board and its "collective symbolism", and technically, to be able to contribute to business discussions. Relationships with peers is crucial and, she advises, "non-executive directors should not become too friendly with executive colleagues".

Though decisions are perceived as being by consensus, the actual politics of power may include the exercise of influence by interest groupings.

The Work of Directors in Reality

The normative viewpoint tends to see the work of the director in terms of roles, responsibilities and duties. The orientation is towards structure, dealing, for example, with the size of boards, attributes of directors, executive and non-executive directors, audit committees and so on.

In the studies of The Corporate Policy Group we have tried to go behind such structural issues, to clarify the work of directors and the activities of boards, as they perceive them. The orientation has been on process rather than structure.

Furthermore, we wanted to probe beyond the roles and responsibilities described in the legal literature, with its emphasis on formal duties and structures, to look at questions such as: —

- how are modern companies governed, at the top and down through layers of subsidiaries?
- what *do* boards of directors actually do?
- who formulates strategy in a complex group?
- why do some companies have subsidiaries and others have divisional management structures?
- who monitors management performance, particularly if the managers form the board?
- what accountability is accepted, for what and to whom?
- what is the role of the Chairman?
- how is the power to govern really derived?

A simple matrix was devised to distinguish areas of activity. Firstly to what extent was the board's focus on the business or businesses being run by the company, as against the focus on the needs of the shareholders, or other stakeholders if the directors thought this important. Secondly a distinction was drawn between matters internal to the business operations, such as the state of the order book, or shorter term divergence from budget or cash flow issues, and longer term considerations of the company's strategic environment (figure 2).

Directors were asked their opinion on the desirable balance of board level activity (figure 3). Then they were asked to compare their ideal with their best estimate of the actual balance of activities in their own board (figure 4).

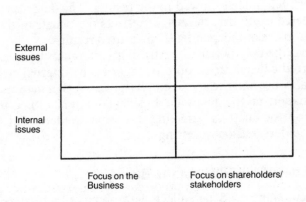

	Focus on the Business	Focus on shareholders/stakeholders
External issues		
Internal issues		

Fig. 2   The conceptual framework for analysis

	Focus on the business	Focus on the shareholders/ stakeholders	
External issues	48	18	66
Internal issues	25	9	34
	73	27	100

Fig. 3   Balance of board activities – DESIRABLE

	Focus on the business	Focus on the shareholders/ stakeholders	
External issues	24	14	38
Internal issues	58	4	62
	82	18	100

Fig. 4   Balance of board activities – ACTUAL

The sample included directors from all four types of company — private and proprietorial, subordinate and public. Consequently one would expect considerable variability in the data, which indeed showed in the results. The data also has to be treated cautiously because it reflects the beliefs of those in the sample, not independently measured results.

Nevertheless, notice the striking difference between the preferred concentration on the longer term, external environmental issues and the actual emphasis on internal matters. The domination of the focus on business matters rather than a concern for matters affecting the shareholders and other stakeholders is also interesting.

A Model of the Work of the Board

The quadrant used to collect data about directors' perceptions, also provides us with a convenient model of corporate governance (figure 5).

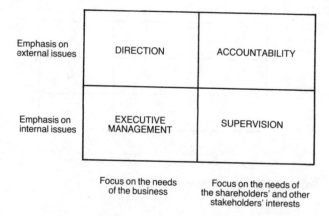

Fig. 5 A conceptual model of the activities of corporate governance

This framework focuses on processes in governance, rather than on the structures through which it is carried out. By determining the activities first, alternative ways of fulfilling them can be evaluated.

The *direction* of a company involves the formulation of strategy and the acquisition and allocation of overall resources, setting policies which guide and constrain management action and, broadly, establishing the direction the company is to take. It emphasises the mission of the business – the shared vision of possible futures and desirable directions for the enterprise.

Setting the corporate direction will inevitably be longer term and orientated towards the commercial, economic, social, technological and political environments in which the business exists. Strategy formulation involves the assessment of the threats and opportunities external to the business and the understanding of the strengths and weaknesses of internal resources. It includes the setting of corporate objectives and the identification, evaluation and choice of strategies to be pursued.

Executive management involves the running of the business – shorter term operational matters of financial, production and market management, keeping an eye on performance throughout the enterprise and taking decisions consistent with the strategies. This is the segment in which governance and management can overlap (see figure 6).

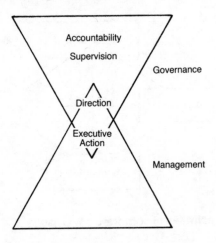

Fig. 6 The overlap of governance and management

It includes planning the ongoing operations, and organising, co-ordinating, motivating and leadership. Industrial relations, procurement, production, marketing, accounting and the control of operations are all part of the executive management task. The orientation will tend to be shorter term.

Supervision, on the other hand, implies a monitoring of executive action, with a view to ensuring it is appropriate to the interests of the shareholders and other groups with legitimate interests in the company. Supervision is an activity carried out to monitor and control executive action.

Accountability is the response to legitimate demands for accountability from shareholders and other interest groups. It includes the disclosure of information required under the Companies Acts, the Stock Exchange and other statutory and mandatory requirements. Accountability is the process by which the legitimacy of the company in society is established and maintained.

Obviously the four areas of activity in the model (figure 7) are interrelated. Setting the corporate direction provides strategies, policies, projects and plans which guide and constrain ongoing executive performance; which can then be monitored, supervised and controlled, with overall accountability, both for longer term strategic direction and current performance.

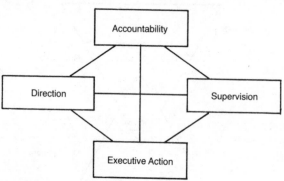

Fig. 7   The activities of corporate governance

How these activities are done, and by whom, will be explored in the next chapters, looking at the private and proprietary companies, the subordinate company and the public company separately.

Suffice it to say, at this stage, that by distinguishing four activities, we will be able to contrast and evaluate the implications of various proposals for governance, such as the two tier supervisory board, the use of independent outside directors, audit committees and representative directors, and the role of the chairman of the board vis-à-vis the chief executive officer.

> For example, in the supervisory board model, both direction and executive action fall to the executive management board, whilst supervision and accountability are the responsibilities of the supervisory board. In the German approach to corporate governance, which formed the basis for the original draft 5th directive[11], the supervisory board have no executive power over direction or executive action, but exercise their authority by the right to appoint, approve or remove the management board. The accountability role is fulfilled by a representative membership of the supervisory board elected by shareholders and employees.

In the unitary board, used on both sides of the North Atlantic, the four activities have all to be fulfilled by the board acting together. Herein lie some of the fascinating aspects of board membership and the potential dilemma of "marking one's own examination papers" or, in more prosaic terms, of separating the functions of executive responsibility from oversight and control.

Conclusions

In the conventional model of corporate governance, the directors, elected by the shareholder members and accountable to them, manage the company. The model emphasises structure and formal procedures. (Fig.1 chapter 2)

In the model proposed in this chapter (figure 7), the director's duty is to ensure effective governance of the company, which entails the four activities of: —

- Direction — formulating strategy, setting policies and approving plans: setting the overall corporate direction
- Executive action — managing the business — typically ensuring that appropriate operational planning, controlling, organising and leadership are fulfilled at the heart of the executive management function.
- Supervision — monitoring and controlling executive actions
- Accountability — disclosing information and responding

to members' and others' legitimate demands for accountability.

The model of corporate governance developed here is based on processes not structure, and emphasises power not procedures.

We can now apply this model of governance to the various types of company. Alternative approaches to governance can be compared and evaluated. Concepts of independence and objectivity, representation, involvement and participation, and corporate regulation can be assessed.

The conceptual framework − differentiating four types of company and the four component activities of governance − provides an opportunity to improve the direction and performance of business; and to influence the development of corporate regulation and company law.

In the earlier, golden days of the corporate concept the single corporate entity facilitated business growth, the formation of capital, the creation of employment and the generation of wealth for society. The new conceptual framework addresses the realities by which companies are governed today, rather than the legal structures which now regulate and constrain. Its adoption could lead to ideas again becoming a prime mover in corporate affairs. The alternative is governance based, at best, on the bureaucracy of regulation, or at worst, on the adversarial pressures of vested interests.

Chapter 11

Corporate Governance in Public Companies
– on objectivity in the boardroom

We turn, first, to governance in the largest of the corporate types in our conceptual framework – the PLC. Fewest in number by far, with less than 1% of all incorporations in Britain, this type of company is highly significant in terms of employment, investment and the creation of wealth.

In this chapter we review the size and structure of boards in PLC's, recognising that they, too, are quite varied. Then we address a key issue in corporate governance – the argument about independence – and consider the many alternative approaches to separating functions of governance.

Size and Structure of Boards – the PLC

In British public companies, the larger the company, the bigger the board tends to be – see table 1.

Company size by turnover	Number of companies in the sample	Average number of directors	Range Lowest	Highest
Up to £50m	66	8	4	24
£50m-£100m	84	8	2	22
£100m-£500m	93	9	4	35
Over £500m	49	12	4	20

Table 1   Board size, 1983, Large UK companies

Source: Korn/Ferry 1983. These data are broadly confirmed by a Heidrick & Struggles study: The UK Chief Executive and his outlook, 1983.

The average number of directors, divided between executive and non-executive, is shown in table 2. Notice that the executives are in the majority, a point made earlier; and that the percentage of non-executives is actually *lower* in the larger companies.

Table 3, however, demonstrates that in some companies the generalisation that roughly one-third of the board tends to be non-executive in the large company is not universally true.

Company size by turnover	Average number of directors			% Non-Executive
	Total	Executive	Non-Executive	
Up to £50m	8.1	4.6	3.5	43.4
£50m-£100m	8.0	5.4	2.6	32.6
£100m-£500m	9.1	6.0	3.1	34.2
Over £500m	11.5	7.5	4.9	34.6

Table 2   Composition of boards, 1983, Large UK companies

Source: Korn/Ferry 1983

Company size by turnover	No Non-Executive directors	Non-Executives in a minority	Equal Numbers of Executive and Non-Executives	Non-Executives in a majority
Up to £50m	6.1	43.2	14.2	36.5
£50m-£100m	19.1	51.1	9.8	20.0
£100m-£500m	6.5	72.0	7.5	14.0
Over £500m	8.2	79.6	–	12.2

Table 3   Structure of boards, 1983, Large UK companies

Source: Korn/Ferry 1983

Again we have to recognise the considerable variability between companies in their approach to corporate governance. Even among PLC's there is little homogeneity in their governance processes. Of course this is not surprising when we remember that PLC's vary from the vast corporate group, with hundreds of subsidiaries held at numerous levels, and the entire equity capital spread throughout tens of thousands of individual and institutional shareholders, to the small PLC whose ownership is in very few hands, with, perhaps no more than 10% of the voting capital available to the public through the unlisted securities market, and that held by very few.

Independence in Governance

Nevertheless, table 3 does show that management direction by executive directors is the norm in British PLC's. By contrast in large United States[1] companies independent direction is the norm, with a majority of outside directors. This focuses attention on two critical issues.

On the one hand, can management directors effectively monitor and control the performance of management and, in terms of accountability, be seen to supervise independently? The executive director is expected, in effect, to "wear two hats", as an executive responsible for his management tasks and as a director for the overall governance of the company.

Of course the problem is not new. Juvenal[2], writing some nineteen centuries earlier, queried "Quis custodes ipsos custodiat?" (Who is to guard the guards?) — although he was worrying about the guard on his wife when he went off to the wars.

On the other hand, with independent outside direction what is the non-executive director's responsibility for setting corporate direction and involvement in executive action? Can outside directors ever know enough about the business to make a real contribution, to accept real responsibility for those segments of governance: or are they, again, really overseeing and approving management thinking and action?

The question is how are the four components of corporate governance (figure 1) to be carried out and by whom?

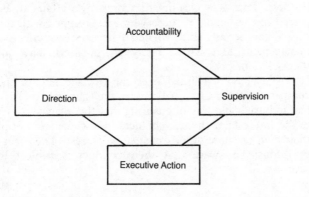

Fig. 1 The function of corporate governance

Another perspective should be noted. Pearce[3] questions whether the "inside" executive director and the "outside" non-executive are misrepresentations of real differences between individual directors. He argues that a dominant coalition of executive and non-executives may be most influential in affecting strategic decision-making. He concludes from his research that the nomination of outside directors may serve neither to provide an external orientation nor even be conducive to corporate profitability.

The Problem as Seen by the European Commission

In making various proposals for separating the functions of

supervision and accountability from direction and executive action, the European Commission outlined the problem as follows[4]

> "The distinctive characteristic of large and medium-sized commercial companies throughout the Community is that such companies are normally owned by a disparate and relatively numerous group. In fact one of the fundamental economic purposes which the 'société anonyme' and analogous corporate organisations have fulfilled is the bringing together of capital from numerous sources for the mutual benefit of those who have contributed and of society as a whole. In the interests of efficiency however, such contributors of capital must necessarily hand over the managemet of the company's affairs to a smaller group capable of relatively quick and continuous decision making. This also permits the company's affairs to be placed in the hands of those who are equipped with the special abilities and skills which are necessary for effective management and which many shareholders may not themselves possess.
>
> However, having handed over the management of the company's affairs to a small group, the shareholders have had to have some way of ensuring that the 'managers' act in the interests of the shareholders as a whole and not in their own or some other extraneous interest. The managers must be aware that their conduct is subject to scrutiny."

The Classical Solution – The Auditors and the AGM

The classical solution to this problem, and the one enshrined in British company law, is for the shareholders (members) to elect a board of directors who run the business and report to the members periodically, with independent auditors, also appointed by the members, to report whether the director's statement of account shows a true and fair view (see figure 2).

The Commission's view of this approach to governance in the large, public company[5] is as follows: –

> "The underlying assumptions of the legislators appear to have been that the members of the board would be personally involved in the management of the company's affairs and that the shareholders, astute in the pursuit of their own interests, would scrutinize the progress of the company's business and if necessary be able and willing to

**Fig. 2 The functions of corporate governance
– the classical solution**

call their managers to account through the power of the
general meeting to replace them. Where these assumptions have been justified, a simple structure of this kind
has worked effectively and in all probability still can.
However, while these assumptions were once justified
perhaps, they are justified increasingly rarely as companies' shares become widely distributed in a society, and
as their operations become complex and technical."

"As for the assumed willingness and ability of shareholders to scrutinize the company's affairs and to call the
managers to account, the problem becomes more difficult
as the number of the shareholders increases. A large,
disparate group of shareholders will not be able to
intervene as effectively as a small, coherent group.
Moreover, the effectiveness of their supervision depends
on the expertise and time which they can devote to the
company's affairs. Small shareholders in a large modern
enterprise often lack sufficient time and expertise to
ensure adequate, continuous control on their behalf."

This opinion does not identify a possible role for institutional shareholders, who might be expected to have the expertise,
the time and the motivation to look after their interests; and,

indeed, there is evidence[6] of their preparedness to do so in certain circumstances. On the other hand institutional intervention may be direct with the chairman and his board, rather than through general meetings of all members: moreover, their interests may not be the same as those of small, individual shareholders.

Attempts have been made by British company law to enhance the position of the shareholder, in successive Companies Acts, by increasing the amount of information which companies are required to disclose to their members. Certain decisions, such as issuing further capital or changing objectives, also need the members' approval.

Some companies, recognising the limitations of the classical approach, have endeavoured to improve the opportunities for the members to use the AGM as a vehicle for exercising some aspects of governance, for example by holding members' meetings in different parts of the country, encouraging financial reporting of company affairs and inviting brokers, analysts and others to learn more about such matters.

Another idea, developed by Charkham[7], is to create the opportunity for the members to form a shareholders' committee, drawn from their membership, if they wish.

Writing in The Financial Times[8] Charkham argues for the use of independent directors, but suggests that any proposal which relies on a proportion or number of such directors is flawed because it says nothing about the calibre and quality of the people elected. He advocates legislation to permit ten percent of the shareholders in a public company to call for the creation of a board membership nominating committee.

Such a committee would be small, should include experts, and would not itself elect. Its task would be to ensure that independent directors of the necessary calibre were proposed. It would report to the members whether those proposed had their approval.

Charkham's proposal attempts to restore power over board appointments to the members' meeting. Unfortunately it could suffer from the same problem that affects the present voluntary approach; who is to form the nominating committee; can a diverse group of shareholders realistically agree on people to represent them?

In the large, complex PLC, with a multitude of shareholders the dilemma remains − the meetings of members is not an adequate vehicle for exercising the accountability of and supervision over the management board which can dominate matters. To elect a shareholders' ginger group could be to shift power to them.

The European Commission concluded that "the (classical) approach needs to be complemented by other techniques".

Other Approaches – 1. The "two hats" solution

One alternative approach to the problem of overseeing and controlling management when all, or a majority, of the board are themselves responsible for management, is to emphasise a separation between the duties of executive action and the other activities of governance (see figure 3).

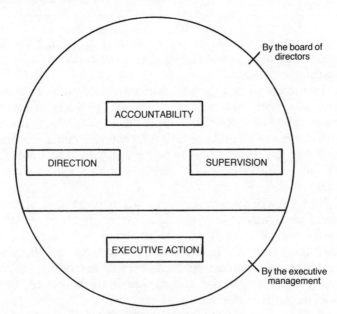

**Fig. 3 The functions of corporate governance
     – the "two hats" solution**

Executives are employees of the company, responsible according to the terms of their service contract, and protected by labour law in matters such as redundancy: as directors of the company the same people are servants of the company with a special status under company law, subject to the company's Articles and any terms in their letter of appointment.

The chairman of a PLC, quoted on the Stock Exchange, writes to newly appointed executive directors as follows:

> "Congratulations on your appointment to the Board.
>
> Whenever a new member joins, I try to outline what my expectations are on the role of the board and the responsibilities of the directors.
>
> I believe the board has a duty to direct: that is why we are called directors. It is different from managing the business.
>
> An executive director must 'wear two hats' – the one as an executive responsible for specific duties within the business; the other as a director responsible with the rest of the board members for directing the company.
>
> In the board room you should not be wearing your executive hat."

The quotation also makes a useful distinction between the individual duties as a manager and the collective task of the board.

In the classical approach the board is seen as running the business, with supervision by the shareholders in members' meetings. The "two hats" approach expects the managers to run the business and the board to exercise control over them and see that the business is being well run. The belief is that executive directors can "wear two hats" and separate the functions.

The drawbacks are obvious. When some area of management performance or a particular management decision comes in for review or criticism the tendency for the management director concerned is to defend himself. In the allocation of scarce resources there will be an inevitable tendency to protect one's existing situation and exploit it to the benefit of one's own managerial interests.

Even if it is claimed that with appropriate attitudes and strong chairmanship such a separation of function can be achieved, it cannot be seen to be acting with total independence from an external viewpoint.

Nevertheless the approach is widely adopted, and held to be successful in many British public companies. Writing about his experience of the board of ICI, Henderson[9] says:—

> "Individual directors on the ICI board each have a number of portfolios to look after — a functional

responsibility, an overview of a particular territory, and a coordinating role internationally for a particular product or group of products."

"Basically the objectives (of the board) should be:—

1. to set and monitor tough but achievable financial targets, including for example profitability, cash flow, return on capital, dividend policy, gearing, retentions, etc.

2. to outline the preferred corporate shape a decade ahead and to ensure that it takes account of both strengths and weaknesses as well as the needs of the environment.

3. to make the most senior appointments and plan carefully succession and career progress.

4. to act as the custodian of the corporate image and to nurture key relationships with the media, the institutions, employees, unions, Government and shareholders."

Other Approaches — 2. The non-executive director

An obvious solution to the problem of separating the functions of executive action and supervision is to appoint non-executive directors to the board. They can also take an objective approach to the direction function.

The appointment of non-executive directors has been encouraged by the CBI, a British Labour government and a Conservative MP as well as the Institute of Directors, the City institutions and the Governor of the Bank of England.

The report of the Company Affairs Committee of the CBI[10] (The Watkinson Report) published in 1973, on the responsibility of the British public company, concluded that "the inclusion on the board of public companies of non-executive directors is highly desirable..... by virtue of the fact that unlike executive directors they are not closely involved in the day to day affairs of the company, and they are in a better position to see the company as a whole and to take a critical view of it".

The Government White Paper on The Conduct of Company Directors[11] argued, in 1977, that

"Non-executive directors can bring to the board a breadth of knowledge and experience which the company's own management may not possess. Even more important, they can increase the element of independence and objectivity in board decision-making. Not being involved in day-to-day management they are able to take a detached look at the way in which the company is being run and at its medium and long-term policies. They should provide independent supervision of the company's management. In order to do this effectively, however, the non-executive directors need free access to management information and there need to be enough of them. One or two non-executive directors on a board which is twenty strong are unlikely to exercise real influence."

Sir Brandon Rhys Williams, in abortive private member's bills[12] later in 1977, called for all companies with more than 1,500 employees or total net assets in excess of £5 million to have not less than three non-executive directors – defined as "not an employee of, nor holding any other office or place of profit under the company or any subsidiary or associated company....."

Sir Brandon also tabled amendments to the Companies Bill 1981[13] which would have required companies that did *not* have three non–executive directors, to bring the matter before the members.

In the debate[14] the Minister announced the formation of an agency to promote and facilitate the election of non-executive directors by companies that have not hitherto appointed non-executive directors to their boards. This became PRO NED (Promotion of Non-Executive Directors), sponsored by the Bank of England, the CBI, the Stock Exchange and other City Institutions[15]. In its booklet on the role of the non-executive director[16], PRO NED explains

"The purpose of appointing non-executive directors is to provide the board with knowledge, expertise, judgement and balance which may not be available if the board consists only of full-time executives.

Some chairmen may consider that all these talents are present without the need for non-executive directors. This would be rare, whatever the qualities of the executive directors, if only because the executives spend virtually all their available time and energy working on the company's business. They will often have done so for many years. Their day-to-day responsibilities may be confined to a limited part of the business. It is unrealistic to expect them also to exhibit the detachment and wider experience that can be brought to bear by a non-executive director from outside.

Thus the essential advantage of non-executive directors is that they bring a fresh and wider view to board discussion and decision taking. In the context of the normal duties of a board of directors, this can involve:

(i) Seeing issues in their totality. An executive director, because of his executive (and sometimes relatively narrow) responsibility, may be less well equipped to give proper weight to the differing aspects of issues faced by the board.

(ii) Giving the external view. Because he is not heavily involved in the day-to-day running of the company, the non-executive director can bring a wider judgement to bear on matters before the board. This is of particular relevance on the context of strategic planning or when events of special importance to the company's future are involved such as mergers and acquisitions and large capital projects. A non-executive director can provide new perspectives, helping the board to think through its underlying strategies and to examine the options.

(iii) Providing special skills. A company that has moved into a new market, overseas location or technology may need board-level counsel from an expert. The addition of a merchant banker, engineer, lawyer or accountant may supplement internal resources.

(iv) Providing an independent view where potential conflicts of interest arise. As a routine this means trying to ensure that the proper balance is struck among the many interests in a company (shareholders, lenders, employees, management, customers, suppliers, the investment community and the public at large). It assumes particular importance where the directors' interests may conflict with those of shareholders (for example where directors have interests in transactions entered into by the company; where the amount or the propriety of benefits to directors is in doubt; on dividend policy; or where a takeover bid is received).

(v) Providing contacts, for example with sources of finance, with potential customers or suppliers, with Government and with sources of professional advice.

(vi) Advising on the public presentation of the company's activities and performance, for example by reviewing the chairman's annual statement and any other documents published in the press or likely to attract press comment."

The Institute of Directors has promoted the inclusion of well qualified and able non-executive directors on the boards of companies, for many years. The Institute's Guidelines for Directors[17] suggests that

> "In the Institute's view, every board of a public company should contain a proportion of suitable non-executive directors with a minimum of two. The same considerations apply to any private company, large or small, which wishes to maintain an active control over its future."

We should remember, of course, that British company law at present recognises no distinction between classes or types of director. All are similarly liable and responsible under the law.

However, the inclusion of non-executive directors on a board, which is otherwise the management team, may well change the corporate culture significantly. The style of the chairman in choosing, introducing and managing the board level processes affected by his non-executive directors can be crucial.

> "The difficulty with the outsider is that he can become the chairman's confidant and mentor: this creates jealousies and uncertainty internally. I had just such an experience recently. The chairman, who likes to hear his own voice, and runs board meetings from 10.30 to 4.30, brought in an outsider to work on corporate strategy – which is the role I had been fulfilling."
>
> Finance Director – British PLC in
> manufacturing industry. Case 004

Even on the boards of American public companies, with a majority of outside directors, the style and culture of the board can be significant.

> "Non-executive directors are not usually seen as a threat by executives, they don't have that much power. It is the independent confidant of the chairman who is the problem. They are rather like the chairman's wife – a person behind him, influencing him – but not really accountable. No-one knows on what criteria, or how, to challenge him."
>
> Finance VP – US Corporation
> Case 007

In focusing on the structure of boards we must not, of course, confuse form with substance. The critical aspects of governance are the processes by which boards govern, rather than their membership. As Jonathan Charkham[18], Director of

PRO NED[19], has put it: —

> "The power of appointment to the board is the fulcrum on which the prosperity of the company is balanced — not the structure of the board."

The role of the non-executive director appointed by a government minister to the board of a nationalised company can be perplexing[20]. Is he to serve a political purpose, intended to influence corporate policy in the direction intended by the government of the day? Should his first loyalty be to the industry itself, as a full-fledged director without thought of political bias?

This confusion seems particularly acute in the case of concerns long subject to strong political direction such as coal, steel and railways. These businesses live in an almost constant conflict between public and politicians on the one hand and a tight-knit, often defensive, management hierarchy on the other. This hierarchy tends to view outsiders — as non-executive directors by definition must be — with deep scepticism. The director is thus encouraged to be an ambassador for the industry outside it rather than a searching critic of its policies and methods.

What should the director's response be to this predicament? Should he attempt to second-guess senior management? Should he be selected with specialist skills relevant to the industry? But can he prevent himself "going native"? Should he set himself up as a buffer between essentially commercial management and essentially political ministers and civil servants?

It is not possible to address these issues here: but the conceptual framework for corporate governance clearly highlights such issues, which have to be resolved if the governance task is to be successfully carried out.

Independence of Non-Executive Directors

Most of the discussions about non-executive directors in British companies have only sought to draw a distinction between the executive directors, who are involved in managing the business, and the others — called, not unreasonably, non-executive.

However, non-executive directors may not be independent of the company. They might be retired executives of that company, representatives of large shareholders, involved in the distribution of the company's products, provide the company with goods, or services and so on[21]. Of course, there may be a good case for including such people on the board for the benefit of their experience and connections. But their involvement cannot be construed as independent, even though it may be constructive and objective.

Of the British commentators on non-executive directors only the Institute of Directors makes recommendations on independence. Their code of practice[22] recommends:—

"That every company board should have a minimum of two non-executive directors who are independent.

At the same time the Institute realises that a company may also choose to appoint non-executive directors who are not independent because their relationship may stem from prior executive responsibilities, association with the company's professional advisors, or from the representation of financial institutions, major shareholders or various sectional interests."

"The non-executive director is independent who does not have either:

(i) A contractual relationship with the company other than the office of director (and therefore is not subject to the control or influence of any other director or group of directors).

(ii) Any other relationship with the company which could affect the exercise of independent judgement."

"It is also recognised that three of the primary contributions of all non-executive directors are:

(i) To improve the decision-making quality of the board.

(ii) To expand the horizons within which the board determines the long-term strategy of its business and to bring into such discussions particular knowledge, experience or skills which are relevant and which the board might otherwise lack.

(iii) To monitor executive performance against agreed objectives."

Independent non-executive directors could find themselves facing difficult problems with an incumbent, executively orientated board. Evidence is sparse, because such matters are typically kept secret; but problems raised by members of the Institute of Chartered Accountants[23], seeking advice on ethical matters, provide some examples:—

	%
Doctoring of figures to support cases for financial support, or in connection with business acquisitions or disposals	22.5
Questions of solvency or possible fraudulent trading	20.5
Tax evasion, PAYE or VAT irregularities	17.5
Window dressing, false transactions, fraud	12.5
Payment of inducements	7.5
Suspected irregularities of subsidiaries in international groups	7.5
Directors' "perks"	7.5
Internal control deficiencies	5.0

Other Approaches – 3. The audit committee

The matter of independence is not trivial. In the United States of America, outside directors (as non-executive directors tend to be called there) often form a majority of the board of listed companies, as we have seen. To obtain a listing on the New York Stock Exchange it is necessary to have an audit committee of the board, with independent directors "genuinely independent of management, free from any relationship, financial or otherwise, which might interfere with the exercise of independent judgement and be able to resign if necessary from the directorship without financial hardship"[24].

In the United States audit committees have been widely used as vehicles for ensuring supervision and accountability at board level. Mautz & Neumann in 1977[25] showed that an audit committee is a main board committee, wholly or mainly composed of independent, outside directors, with the main responsibility to:

- discuss with independent auditors any problems and experience in completing the audit
- discuss scope and timing of independent audit work
- discuss effectiveness of internal controls
- discuss meaning and significance of audited figures
- approve or nominate independent auditors

- discuss adequacy of staffing for internal audit
- discuss findings and recommendations of internal audit
- discuss adequacy of staffing for accounting and financial responsibilities
- discuss organisation and independence of internal auditors
- discuss plans of internal audit function
- review accounting principles and practices followed by the company
- discuss effectiveness of procedures to prevent conflicts of interest, political contributions, bribes or other improper payments
- discuss effectiveness of use and control of data processing.

Audit committees of the board have also been recommended for British companies[26].

The White Paper on the Conduct of Company Directors[27] outlines the nature and purpose of such committees:

"In the United States and Canada a practice has developed in recent years whereby the boards of public companies appoint *an audit committee* composed wholly or mainly of non-executive directors. The duties of the audit committee are flexible depending on the needs of the company, but the core functions are to review the financial statements and to review the audit arrangements and the company's internal financial controls. The audit committee works closely with the auditors who are normally invited to attend its meetings. It has been found in the United States and Canada that audit committees play a useful role in strengthening the influence of non-executive directors and the position of the auditors..... The time may come when it will be appropriate to legislate in this field, but the government believes initially at least it will be better for companies, investors and their representative bodies to work out schemes which can benefit from a degree of flexibility which the law could not provide. It has been found in North America that one of the conditions for the successful operation of audit committees is that the board should contain a suffcient number of strong and independent non-executive directors to serve on them. This means that companies must be willing to allow members of their senior management or directors to serve as non-executive directors on the boards of other companies, to the general advantage of industry. The

Consultative Committee of Accountancy Bodies, in a memorandum to the Secretary of State for Trade, has supported experiments with audit committees by UK companies. The Government welcomes this and also the consideration which is currently being given to them by the Confederation of British Industries and The Stock Exchange."

The Bank of England Quarterly Bulletin[28] in 1983 showed an increasing use of non-executive directors and audit committees.

In the 1981 survey by the Company Secretary's Review[29] 13% of listed companies, 4% of private companies and 3% of subsidiary companies in the sample of 380 UK companies had audit committees. The majority of them had been created within the previous decade. Korn/Ferry[30] also report on the use of audit committees (table 4). Those data give a broad picture of the use of audit committees; but care must be exercised in deducing trends because of the sample size and distortions produced by different firms responding to the questionnaires in each year.

Company Size by Turnover	Number of Companies in sample	% with Audit Committees
£20m-£50m	66 (59)	24.2 (11.86)
£50m-£100m	84 (101)	17.6 (4.95)
£100m-£500m	93 (112)	22.6 (13.39)
Over £500m	49 (36)	34.7 (36.11)

Table 4 Use of predominantly non-executive audit committees 1983 (compared with 1980)

Source: Korn/Ferry: 1983 and 1980

In a previous study, the author[31] made the following comments on the development of audit committees in UK governance:

"With classical British empiricism we may expect leading companies to experiment with audit committees, learning as they go, and ultimately legislation being enacted to reflect the then perceived good practice. But do such companies really need the audit committee in the first place? Inevitably one is drawn to the conclusion that in British companies audit committees are most likely where they are least needed.

Given the enthusiastic support of the Chairman, the cooperation of the entire board, and high calibre, independent directors, there seems little doubt that an audit committee can make useful contributions. It is one way for a Chairman to use his independent directors and to secure open communication with the external auditors. But that is insufficient to give it universal acclaim.

If we want to reinforce the auditors' position and ensure that shareholders' interests are adequately represented there are ways other than by an audit committee – a return to practices prevalent fifty years ago, for example. Auditors could be required to attend, to report and be open to questions at any meeting of the board of directors at which published financial reports were to be considered. They might be expected to attend, to report in person and be open to question at every annual and other meeting of the company. The routine management letter prepared at the conclusion of an audit might become the vehicle for communicating with non-executive directors or the chairman about outstanding matters of financial reporting, financial controls, accounting policies or other pertinent issues about the audit, creating the opportunity and expectation for discussion and follow-up.

Of course, where conflicts of opinion or other disputes do arise with a strong executive management the auditor needs intellectual authority and tough moral fibre to stand out against them. An argument in favour of the audit committee is that such situations might be eased. But care must be taken with the argument – it is surely better to increase the resolve within the accounting profession than to provide the weak auditor with an escape route.

But above all the detailed discussion of the pros and cons of audit committees in Britain there towers another issue of considerable significance. The audit committee is a North American concept. Britain is part of the European Community. An audit committee, seen as a surrogate for shareholders, creating a channel with external auditors, increasingly looks like a committee of independent directors to monitor the management and begins to resemble a second tier for the board. They do not have audit committees elsewhere in Europe: perhaps because they are not necessary with alternative forms of corporate governance."

Other Approaches – 4. The two tier board

The experience of two tier boards, with an absolute separation of supervision from executive management lies in continental European countries. Advocacy for the concept has come from the European Commission in Brussels.

The original draft 5th directive from the Commission, published in 1972, concerned board structures and employee participation, and proposed that all large companies should have two-tier boards. The upper, supervisory board would be responsible for generally overseeing the company, monitoring and supervising the executive actions of the lower, management board, with the duty, and the sanction, of appointing and, if necessary, removing the members of the management board, who are responsible for running the business (see figure 4).

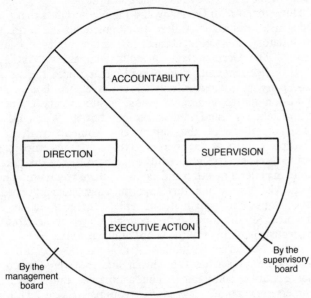

**Fig. 4   The functions of corporate governance
– the supervisory board**

In explaining the idea of a supervisory board, and contrasting it with the classical approaches, the Commission[32] explained that

"Legislators in many Member States have attempted to solve the problem of supervision more radically by introducing into the company's structure a new element: a body distinct from either the general meeting or the managing board or council which has as its function the supervision and control on behalf of the shareholders of those managing the company."

"The earliest form which this solution took may well have been the commissioners ('commissarissen') of Dutch law and practice, who might be appointed by the shareholders to supervise the executive directors' conduct. In forms more limited in practice, the idea was also given expression in Belgium, France, Italy and Luxembourg. In these countries, the law has required the appointment of commissioners ('commissionaires' or 'sindaci') but their function has normally been limited to controlling the accuracy of the company accounts and the legality of the company's activities. The Scandinavian shareholders' committee is also the same basic concept."

"However, it is in Germany and the Netherlands that the idea has received its fullest development in the form of mandatory 'dualist' structures for certain kinds of company. The German law on stock companies ('Aktienrecht', 'Aktiengesetz') since 1870 has required the stock company ('Aktiengesellschaft') to have two bodies in addition to the general meeting: a supervisory council ('Aufsichtsrat') and a management board ('Vorstand'). The members of the supervisory council, with the exception of those members who represent the company's employees, are today normally appointed by the shareholders in general meeting and can be removed by them. The supervisory council in turn appoints a management board, the members of which it can replace for good cause. A member of the supervisory council may not be simultaneously a member of the board of management."

"In the Netherlands, the law of 1971 on the structure of companies prescribes a somewhat similar system for most large public companies. The companies must have a supervisory council ('raad van commissarissen') and a management board ('bestuur'), the latter being appointed and removed by the former. The supervisory council is self perpetuating, but the shareholders and the employees have the right to challenge a proposal to nominate a member on the ground that the appointee is not qualified or that the council would not be properly composed if he were nominated."

"The distinctive feature of these systems is that the shareholders have an opportunity to influence the composition of a body which has as its function the exercise of general and relatively continuous control and supervision over the activities of those managing the company's affairs. The members of the supervisory body have the opportunity of scrutinizing the management of the company on behalf of the shareholders in a way that shareholders themselves, particularly small shareholders, normally cannot."

"Even when companies do not have a formal dualist structure, the division of directors into executive and non-executive groups can operate so as to produce a similar separation of function, with the non-executive directors exercising a supervisory function in relation to the conduct of the executives. This phenomenon has been observed in France, Italy, Ireland and the United Kingdom. However, it is clear that an informal separation of function does not provide the same guarantees as a formal separation. Moreover, in many cases non-executive directors do not have supervisory functions at all, and could find it very difficult to exercise such functions even if they wished to do so, by reason for example of their minority position, their lack of time and information, or their dependence in fact upon the executive directors' good-will."

The conceptual argument behind the Commission's thinking is well understood in political theory; the need for checks and balances. John Stuart Mill commented that:—

"A majority in a single assembly.... easily becomes despotic and over weaning if released from the necessity of considering whether its acts will be concurred in by another constituted authority. The same reason which induced the Romans to have two consuls makes it desirable that there should be two chambers; that neither of them may be exposed to the corrupting influence of undivided power...."

The State of Play on the Draft 5th Directive

The original proposals for the separation of function with a supervisory board from the European Commission[33] was published in 1972.

The British government, then a Labour administration, formed a committee of enquiry, under the chairmanship of Lord Bullock, in 1975, to consider aspects of industrial democracy. Their report[34] advocated the continuation of the unitary board, but with a statutorily enforced tripartite representation of shareholders and employees (appointed through trades union mechanisms) in equal proportions and a third, balancing element of independent members. This was referred to as the $2x + y$ formula.

However, the business members of the Bullock Committee produced a minority report which rejected the trades union nominated employee component and proposed a separation of function between executive and independent supervision.

Both the original draft 5th directive and the Bullock Report were attacked by management and directors of British companies, but the debate focused principally on the ideas for worker involvement at board level rather than on the structure of boards.

The Commission produced a further consultative document in 1975, submitted a working paper to the European Parliament in 1978, and in May 1982 the Parliament adopted an opinion on the directive and a further draft was produced in 1983.

These proposals[35] introduced two alternative forms of governance for all PLC's: either a two-tier board structure or a one-tier unitary board, called the administrative organ, with the following provisions (Article 21A): –

"The one-tier system – the administrative organ

1. (a) The company shall be managed by the executive members of an administrative organ under the supervision of the non-executive members of that organ. The number of non-executive members shall be divisible by three and greater than the number of executive members.

   (b) The executive members of the administrative organ shall be appointed by the non-executive members acting if necessary by a majority. However, the executive members of the first administrative organ may be appointed in the memorandum or articles of association.

2. Where the administrative organ has more than one executive member, the non-executive members, acting if necessary by a majority, shall specify which executive member is more particularly responsible for questions of personnel and employee relations."

In addition to this fundamental shift of power from the board as a whole to the non-executive members, the proposals would also require changes to the duties of directors and penalties for failing to fulfil them, the conduct and powers of members' meetings, and the function and liability of auditors.

Member states are to be left free[36] to choose whether to introduce either or both of the approved models of board structure. Thus any legislation could take one of the following forms:

.. a requirement for a unitary, single tier board along the lines of the description above,

.. a requirement for a two-tier board on the directive's model,

or .. the right for a company to choose either model.

In any case fundamental changes to corporate governance and law would be required in Britain.

The original 5th directive had two primary aims — to separate the executive function from an independent supervisory activity; and to provide for wider employee involvement in key decisions.

The revised proposals for employee participation have to be read in conjunction with the "Vredeling" proposals[37]. Mandatory participation would be required in all groups of public companies employing 1000 or more people: to be provided by either: —

1. a supervisory board with representative worker directors,
2. elected "non-executive" worker directors on a unitary board,
3. a works council,
4. or some other system established by collective agreement.

The intention is to give the employees' representatives the same rights to information and consultation, under each of the schemes. These would include quarterly reports of company affairs, advance copies of the annual financial report and accounts, the right to call for special reports, and the need to be consulted on major decisions such as plant closures or significant restructuring.

The Vredeling draft would further give the employees' representatives access to substantial general information on their local company or division and on the group as a whole. Where local management failed to communicate adequately, there would be a right to approach the group corporate office directly[38].

The response of the British Government to these proposals was provided by Mr. Tom King[39], the Employment Secretary, in November 1983: —

> "It is difficult to see how legislation that imposes the rigid set of procedures set out in the draft "Vredeling" and Fifth Directive contributes to the creation of a 'common market' of goods and services. Instead of strengthening trade links between Member States these Directives look likely to reduce the competitiveness of industry in the Community.
>
> The Government welcomes moves to promote the involvement of employees in the enterprises for which they work, but it believes that the main initiative is best left to employers and employees, who are in the best position to judge what best suits their particular circumstances. European Community law in this field would be cumbersome, would increase costs for employers and would harm industrial relations by disrupting the many flexible and effective arrangements which have evolved in the UK voluntarily."

From the perspective of our research studies the latest European Commission ideas have two weaknesses.

Firstly, by encouraging employee participation at board level, the Commission fails to draw the essential distinction between governance and management. Though the creation of harmonious working conditions and obtaining fair play for all employees are undoubtedly worthy objectives, to seek them through power in the governance of the enterprise, rather than through the management structure, would be to encourage adversarial relations.

Secondly, the ideas apparently fail to appreciate the complexity of large groups, as described in chapter 5. They also ignore the potential power of institutional investors in the public company, overlook the significance of joint ventures, associations and federations between groups, and totally exclude private groups which, in the UK, include enterprises much larger than many public companies (see chapter 4).

Other Approaches — 5. Using the courts or a state agency

The underlying principal in the exercise of corporate governance in Britain is that, as far as possible, regulation should be in the hands of those directly involved. Self-regulation is preferable to state-regulation. The role of the law is to facilitate and legitimise activities, providing for essential disclosure and controls. The role of the courts is to prevent abuses and to provide an avenue of appeal for the resolution of conflicts.

The alternative concept, practised in many continental European countries is for regulation and codification of corporate behaviour by the law. The director in France, for example, is exposed to penalties for offences against a multiplicity of rules, regulations and statutes. As a result the chief executive must clearly define actions delegated to subordinates.

In the United States, a broadly Anglo-Saxon attitude to self-regulation is adopted; but the States laws, under which companies are incorporated, differ in the extent of their definition of governance duties, and the courts are more widely used to resolve conflicts. Litigation can become a surrogate for regulation.

The regulation of the stock market in Britain is similarly regulated under the traditions of self-regulation. The Council for the Securities Industry and the Take-Over Panel are vehicles of the City institutions not of State regulatory mechanisms[40].

In America many of these activities are undertaken by a Federal agency – the Securities and Exchange Commission which thus exerts considerable power in the processes of governance – particularly of accountability.

Summary

We have seen how public companies compare in terms of the size and structure of their boards. Since outside capital is involved in the PLC a crucial issue is how governance is to be exercised for the benefit of the company.

Various alternative approaches were explored:–
- the classical solution relying on the members' meeting and independent auditors,
- the "two hats" solution in which predominantly executive directors are expected to be able to take an objective, corporate view as well as act managerially,
- the use of non-executive directors, and the discussions

about their independence,
- the use of an audit committee of outside directors to exercise some supervision,
- the idea of two tier boards and
- the reliance on the courts or State agencies like the SEC.

The tendency of the European Commission, in their search for company law harmonisation, seems to be towards codification and regulation of corporate governance by law: albeit the later drafts of the 5th directive allow more alternative forms of structure. The United States approach is to favour self-regulation, with independent, outside directors, but with tough demands for disclosure and supervision by the SEC. In Britain, though there have been plenty of ideas, we have yet to face up to the conceptual issue of how we do want our public companies to be governed – for the protection and benefit of *all* concerned. We shall be making some suggestions in the last chaper.

Chapter 12

Corporate Governance in Private and Proprietorial Companies
– the significance of style

In this chapter we look first at the appointment of directors. Although company law does not differentiate between types of company, we see how the composition of boards produce different styles of governance.

We look specifically at the size, structure and style of boards in private and proprietorial companies.

The Appointment of Directors

Under British company law, and subject to the company's Articles of Association, the directors are formally nominated and appointed by the members acting together, either in general meeting or by proxy vote.

The number and names of the first directors are usually determined by the subscribers who originally form the company[1]. At the first annual general meeting all directors retire and the members then elect or re-elect their board. Thereafter one-third retire annually. But as Thomas[2] reminds us: –

> "What are perhaps less, well known are the other restrictions in Articles that private companies can make. One important topic is the balance of power both in the board and among the shareholders. Thus the first directors may be relieved of any obligation to rotate and may even be made life directors. The requirement that directors retire automatically at 70, unless re-elected by special resolution, does not apply to private companies. All the directors can be re-elected by special resolution at the Annual General Meeting. There may be a provision that in the event of any further issue of shares being made, it must be offered in the first instance to existing members, even in the proportions of their existing

holdings. Lastly it is still the case that a private company need only have one director and a secretary."

Normally any member may, with proper notice in writing, and with the approval of the person concerned, nominate someone for election to the board. Share qualifications for directors may be fixed by the company in general meeting, but otherwise no qualification is required. The members may from time to time increase or decrease the number of directors. The board usually has the power to fill casual vacancies, and to make new appointments up to the limit; such directors holding office until the next general meeting, when the members decide on the election to the board[3].

Such is the de jure position. Of course, in the closely held company, such as the PTY and many PTE's, the directors, being significant shareholders, are in a position to determine the structure and actual membership of the board.

But in the larger company with diverse shareholdings, such as many PLC's and some PTE's, the incumbent chairman and his board colleagues can exercise considerable influence in making board appointments. Although the board's discretion to make appointments is subject to members' approval, challenges to board nominations are sufficiently rare to be newsworthy[4].

Obviously the widespread discretion available, de jure, to the members and, de facto, to the incumbent directors to determine the structure of the board and to choose its members would be eroded if initiatives such as the draft 5th directive[5], to have a supervisory board or independent non-executive directors, became statutory.

Styles of Corporate Governance

The structure and membership of a board will, obviously, affect the way in which it carries out the functions of corporate governance – direction, executive action, supervision and accountability. Where the owners of the company also manage and direct its affairs, as in PTY's and many PTE's, the style of governance is likely to be different from the company with a mainly managerial board, and different yet again from one with a largely independent board.

In an attempt to distinguish different styles of corporate governance, a form of analysis by ownership and board structure has been devised. The initial work was reported in The Independent Director[6] and amplified in recent work by The Corporate Policy Group.

A sample of British companies was plotted on a simple matrix (figure 1). The horizontal axis plots the extent of separation of management from ownership. At the left of the axis there is no separation; at the other pole there is total separation, with management shareholders, if any, quite minimal and owners playing no part in management. This separation, of course, has been well recognised since the 1930's[7].

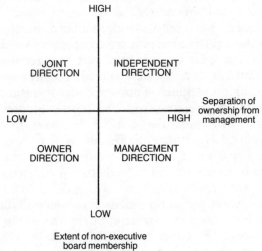

HIGH

JOINT DIRECTION

INDEPENDENT DIRECTION

Separation of ownership from management

LOW   HIGH

OWNER DIRECTION

MANAGEMENT DIRECTION

LOW

Extent of non-executive board membership

Fig. 1   Styles of corporate governance

The vertical axis is a more original dimension, plotting the structure of the board in terms of executive and non-executive membership. At the base are companies with all executive boards; at the top are boards comprised totally of non-executive members.

The four quadrants now distinguish alternative styles of corporate governance.

In the bottom left quadrant are owner-directed companies, in which the owner(s) control the members' voting and dominate the board. All PTY's are, by definition, in this quadrant; so, in fact, are most PTE's and a few PLC's, particularly those traded on the unlisted securities market, in which the majority of equity voting power is still in the executive directors' hands.

In the bottom right quadrant are management directed companies. Their boards have a majority of executive directors, though the ownership is diffused and the directors, themselves, hold only a minority proportion, if any. Most PLC's, and some PTE's are in this sector.

Public companies in the United States tend to have boards with a majority of outside directors[8]. Hence they would be in the top right quadrant, being independently directed. The boards of some major British banks and insurance companies also fall into this sector, as do a few other PLC's. British building societies are also independently directed.

In the top left quadrant are companies in which the owners are able to play a significant part in direction, because the shareholding is not widely spread, but who appoint a board with a preponderance of non-executive members.

Examples are found in the boards of nationalised companies. The potential conflict between the "owners" – personified by Treasury officials or the sponsoring government department – and the independent chairman and his board is apparent: and indeed confirmed by the comments of various nationalised industry chairmen[9].

But where do subordinate companies fit on the matrix? They have dominant owners; but is ownership separate from management? They are likely to have a predominantly executive board; but is de facto power over the company exercised through the group management processes, thus diluting the power of the subordinate board to govern?

The governance of subordinate companies presents some difficulty – a matter highlighted by the diagram and confirmed in practice, as we shall see in the next chapter.

Background to Board Membership

Further consideration of the classification of styles in corporate governance will show that we have identified three distinct categories of person – owners, managers and directors.

It is pertinent, at this stage, to recognise that this provides an insight into four different backgrounds for board membership (figure 2).

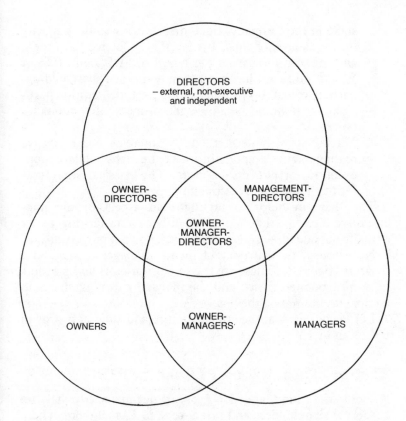

Fig. 2 Backgrounds to board membership

Thus we have the following categories of director depicted in the director circle of figure 2:–

1. Owner-manager-directors, who own the company and who tend to dominate corporate governance. All PTY's, by definition, are run by such people, as are many PTE's and a few PLC's.
2. Owner-directors, who have no hand in executive management. Examples are found in PTE's and PTY's where ownership has moved to distant branches of the founder's family, who retain seats on the board reflecting their shareholding; also in PTE's which have a significant (but not dominating) part of their voting equity capital held by other companies, who thus obtain board representation.
3. Management-directors, who have no significant equity

stake in the company. Such directors are in the majority on the boards of most British PLC's, as we have seen; and are also typical on the board of SUB's and PTE's. Where a director has more than a minimal shareholding, particularly if his remuneration includes equity participation, it would be a question of materiality about his power.

4. Directors, with neither equity interests nor executive management responsibilities. Perhaps called non-executive or outside directors. The classical arguments for the non-executive director apply.

The diagram helps to highlight an aspect of the non-executive director, that he may be either an owner-director or a totally outside director — being neither owner nor executive.

Notice also, the category of owner manager in the Venn diagram (figure 2). These are the sole proprietors and partners in unincorporated firms; and the managers owning shares in companies but not on the board.

Let us look now at the size, structure and style of boards in PTE's and PTY's.

The Size of Boards — the PTE and the PTY

By our definition the PTY is owner-managed, has no corporate shareholders and no more than 10 members. There is no separation between owners and managers: the owners are themselves running the business.

Our studies show that the boards of PTY's are also relatively small (figure 3).

Where a PTY is run by a sole proprietor, he will often be the sole director, or be joined, nominally, by his wife or another family member where the Articles require two directors. In fewer cases the owner-manager(s) are joined on the board by other directors drawn from the business' top management, members of the owner's families or, occasionally, outside business associates. Of course, to remain within our definition of a PTY, the board must be dominated by the owner-management, and have no dominant external or corporate holding.

Many private companies (PTE's), we also find, have relatively few directors. However, as a company becomes well established and mature, owners may tend to become more

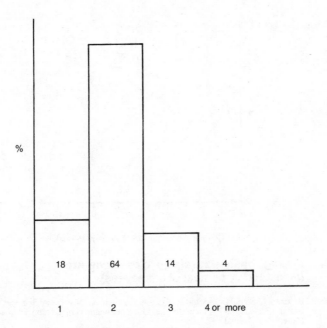

Fig. 3   Number of Directors in PTY's

Source: Corporate Policy Group
Sample: 50

remote from management. For example, in the second generation of a family business shares may pass on inheritance to distant members; or the size and geographical spread of the business may require echelons of professional management who join the board; or further finance may be introduced by friends, business contacts, other companies or financial institutions who acquire board representation; and separation between the original owners as management activities develop.

In the larger PTE's the size of the board tends to reflect the growing significance of their corporate affairs (figure 4).

The Structure of Boards – PTE and PTY

Corporate governance in the PTY will be undertaken by the owner-manager-director(s): that is part of the definition of the proprietory company. Consequently the board will consist entirely of, or be dominated by, such directors. Governance in many PTE's is also, principally, by owner-manager-directors.

We have also seen that, as companies grow, management-

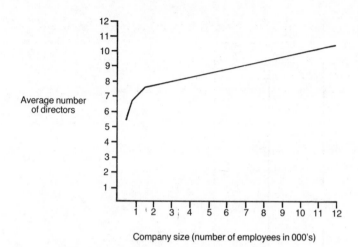

**Fig. 4   Average board size related to company size
(measured by number of employees)**

Source: Brookes, Christopher: Boards of Directors in British Industry; Social Science
Branch; Research & Planning Division; Dept. of Employment, London: Research
Paper No. 7, August 1979.

Sample size: 296 independent and subsidiary companies

directors, who are not themselves shareholders, are sometimes appointed, recognising their status and functional importance to the running of the business.

However, as the company matures and expands, a case can be argued for having directors on the board who are not, themselves, directly involved in executive management. Such directors may be owner-directors, reflecting the interests of shareholders but not themselves involved in management, thus reducing the risk of domination by the executive owner-directors.

A company can also reach a stage of development at which additional expertise and knowledge may be valuable at board level. However, the use of non-executive directors is not

Number of Non-Executive Directors	%
0	46
1-2	39
3-5	13
Over 5	2

**Table 1   Percentage of non-executive directors in smaller UK
companies with sales £2-£5 million**

Source: Booz, Allen & Hamilton and the Institute of Directors, 1972.

particularly widespread in the smaller UK companies — see table 1.

Directors without executive responsibilities may be appointed for a variety of reasons: —

— because a second director is required by the company's Articles: frequently this is the owner-manager's spouse who becomes a supernumerary director for legal reasons, but playing little, if any, role in governance.

— because they have a financial stake in the company, either on formation, a subsequent investment or shares passing on succession. Such directors may be content to leave the running of the business to the executive director(s) provided results are satisfactory. However, their support and approval will be necessary for any decisions with implications for their holding. Considerable power can be exercised over matters of corporate direction by such directors exerting moral pressure, or, in the ultimate, voting power.

— because a retired executive director has been reappointed as a non-executive director. Such an appointment is a mark of recognition and may provide the chance for a continuing contribution based on experience and knowledge of the business. The obvious drawback lies in the director not keeping in touch with a fast changing business environment and the "voice of experience" becoming the brake on progress and adaptation. By definition such non-executive directors cannot be considered independent: it is their very involvement which gives them their value to the board.

— because the chairman and other board members see the benefit in having independent outside membership on the board. Typical benefits ascribed to such appointments include:

.. obtaining independent advice, information and insights,

.. adding knowledge and expertise lacking in the board,

.. bringing in business contacts – in the market place, financial sector or elsewhere.

The outside director may well find that he is fulfilling a quasi-executive role on the board of the PTE or PTY. A non-executive director to to a number of such companies, offering an independent service to smaller companies as a business venture, commented in evidence:–

"The non-executive director is both insider and outsider.

He is an insider in that he has an intimate knowledge of
your business and understands the environment in which
you have to operate. But, unlike the employees and
full-time directors, he is a person who spends most of his
time in a different environment. This means that he
arrives at your problems and discussions with a far less
conditioned outlook."

Another perspective was offered by an owner-manager
director of a publishing and printing company:–

"On the board of a private company people have great
difficulty in separating the ownership role from the
management role. There is a genuine need for independent advice."

The Style of Boards – PTE and PTY

In studying PTY's we draw evidence mainly from their
professional advisers – particularly their auditors. In many
proprietary companies, and especially in the hundreds of
thousands of really small owner-managed enterprises, it is
apparent that little or no distinction is given to the role of
director, which is seen as a surrogate title for those who own
and run the business. Regular board meetings are not held and
the statutorily required meetings of directors and members are
rituals created by the professional advisers. Formal approval
of accounts or of the use of the company seal, for example, are
authorised after informal discussion, sometimes over the
telephone, and the minutes written up subsequently.

Obviously where there is the possibility of a conflict of
interest, with a wider spread of voting shares beyond the
single owner-manager-director, more formality in meetings
and their minutes is necessary.

There are various reasons for the original incorporation of a
company: –

   – for taxation benefits[10]
   – to gain the apparent status of trading as a limited
     company,
   – to separate the business from personal finances,
   – to limit personal liability for business debts[11],
 or – to create an identifiable corporate value.

The fact that some of these supposed benefits could be
achieved by sole trading or in partnership, or that they are
illusory, is immaterial. The owner-manager-director tends to

be totally involved with *his* company. His role as a director and the function of his board and the meeting of the members are legal formalities. It is the running of the business which predominates.

However, where the board of a PTE or PTY includes owner-directors, management directors or independent directors, a need arises for greater formality, because matters are no longer solely in the hands of the owner-manager.

In the case of management directors, our evidence showed that the formality of the board meetings often requires a different interpersonal style and manner of presentation than exists in day to day interaction between the same people. The process of the board meeting is given a special place in the culture; it provides a ritualistic formalisation of executive actions. Even the furnishing of the board room and its occasional use for board meetings emphasises the distinctive role of the board meetings in corporate culture.

Comments of manager-directors in PTE's are instructive. Broadly they perceived three basic roles for the board: —

1. To run the business

   "The job of the directors is to run the business, as a whole, successfully."

   "Our job is to maintain and improve the bottom line performance."

   "We spend a lot of time and effort on sales plans and expenditure budgets. We keep our eye on the financial figures and on the cash flow. It is also important for the board to be seen to be right on top of things like stock control. In a business things will always run away, unless a tight rein is held. There are always some savings to be made."

2. Communication within the top management

   "We find the board meetings help to keep the executive directors in touch with the way the business is going."

   "I use the board to test out ideas with the functional directors and tell them of my decisions."

   "I do a lot of listening at board meetings. It is surprising what you find out."

3. To comply with corporate formalities

   "The board, as a whole, has to approve the use of the company seal on contracts."

   "There are things like bank mandates and getting credit cards for reps, and hire purchase agreements that need formal board resolutions."

Contrast this perception of the directors' role with the model of corporate governance developed in the last chapter. In the PTY and PTE there is a major emphasis on executive management, with accountability seen as a corporate formality. Exceptions were, however, found in the larger PTE, with external equity holders and non-equity financing; in which separation of executive function has occurred.

The need for the board to emphasise supervision of executive management as an independent activity is seen to be less important where the directors are, themselves, closely involved in the management process.

Notice, too, the lack of emphasis on longer term strategic thinking. Our discussions with the proprietors and managing directors of PTY's and PTE's showed how difficult they found the process of strategy formulation. In some cases the uncertainty of the business situation and the perceived need to react to changes rather than cause them limited any interest in setting corporate direction: in other cases, the entrepreneurial proprietor felt that this was fundamentally his role, with the board, at best, passively confirming and facilitating his plans. Exceptions again occurred in the large PTE with external interests, in which all four dimensions of the governance process — direction, executive action, supervision and accountability — were described.

The Board in the Management Buy-Out

A significant development in Britain in recent years has been the restructuring of PTE's from management buy-outs. Prompted by the 1979 budget, which reduced top rates of tax, and facilitated by funds from specialist institutions such as ICFC, Candover Investments and some merchant banks, existing top management teams have been encouraged to acquire the majority equity stake in their business.

Typically the buy-outs have been of existing subsidiaries in groups which no longer felt they were consistent with group strategy or units which were not performing well within a group. Coyne & Wright[12] provide a useful summary of the possible ownership categories (figure 5).

The financial institutions behind many of the deals have agreed to retain an equity stake themselves, being sleeping partners in the venture, but usually maintaining a supervisory oversight.

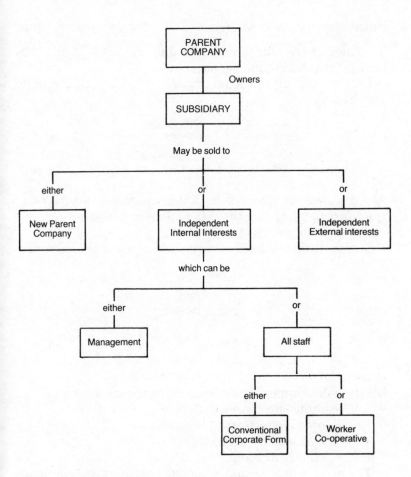

Fig. 5   Ownership transfers on buy-out

Source: Coyne & Wright 1982

Commenting on the apparent success of the management buy-out movement, The Telegraph[13] commented that:—

"(it) speaks volumes for the inhibiting effects of many existing boards of directors and their shareholders, particularly institutional shareholders with the muscle to put pressure on the board.

It is also a sharp commentary on the qualities of managements who seem able to perform miracles when motivated by personal reward which they seemed quite incapable of when they were merely doing a job."

Summary

Two models relevant to understanding the work of directors were introduced in this chapter.

Firstly, the classification model of styles in corporate governance:

Joint direction	Independent direction
Owner direction	Management direction

which shows the effect of both the separation of ownership from management and the differentiation between executive and non-executive directors.

Secondly, the model of backgrounds to board membership:

which enables important distinctions to be drawn between:
- owner-manager-directors
- owner-directors
- management directors

and - outside directors

The size, structure and styles of boards in private companies (PTE's) and proprietary companies (PTY's) were reviewed. The tendency to focus on the executive role, with accountability as a legal formality, and the failure to emphasise either the supervisory or the direction roles, were noted in PTY's and many PTE's. The potentially motivating effect of management buy-outs was suggested, with their mainly executive boards.

Chapter 13

Corporate Governance in Subordinate Companies
– the dilemma of the dominated company

Now we turn to corporate governance in the subordinate company. Here, by our definition, we are looking at companies in a subsidiary or associate relationship within a group of companies, in which one or more corporate entities are able to exercise power over its affairs. Direction can thus come through management lines, as well as via the corporate board of the SUB. This introduces an important new element into corporate governance.

In this chapter we look at some examples of group structures and see how varied the position of SUB's can be in practice. A means of identifying a profile of the extent of domination by the holding company(ies) or autonomy for the SUB is introduced. We also look at the size, structures and styles of corporate governance in SUB's.

Dilemmas in Governing SUB's

The majority of companies included in The Corporate Policy Group's studies operate in groups. Initial examination of the voluminous case notes shows, more than anything else, just how differently groups are structured and how variable are their styles of governance.

Consequently generalisations about corporate governance in SUB's must be treated with care. The dilemma is how to assess the autonomy to govern available to the board of the SUB, as against authority assumed by the holding company(ies); also how far governance is practised through the board of the legal corporate entity and how much through a different managerial or divisional business structure.

To illustrate the problem seven case examples have been chosen. These cases are neither exhaustive nor mutually exclusive in their methods of governance; but they do illustrate the range of possibilities and the dilemmas for those who would understand governance in subordinate companies.

1. *Governance through the corporate structure: Case 059*
   The holding company of this group is a large PLC
   quoted on the London Stock Exchange. At the time of
   the study the corporate organisation structure had
   evolved to the following (figure 1)

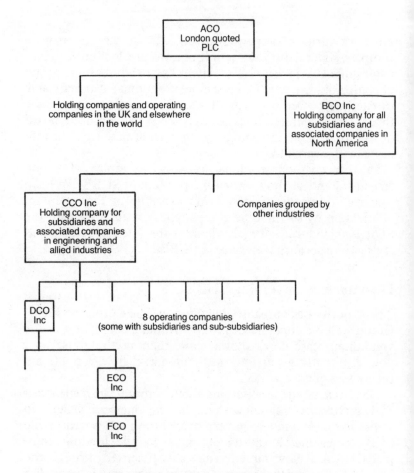

**Fig. 1 Governance through the corporate structure
Case 059**

Here was an example of a typical large multinational
with nearly 200 subsidiaries at six levels, as well as over
50 associate companies. Governance was exercised

through the corporate structure. In other words there was no divisional structure cutting across corporate lines and the staff at head office was relatively small and mainly advisory.

The holding company – ACO PLC – had a board of about 20 members (just over half executive)[1].

The operations in North America had grown very significantly over the past seven or eight years, largely due to an aggressive acquisitions policy.

The holding company for the North American interests – BCO Inc. – had a predominantly executive board with a president/chief executive officer, 5 vice presidents and 4 senior directors from various subsidiaries, plus two independent outside directors.

"The two outside directors are good, but not really making their presence felt", commented the VP (Finance). "I wonder whether there really is a role for them. We can tell London all they need to know about the US business situation. If anything, they are used by the chief executive to bolster his decisions and protect him from too much interference from London".

He also outlined problems he had as VP (Finance) for BCO Inc.

"Is BCO responsible for the finances of its subsidiaries such as CCO? Am I, as finance vice president, responsible and accountable for investment appraisal, cash controls and performance measurements? Or is the financial controller of CCO right when he says that he has his own board to which he is responsible – not a company interposed between him and head office?"

The style of governance throughout the group was to give operating companies, having acquired them, considerable autonomy and executive compensation based on results. However BCO had been created to coordinate US activities; although the chairmen and presidents of CCO and other subsidiaries continued to refer matters directly to the chief executive officer in London.

Another issue of relevance was outlined by the chairman of CCO – the original entrepreneurial owner of that company prior to acquisition – and himself a member of the BCO board.

"Do you know what they (meaning the London head office) have done now? They acquired the XYZ group of companies in the Far East — and in the process have bought my main competitor in Chicago: and I found out from my salesman!"

2. *Governance through the management structure: Case 136*

Lemon Ltd., incorporated in Britain, is the wholly owned subsidiary of Orange Incorporated, a public company based in the United States.

Orange Inc. is a major trading entity, as well as being the holding company for group subsidiaries. The board of Orange has 19 members — 9 executive and 10 non-executive.

The board of Lemon Ltd. has 8 members — the Lemon managing director, 3 corporate executives of Orange and 4 UK non-executive directors. The Lemon board publish a detailed and illustrated annual report and accounts of the activities in the UK. Sales are in excess of £150 million and profit before tax about £13 million. There are three manufacturing plants in Britain.

Yet, in fact, the board of Lemon has little control over, or real business responsibility for, corporate activities in the UK. The Orange group is organised by product divisions, grouped under three broad product and market sectors, which are responsible for business activities worldwide. The top executives of the product divisions are based in the United States.

Basic research and product development are undertaken by group laboratories around the world, reporting to, and coordinated by, group sales executives. The managers of the production plants also report to their respective product group executives in the United States. Sales activities report through five regional sales executives to the top executives in America.

Lemon Ltd. is the legal entity under which all Orange Group activities are carried on in Britain. It provides the taxation base and is the focus for customers, employees, suppliers and other interests affected by the business locally and nationally.

The board of Lemon, clearly, fulfil the accountability role. But corporate direction, executive action and supervision, though influenced by UK managers, are effectively undertaken by executives based outside Britain.

3. *Governance through divisions: Case 111*
"A" PLC is a large group quoted in London. It is organised by divisions each in a distinctive market/ product area. The divisions are not incorporated, although the group does have subsidiary and associate companies in many countries.

The underlying philosophy in corporate direction and control is one of considerable decentralisation, derogation and autonomy for the divisions. Implicit in a structure like this is the need to avoid duplication of administrative services.

The main board has a full-time chairman and a majority of executive directors who have a mixed portfolio, being responsible for a combination of functional, product and regional matters; for example, one director is responsible for personnel, certain products and one of the regions of the world.

The main board exercises its authority by reserving powers over finance, investment and top management appointments. The executive directors form the executive committee, meeting twice a month with considerable delegated power. In addition there are main board policy committees for products, regions and capital programmes.

Below the main board are the divisions, each with a chairman and executive board, even though they are not constituted as legal entities. These operating units are sub-divided into product groups.

The responsibility for setting direction was explained as follows:—

"In most cases product divisions have considerable autonomy to develop products, manufacture and market in their broad area. The Product Committee monitors performance and makes recommendations to the committee on capital programmes: it also agrees the sub-strategy of the product group in the context of the overall strategy."

"Some businesses need a global strategy — others need a local strategy where manufacture and marketing takes place entirely locally and there is no inter-trading. We have examples of each type of strategy formulation."

4. *Governance through partly owned subsidiaries and associates: Case 300*
"B" PLC has wholly owned subsidiaries in the UK and abroad, subsidiary companies abroad in which they hold the majority shareholding, and other companies abroad with a minority stake. In many cases the wholly owned subsidiaries are sales companies.

The major overseas investments tend to be public companies, quoted locally, with a minority public holding. They can borrow independently but this can concern "B" PLC because it can change the debt/equity ratio of the parent company when the accounts are consolidated.

The main board can exercise influence over the subsidiary company board in the appointment of the chairman or president, by influencing the selection of the chief executive officer, by having their own members on the board and by influencing the appointment of non-executive directors. As a main board director explained: "We try to act as a sensible shareholder".

Problems can arise in the course of consultations on the investment policies of overseas subsidiaries. The large, successful overseas companies, particularly those with minority outside shareholders, may put forward investment plans for strategies that are not wholly in line with the overall strategy of "B" PLC. If an overseas company can raise funds locally, their board is in a better position to apply pressure on the main board to support a particular plant or facility.

Where the strategic plans of a subsidiary seem to be out of line with overall strategy, the main board's policy committees try to influence the local board's thinking.

Many of the overseas companies, both wholly and partly owned, have non-executive directors. Often they are prestigious local figures whose independent advice and outside experience is particularly valued both by the subsidiary and the parent company. It was emphasised that the outside directors were not expected to play a specific supervisory role.

In some cases a main board director serves as a non-executive on a subsidiary company board. In such cases the main board director has to be able to distinguish his two separate roles, as a director of the subsidiary and as a director of the main board; and be able to help resolve any conflict that may arise.

5. *A choice of governance: Case 069*
This relatively small public company is in the transport field and operates through subsidiary companies which run the business in twelve regional areas throughout Britain.

Each wholly owned subsidiary has a chairman, who is a member of the main board. Such chairmen may have three or four companies each. Then each subsidiary has a managing director who is not on the main board.

A member of the board explained this company's approach to governance:

"The managing director of each subsidiary can choose the form of direction he wants. On the one hand he may create a board of his top management team, letting them take strategic decisions and exercise control: or on the other hand he may have a purely nominal board for statutory purposes only.

Which is appropriate depends on the business circumstances and the personality of the managing director. I call the former the 'participative executive team' approach, and the latter 'the autocratic hierarchy'. Both seem to work in practice. What we need at head office are results: how the local companies manage their affairs is up to them."

6. *Governance with strong financial control: Case 143*
Another relatively small PLC has five subsidiaries, all held at one level. The board of the holding company has the managing director and 3 executive directors, a non-executive chairman who was previously the managing director, an outside director who is also on the board of another company with an important equity holding in this one, and 2 independent outside directors — 8 in all.

The boards of the SUB's are entirely executive with the exception of their chairmen, who are main board executive directors.

The boards of the SUB's have considerable responsibility for direction and executive action. But none of them have a finance or controllership function, this activity being undertaken by the holding company. Consequently their financial strategy and supervision over their executive activities is carried out by the holding company, who also undertake the bulk of the accountability element in the governance of the SUB's.

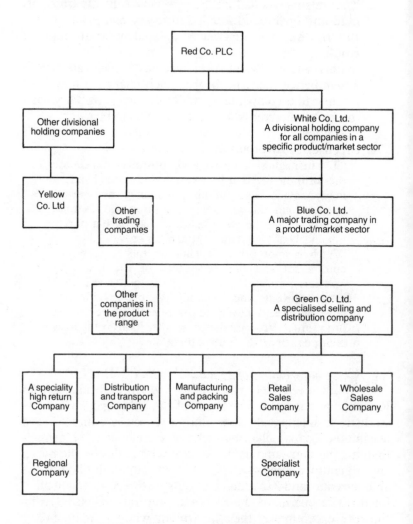

Fig. 2 Governance with group inter-trading   Case 139

7. *Governance with group inter-trading: Case 139*
Green Co. Ltd. is a third level subsidiary, wholly owned, of a large PLC. Green Co. has five subsidiaries itself and two sub-subsidiaries.

Green Co. Ltd. has an executive board with a non-executive chairman, who is managing director of Blue Co. Ltd. and on the board of White Co. Ltd. The Green Co. board are expected to formulate strategies for their business consistent with the direction set up by the corporate group. Executive management is entirely in the hands of the local management, subject to superior company policies. Supervision is exercised by Blue Co., in line with group wide accounting standards and performance measures.

Difficulties have recently arisen because Green Co. inter-trades with other group companies. To give two examples:—

● Green Co. buy products from another Blue Co. subsidiary. Naturally the supplying company want Green to promote their product; but Green makes a better return on competitive lines bought outside the group. The chairman of Green has recently overruled the board and instructed them to promote the group product.

● Green Co. supply retail outlets owned by the Yellow Co. — which is in another divisional product/market sector entirely. The retailers have just been permitted by Yellow to buy their supplies from discount stores, which undercut Green's prices. Green claims that it is no longer profitable to distribute any goods to Yellow Co. retail outlets, but are forced to do so by group policy.

The Range of Alternatives

Reviewing these case examples, and the many more cases studied, it is apparent that many forms of governance are feasible in SUB's. At one extreme the SUB may be no more than a legal convenience, its board having no real power for any aspect of governance; at the other it may have considerable autonomy, be able to stand alone, its board responsible for direction, execution, supervision and accountability, with the owning company acting, in effect, as a remote outside shareholder.

In between these polarities lie a wide range of alternatives.
The board of the SUB may be responsible for the accountability of their company, whilst the direction, execution and
supervision is run on global product lines (as in case 136). Or
the SUB board may be responsible for executive action, whilst
direction, supervision and accountability are assumed by the
dominating company. Alternatively the SUB board may be
able to develop strategy, run their business, supervise and be
accountable, but strictly within the constraints of direction,
supervision and accountability laid down by the dominating
company.

The Locus of Decision-Making Power

In an attempt to differentiate between such varying forms of
governance, we recognised the need to determine the locus
and extent of decision-making power within a group of
companies. Again our sights were aimed at the processes by
which companies are run, rather than on the structures or
procedures adopted.

A simple method of profiling SUB's was developed[2].
Opinions were sought on the locus of power to make various
decisions, using a scale from 1-10, between autonomy lying
with the SUB to power held by the dominating company. An
example follows on page 229.

The method has been valuable in confirming the conclusions of this study that governance in SUB's is very variable.
Consequently generalisations, and normative statements of
preferred behaviour, are potentially misleading. Indeed using
the profiles caused some executives to reappraise the assumptions they had held about the governance of SUB's. Some
groups tend to treat all their SUB's in a similar way: others
discriminate exerting greater power over some than others,
perhaps because of their performance and maturity of
management.

The method has also proved useful as a diagnostic tool to
compare governance of SUB's in a group and between groups.
The detailed questions can obviously be adjusted to fit the
circumstances.

Size, Structure and Style of Boards – SUB

One would expect the size, structure and size of the board in a SUB, broadly, to reflect the power profile. In a SUB with minimal power the board can be small, without regard for representation or independence in its membership. Where more widespread governance is expected concern has to be paid to such matters.

	Autonomy Power to decide with the SUB	Domination Power to decide with the dominating co.

Direction   1 2 3 4 5 6 7 8 9 10

Product & market strategy
Production & distribution strategy
Organisational development
Management development
Product development & research
Manpower planning
Information systems strategy
Acquisition & divestment strategy
Financial strategy
  – capital investment
  – working capital
  – raising funds
  – raising equity capital

Executive action

Responsibility for:
        Major capital projects
        Cash flow
        Industrial relations
        Sales & the order book
        Manufacturing & productivity
        Profitability
        Top management remuneration

Supervision

Monitoring & control over:
        Expenditure
        Profit
        Profitability
        Other performance measures
          (defined)

Accountability

Board size & structure
Board membership
Corporate reporting
Corporate social responsibility
Accounting policies

In this example company A has a higher degree of autonomy, and responsibility for corporate governance, than company B.

Table 1 presents some research evidence on the size of SUB boards.

Number of Companies in sample	Average Size of Board	Average Board Membership		% Non-Executive
		Executive	Non-Executive	
108	5.6	4.0	1.6	28.6%

Table 1   **Board size and composition at 1980 of subsidiary companies**

Source: Company Secretary's Review: 1981

The wholly owned British SUB's of British companies that were studied showed a preference for a majority of executive directors, drawn from the top management of the SUB, often with a non-executive chairman or other directors drawn from the holding company or elsewhere in the group. Others had wholly executive boards, and a few had non-executive directors such as retired executives, members resulting from acquisitions and the genuinely, independent outside director.

In overseas SUB's one finds a greater use of outside non-executive directors and in some countries, such as Brazil and India, they are mandatory.

Where there are minority interests in the SUB, a further case can be advanced for the independent director to ensure that the minority interests are recognised.

Background to Board Membership in the SUB

In fact the possible backgrounds — or rather basis of power — for directors in SUB's are surprisingly varied. Figure 3 attempts to depict all the alternatives. The Venn diagram covers a SUB with minority, outside shareholders.

By distinguishing the dominant owner from any other outside shareholders we find six possible backgrounds for directors of a SUB; viz:

A — a director drawn from the top management of the SUB,

B — a director from the dominant company(ies) or part of the holding group,

C — a director holding significant shares or someone representing an outside shareholder(s),

D — a genuinely independent, outside director,

E — a director who is both an executive of the SUB and on

the board of the dominant company,

F   – a director holding significant shares, or representing those who do, and also a member of the SUB management.

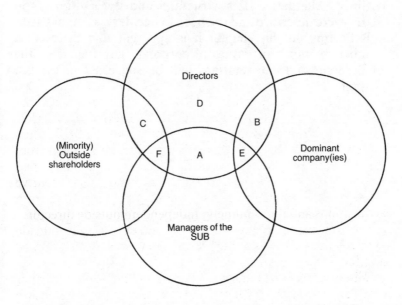

Fig. 3   Background to board membership in the SUB

Which board structure, size and style is preferable, and likely to be the most cost effective, depends on the power profile and the intentions of the dominating companies about the governance of the SUB. The important aspect of this analysis is to recognise the alternatives and to appreciate the need to determine, in a given situation, what the intentions are about the style of governance.

Conclusion

Corporate governance in the SUB cannot be readily categorised. There is a wide range of power profiles feasible in a group of companies; from the SUB with very considerable responsibility for its own governance – that is very much involved in setting direction, running the business, supervision of executive action and accountability; to the SUB with little, if any, de facto power, governed by the dominant board, and only de jure existence.

A method for depicting the locus of power in a SUB was outlined. Alternative sizes, structures and styles of boards in SUB's were described and the need to decide was emphasised.

Reflecting on this chapter it is apparent that there are a number of important issues of corporate governance in the SUB. Some possible solutions will be suggested in the last chapter.

Chapter 14

The Corporation Tomorrow
— some implications and suggestions

In the first part of this book we traced the evolution of the corporate concept from its simple and successful origins to the diversity and complexity of today. On the one hand we saw how the massive increase in the incorporation of owner-managed companies had raised questions about regulatory constraints to entrepreneurial enthusiasms: whilst, on the other hand, the development of giant groups had focused attention on the outward legitimacy of their activities and the internal effectiveness of their processes.

In the second part we examined the threads of corporate governance that tie the company into contemporary society, looking at constraints on corporate power and reappraising concepts of accountability, liability and regulation of companies.

Then, in the third part, we have endeavoured to unravel some of the threads in the processes and practices of corporate governance at the level of the individual firm.

Now, finally, we will try to weave these macro and micro threads into the fabric of corporate governance.

The earlier descriptions of governance practices, and the models that were derived from them, are essentially value free; that is they are independent of any assumptions or expectations about the "proper" role for companies in society. In this chapter we take the stance that the underlying rationale for corporate entities should be to facilitate the provision of capital and the effective operation of business enterprise, primarily to create wealth: the principal purposes are not to provide a vehicle for tax planning or the minimisation of business risk.

We also take a position on employee participation. Although the European Commission, in the 5th directive and Vredeling drafts, combine the ideas of independent supervision of executive action with worker involvement in business

233

decision-making, we believe those to be separate issues that should be studied independently. To combine them is to confuse governance with management. Governance involves the balance of power with which the entity is directed, monitored and held accountable: whether employees have rights is a matter of political philosophy and judgement. The integration of employees harmoniously into the business, and the protection of their legitimate interests, is of vital importance, but to management.

Let us begin with a brief recapitulation of the principal themes and specific proposals that have been developed so far.

Recapitulation – The Key Ideas

The basic theme is of the need for a new conceptual framework to describe companies in modern society. It should be based on the reality of corporate governance, which is distinguishable from management. (Chapter 1)

The conceptual framework must identify different types of corporate entity, particularly recognising the myriad of small owner-managed companies and the complexity in corporate groups. Consideration has to be given to governance in groups with subsidiaries at various levels, and where there is a mismatch between the corporate structure and the management organisation. (Chapters 2 to 5)

The power to govern can stem from a number of sources – ownership, incumbent board membership, the management line in a group of companies and from financial institutions. (Chapter 6)

A framework for distinguishing different types of company was proposed –

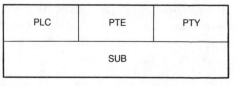

proprietary, private, public and subordinate companies.

Constraints to the power of boards come from the legal processes, self-regulatory processes and from the position in the business market place. The implications vary for different types of company. (Chapter 7)

Accountability is a key element in governance. It was precisely defined in terms of a party's right to enforce accountability and the company's countervailing duty to provide it. (Chapter 8)

In complex groups, in which the corporate structure does not mirror the organisational/decision-making structure, Accountable Business Activities should be identified as the accountable entities for governance. (Chapter 9)

Four crucial components of the governance task were identified – setting corporate direction, involvement in executive action,

DIRECTION	ACCOUNTABILITY
EXECUTIVE MANAGEMENT	SUPERVISION

supervision of management and accountability. (Chapter 10)

In the public company the importance of separating functions of executive action and supervision was discussed. Various approaches were compared – the classical approach, directors "wearing two hats", non-executive and independent directors, the audit committee, two tier boards and the use of the courts or a state agency. (Chapter 11)

Different styles of governance and structures of boards were identified – owner directed, management directed, independently directed and joint direction.

A three part model enabled four categories of director to be identified:

1. the owner/director
2. the owner/manager/director
3. the management director

and 4. the independent director

(Chapter 12)

The particular issues of governance in a subordinate company were considered and a method for distinguishing the locus of power was suggested. In a dominated company, with outside shareholders, additional categories of director were feasible; representing the outside shareholders or the holding company

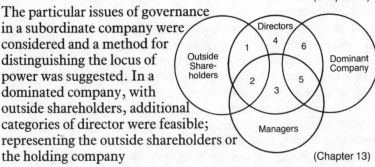

(Chapter 13)

Two principal propositions have emerged from our study of corporate governance in practice:

1. That companies need governing; whilst businesses need managing,
2. That companies can be different and need governing appropriately.

Let us now reflect on the implications and consider some proposals.

Companies Need Governing: Businesses Need Managing

By virtue of their constitution as independent, legal entities, the nature of ownership, and the reality of power in and around the board of directors, companies need to be governed as well as managed. In the light of the issues raised in the third section of this book we believe these processes of ruling should be made explicit.

Corporate governance is a specific role, with activities that should be distinguished from the management of the business. This applies to the simple enterprise as well as the vast, complex group with a multitude of different businesses.

Management textbooks classically presuppose that the prerogative of management is to manage, and do not consider matters of governance. Typically management is depicted as a hierarchical command structure in the shape of a pyramid or similar vertical model.

Corporate governance, by contrast, can be depicted as an inverted triangle superimposed on the top of the management pyramid (see figure 1). The key elements of corporate governance are the *supervision* of executive activity, *accountability* to legitimate interests, the setting of corporate *direction*, and involvement in the *executive action*.

The extent of that participation in general management will depend on the style of corporate governance adopted; and is crucial to an appreciation of the reality of the process. In effect it involves the extent of overlap between the two triangles of governance and management.

In an owner-managed proprietorial company the same individuals will be fulfilling both governance and management roles: in which case the two triangles will have considerable common ground. Notice, however, that the essential roles

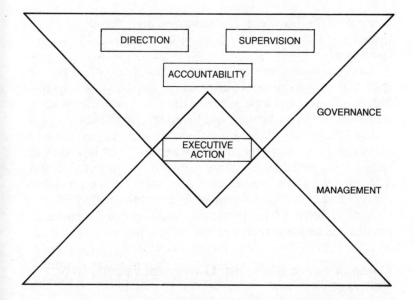

Fig. 1 The governance and management of companies in principal

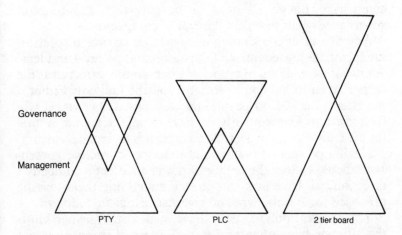

Fig. 2 The governance and management of companies in practice

have still to be fulfilled (see figure 2)

In a British PLC, with independent, non-executive directors, but a majority of executives on the board, the two triangles have some commonality, and separating the roles becomes very important; whilst in the supervisory board concept of the European Communities draft 5th directive the triangles touch only at the point, with a complete separation of functions.

The distinction between the processes of corporate governance and of management, in practice, can be very helpful in highlighting crucial aspects of the director's job, the structure and membership of boards, and board level activities.

The four principal elements of governance are performed in every company, to a greater or lesser extent. But how they are carried out, and how effective they are, varies considerably. The model of the governance processes reflects corporate reality, and is not dependent on nineteenth-century ideas of authority, derived from ownership and expressed through the members acting together.

Companies are Different: Governance needs to be Relevant

The second proposition is that fundamental differences exist in the way power is exercised between the various categories of company. Though all need to be governed, the form of governance needs to reflect the type of company.

Any theory of corporate governance must have respect for the historical precedents and the economic, political and legal realities, as well as the social (that is the effects of the corporate entity on and in society) and the individual (that is the effects for and on people) implications. Otherwise it will be irrelevant. Consequently we have to appreciate the setting for the entity; and the possible changes it is facing.

Having postulated that a valid theory of corporate governance should reflect the reality of power to affect a company's direction, we have now to state the underlying thesis for the proposals for specific types of governance that are to follow.

The classical notion, as we have seen, is that ownership is the ultimate basis of authority in all types of company under British law. Capitalism is the underlying political philosophy. By contrast the continental European view tends to be of the company as a joint relationship between capital and labour, at least in terms of public companies.

We reject both these philosophies because they do not adequately reflect the reality in all types of British company. True, in all proprietorial and some private companies ownership wields power, but that is due to the congruence of owners, directors and managers. Similarly in subordinate companies ownership is the root of authority to act but it is often pursued along the management lines.

Other philosophical underpinnings include nationalisation, with the state usurping the capitalists' role, and cooperatives – of customers, suppliers or workers. But neither are pursued further here because they are not the principal forms of governance adopted in Britain: although certainly the model of corporate governance developed in this book could be applied to a better understanding of the governance in nationalised industries, cooperatives, building societies and other entities which trade for a profit.

Instead of the ownership of capital as the basis of power, we propose a model of collaboration of those able to exert power – that is owners, the incumbent directors, management and the financial institutions (as elaborated in chapter 6). Consequently the company is seen as a collaboration between the forces of capital, direction and management. In future labour could be added, if and when this dimension wields significant power at the corporate level. For the moment the protection and enhancement of the employees' position is developed at the level of the ABA (Accountable Business Activity).

The collaborative philosophy emphasises that governance involves a proper political process. Typically this involves a consensus being reached between the participating powers, but, rarely, can lead to the differences being battled out between factions at variance.

Inevitably the collaborative view provides a transient vehicle for governing a company. In this it reflects corporate experience and exposes a fundamental flaw in the classical model, which postulates a company as a legal entity created in perpetuity. But companies are observably not permanent – they grow, evolve, split, merge and die. A model that mirrors such changes is clearly better than one that is static.

Cultural Assumptions in Corporate Governance

The practice of corporate governance is set within the cultural norms, the expectations of behaviour, of society. What people believe influences how they think and, thus, behave in all matters – including the governance of companies. There are historical and cultural determinants in developing such frameworks. As Hofstede[1] puts it:

"Culture is the collective programming of the human mind, obtained in the course of life, which is common to the members of one group as opposed to another."

Nineteenth-century England recognised great virtue in the self-made man. A work ethic, rooted in individualism[2] and a protestant, non-conformity[3], believed firmly in self-help[4]. "God helps them as helps themselves", as the contemporary adage put it, reflected a commitment to business freedom with a minimum of controls. Businessmen mistrusted central authority, abhored bureaucracy and had a Spencerian conviction of the survival of the fittest. The English middle class projected a professionalism rooted in self-interest and a commitment to individual freedoms within their social classes.

Such attitudes contrasted sharply with those in post-Napoleonic, and catholic continental Europe in which many aspects of life were centrally codified, coordinated and controlled.

The old business ethic, though seldom articulated with such detail, still permeates the thinking of present day entrepreneurs, owner-managers and supporters of the smaller firm in Britain to this day. The underlying motivation to attain and preserve their independence is clearly described in the Report of the Committee of Inquiry on Small Firms in 1978[5].

But in other companies and, particularly in large international groups, attitudes may have changed. Moreover, there seems to be significant differences between cultures.

Wiener[6] shows an English frame of mind conditioned by an aristocratic and rural idyll, anti-industrial prejudice in education and amongst intellectuals: a way of life in which, even the successful businessman becomes "gentrified". He contrasts such attitudes with pro-business ideologies in Germany and the United States. Cole[7] confirms the British pretension to gentility based on squirearchy with engagement in commerce or industry being degrading, save only by "ornamenting a board" rather than participating directly in its affairs.

Consequently attempts to harmonise company law, or to develop common international standards, are destined to create conflict, unless an attempt is made to understand the underlying ideological assumptions about company behaviour.

As J.B.H. Jackson[8] has put it: —
"We are peculiarly good in this country at self-regulation, but we have the greatest difficulty in persuading the people of continental Europe that such systems are workable or have any merits whatsoever."

Firms of the Future

Before we conclude with the proposals for the form and methods of governance in each of the types of company, we should remind ourselves of possible developments in the way businesses may be built and financed in the future.

The availability of funds from the financial institutions, fuelled by the cash flow from pension contributions, is likely to continue the support for the large public company — though not necessarily at present prices nor in UK based companies — and with greater interest in performance.

At the other end of the scale for public companies there is evidence of continuing support for the venture company — with, perhaps, only a small proportion of its equity available to the public and that in the hands of a few institutions. The availability of such funding, to encourage viable, independent companies involved in vigorous competition, is clearly in the interests of the economy. It is, perhaps, more likely to develop a strong corporate infrastructure than the growth of huge, potentially conglomerate, groups seen in the 60's and 70's.

That is not to imply that scale and concentration are things of the past. On the contrary the potential exists to build even larger and more massive corporate groups internationally. But the likelihood is that rationalisation in corporate direction, rather than conglomeration, will be the emphasis. Mergers are inevitable, and indeed indispensible, in a flexible, capitalist economy. The ability to sell ailing companies gives creditors and shareholders a life-line. The opportunity to aggregate commercial entities, subject to monopoly controls, offering possible synergies and economies of scale, is potentially valuable. The danger lies in stagnating giant corporations, already highly diversified, too bureaucratic to sponsor new businesses, but with the bidding advantage of large cash resources, realising that their standing can only be maintained by a major acquisition strategy.

External venture capital funds are also likely to promote

new private companies, particularly in high technology "start-up" situations and where there are opportunities to bid for a franchise such as a new television, local radio or cable television licence. Local authorities could also become a source of capital for development of companies at the local level[9]. The shift towards more bank financing may also reflect structural changes in methods of financing and more financial innovation[10].

With the developments in new sources of capital – venture funds, the Unlisted Securities Market, and individual investors attracted by the business expansion schemes; with the potential of leveraged management buy-outs; with public companies reregistering as private; with demerges and reconstructions: we could be facing a fundamental change in the nature and structure of the equity market. If so we need to rethink the processes by which the entities shall be governed to meet the needs of the new situation.

In the absence of any legislative alternative the small company is likely to remain an attractive entity for the owner-managed business: but if the additional benefits of the proprietary company, to be proposed, are enacted it could become an even greater encouragement to innovation and stimulus for new business.

Against this background let us now consider some possible avenues for achieving effective corporate governance in the different types of company.

Governance in the Public Company (PLC)

The public company is one in which the outside public can be invited to subscribe. These investors may be individuals, corporate bodies and financial institutions; and they may also include internal management shareholders. In some cases the number of members will be large with the shares widely held; but it should be remembered that in other PLC's the shares may be narrowly held in few hands.

Under the definition of the PLC developed in this book a PLC may not be dominated by another company – otherwise its status is that of a SUB and the outside investors need to be aware of the fact.

Existing company law requires a PLC to have a minimum paid-up share capital of £50,000. In our definition we would extend this to a minimum authorised and paid-up capital plus reserves of at least 50% of the net worth; thus providing additional cover against the limitation of further liability.

Even though members have an independent auditor's report that the directors' report and accounts show a true and fair view of the state of the company, we have recognised that the members alone cannot exercise adequate governance over a PLC; neither can an incumbent board with a majority of executive directors.

What is needed, we argue, is a body capable of exercising professional supervision over executive actions and demonstrating the legitimacy of corporate activities to outside interests.

The proposal is that all PLC's should have a *Governing Body*.

The members would elect a group of *Governors*, who would be totally independent of the company's business – neither they, nor their associates, would have material financial or other related interests in the company; neither would they be employees, or past employees, of the company. Governors would be paid reasonable fees, but no governor should be so dependent on such a source of income as to prejudice the exercise of independent judgement.

When a Governing Body was being set up for the first time, the governors could be nominated by the existing directors for approval by the members. Thereafter the governors themselves would form the nominating committee for additions to their ranks. The members would, as now with the appointment of directors, have to approve and would always have the right to make other nominations.

In the early stages there could be a shortage of people of appropriate standing and detachment suitable to be governors. In the longer term the creation of the need would undoubtedly enhance the supply to the benefit of all.

The Governing Body would also include the directors, nominated and elected by the shareholders. A governor, of course, could not also be a director of the company. But directors could be full time executives, with top management responsibilities or part time outside directors contributing knowledge and expertise to the directors' activities.

The governors would meet both as part of the unitary Governing Body and separately as a meeting of governors.

Likewise the directors would meet as part of the Governing Body and also separately as the Board of Directors.

The Chairman of the Governing Body

Another idea, which would enhance the separation of executive and supervisory functions in the PLC, would be to formalise the position of the chairman.

Though, in law, the role of the chairman is relatively simple, being concerned with the management of meetings and the company and the board, practices have developed in which the chairman plays a much wider role in overseeing the top executive management, stimulating strategy and becoming the "public face" of the corporation.

This leads to the specific proposal that, in PLC's, the statutory position of *Chairman of the Governing Body* be created. He would also be chairman of the governors. The chairman could not also be the chief executive.

He would be required to be independent of the executive decision-makers in the company. His primary duty, defined by statute, would be to ensure that the company's duty to be specifically accountable was fulfilled. He would be the primary focus for those who wished to exercise their rights to accountability. In other words, the external interest groups with a specific right to accountability would look to the Chairman of the Governing Body for the satisfaction of that right.

The creation of the role of Chairman of the Governing Body, with a statutory duty to ensure that accountability was properly fulfilled would be new to British law. The task would be much wider than that of the Chairman of the Board at present.

In some existing public companies, where the roles of chairman and chief executive are already clearly separated, the positions would scarcely require any change. In companies where the roles are combined, so that the chairman wields direct executive decision-making power, a rethink of the processes of governance would be needed. Some people will undoubtedly argue for the continuation of the existing flexible arrangements, catering for the dominant personality. Others will argue that, with external investors involved, some separate supervision is desirable: not least to protect the entrepreneurial enthusiasms of the chief executive.

Figure 3 attempts to depict the proposals in their entirety.

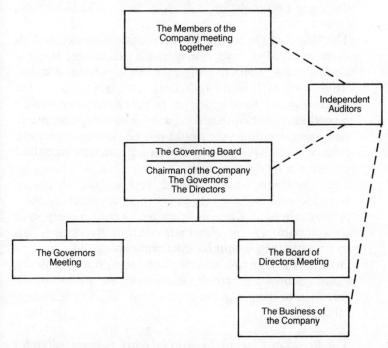

Fig. 3 Basis for governance in the PLC

No prerequisite number or proportion of either governors or directors is suggested. Circumstances vary between companies, as we have seen; and this way the freedom of choice, flexibility and robustness, which has typified the British approach to governance is maintained. The only requirement would be that there should be at least two governors and two directors plus a company chairman. Since both governors and directors meet and act separately, as well as jointly in the Governing Body, the power is not solely dependent on votes in a single meeting. Governors and directors would be nominated by the governors, approved by the Governing Body and, finally, elected by the members.

Let us now consider how the four dimensions of the governance task would be carried out in this framework.

1. *Direction*

The primary role in the strategic leadership of the

enterprise would fall to the directors. It would be their responsibility to formulate strategy and bring fundamental proposals for shifts in policy to the Governing Body.

The Board of Directors would, as now, typically include some or all of the top management executives. It could also have non-executive directors with particular knowledge or contacts in the industry, the market place or the technology; or have special experience, such as being a retired executive of that company. The independence of non-executive directors would not be an issue, since the roles which require a separation of function would be carried out by the governors.

The Governing Body would receive the directors' strategic proposals, question them and, when satisfied, approve them. If the governors felt that the direction of the company was inappropriate, then both as individuals and jointly they would have to bring about the necessary changes through the meetings of the Governing Body. Consequently the governors would be party to the direction of the company and able to fulfil the accountability role.

2. *Executive Action*

The Board of Directors would be entirely responsible for executive action. The directors are, in effect, at the pinnacle of the management command structure.

In other words the responsibility for running the business lies with the board. The extent to which it delegates this responsibility to functional executives, a chief executive officer or managing director, the boards of subordinate companies, or the management teams of divisions, is a matter of choice in management style and structure.

3. *Supervision*

The responsibility for supervising the performance of the executive lies with the governors. The governors meeting would act in this capacity, setting appropriate objectives, reviewing and approving operating plans and monitoring the performance regularly against those plans. The governors would receive regular information on the material aspects of corporate performance and on the company's position. The governors would also be concerned about the adequacy of the management information and control systems, the security of corporate assets and, most importantly, about the calibre of top management staff.

Thus the board of directors would be continuously accountable to a separate, and independent group of professionals, who would be well informed about and understand the businesses being managed. One of the roles of the governors would be to ensure that the business was being well run.

There are, obviously, parallels in this proposal with the attempt to separate executive and supervisory functions in the two-tier board. The advantage of the Governing Body is that it perpetuates the unitary perspective, whilst formalising and legitimising the separation of functions between its constituent parts – the directors to take executive responsibility and the governors to oversee their performance.

Some people might fear that the Governing Body could be institutionalising what they see happening informally in Germany, when the Aufsichtsrat meets with the Vorstand. It should be emphasised, therefore, that the governors are also to be closely involved with, and jointly responsible for, the setting of objectives, the formulating of strategy and the overall direction of the enterprise.

4. *Accountability*

The Governing Body would be responsible for demonstrating accountability for the company to the members. Given the special roles of the governors and the company chairman in the field of supervision and accountability new approaches could be adopted to the meetings of members and the form in which information was provided to them; for example, a governors' report, under the signature of the chairman of the Governing Body could provide an independent assessment of the corporate performance and prospects.

The auditors would continue to be appointed by the members and report to them as now; but the governors would have a direct contact with the auditors. The governors meeting would, consequently, be able to discuss the audit findings, report and any recommendations.

It is sometimes argued that by recommending auditors and

approving their remuneration, executive management may not be, and be seen to be, totally impartial: and auditors may not be seen to be completely independent. If the governors are responsible for appointing and agreeing the remuneration of auditors this dilemma would be solved. In this context the governors would be adopting the guise frequently recommended in an audit committee.

The governors would also act as the independent nominating committee for all appointments to the Governing Body: thereby exercising real power, subject, of course, to the members' ultimate approval.

In all other matters of registration, the limitation of liability, filing, registration of charges, disclosure in accounting and overall company regulation, the governance proposals now developed would call for no further changes.

On Governors

Before we leave the idea of governors and a Governing Body in PLC's, it might be useful to note that the concept is hardly new. Long before the 1855 Companies Act, the Crown appointed governors to oversee the work of the great trading corporations, and even today independent governors are found in various institutions.

Some public companies already have boards, with good independent non-executives, which act very much in the way envisaged with the Governing Body. No new appointments may be needed. The big advantage would be in the formalisation of the role of the governor and its differentiation from that of director. The creation of the Governing Body would enable a unified responsibility to be accepted, avoiding unhelpful adversarial roles. But the existence of a separate meeting of the governors could legitimise the supervisory and accountability activities.

The importance of independence, both of the governors and the outside auditors, has been stressed. The intention is obvious – to demonstrate that those entrusted with the duty of monitoring performance are not affected by vested interests. In addition the proposal for electing professional, experienced people as governors would have the merit of adding objectivity to independence.

A further advantage of a group of governors would arise

where the existing chairman and/or chief executive had a tendency to dominate board meetings or, worse, to treat the company as his private fiefdom. Had they had governors and Governing Bodies at the time, many of the public companies criticised in Department of Trade Inspectors' Reports would not have been investigated.

On the other hand, by permitting the entrepreneurial executive to lead his board of directors there need be no diminution of the flair and executive risk taking attributes often essential to business success.

A proper question, before we leave this proposal for independent governors and a unifying Governing Body of governors and directors, is, what happens if there are basic disagreements?

As has already been explained, the approach to corporate governance advanced here is that it is a political process primarily. Consequently we anticipate differences of opinion and the need to resolve conflicts. The Governing Body is the vehicle for identifying and airing such issues and achieving their solution. The role of chairman, now quite separate from that of the chief executive or managing director, is likely to be crucial in such circumstances.

The ultimate sanction lies with the governors' ability to report to the members (and since the report is published, to the world at large), and to nominate membership of the Governing Body to the members. Considerable pressure would, therefore, exist to find a mutually acceptable consensus. Where that is impossible (for example where the governors are dissatisfied with the company results and doubt the ability of the existing directors to put matters right), it is entirely proper for the governors to tell the members and to make proposals for correcting the problem.

Governance of the Private Company (PTE)

By definition there can be no public invitation to subscribe for shares in a PTE. Neither can the company be dominated by another – otherwise it would be a SUB.

However there must be some separation of ownership from management, some "outside" investors – otherwise the company would be an owner-managed PTY. Such outside shareholders could be dormant investors, non-executive members of the founding family, a financial institution providing venture capital, a joint venture partner and so on. This variability suggests that flexibility in the structure and processes of governance would be desirable; whilst protecting the interests of the outside investors and others affected by the company.

We do suggest that PTE's should have a minimum authorised capital of £10,000 with at least £5,000 paid-up.

The proposal for governance in the PTE is quite similar to existing arrangements — a board of directors, an independent audit and periodic meetings of the members. It is recommended that such boards have a proportion of non-executive directors, and that consideration be given to creating an audit committee: but such matters are at the discretion of the incumbent board, depending on the circumstances. Chairman and chief executive roles should also be separated.

However, with the four part model of corporate governance, we can highlight responsibilities for specific activities: —

1. *Direction*

   The board as a whole would be responsible for establishing the strategic direction for the company. The benefits of outside directors in stimulating strategic thinking and avoiding the tunnel vision and self-delusion of an entirely executive board is emphasised.

2. *Executive Action*

   Basically the business is run by the executive members of the board, and the rest of top management.

3. *Supervision*

   The board exercises supervision over the executive actions. With independent non-executive directors and an audit committee, as recommended, the separation of function will be clear. Otherwise the executive members will have to "wear two hats". This is a matter to be borne in mind by the chairman and the members of the company when considering the structure of the board.

   What is really needed is "hands on" supervision. A balanced board membership with informed, experienced and capable non-executives helping to drive the business forward whilst keeping a strict eye on performanced. Directors who merely turn up for meetings are inappropriate.

4. *Accountability*

As presently the board will report to the members in annual meetings on the performance of the company, with independent auditors reporting whether such accounts show a true and fair view. Remember we are not dealing here with widespread, public investors, but with shareholders who can be expected to have a closer interest in their company. It is up to them, using their power in the members' meeting to question the board structure and processes. There seems no obvious case to increase the power of dissatisfied minorities to call for special meetings of members or, even, to call for an inquiry into the company's affairs.

It is suggested that all other regulatory matters – such as initial registration, the limitation of shareholders' liability, the publication of accounts, filing, the registration of charges, etc. – remain as at present.

Figure 4 attempts to depict the proposed form of governance in the PTE.

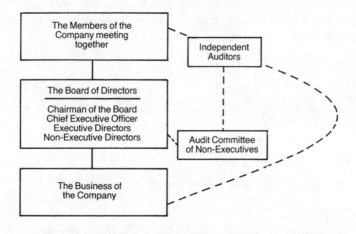

Fig. 4 Basis for governance in the PTE

Governance of the Proprietary Company (PTY)

By our definition the proprietary company is entirely owner directed and managed. All the investors are insiders, involved in the business; and there are no corporate members. (If there were the company would be a PTE).

In the PTY we are dealing with a specific type of entity and consequently propose that such companies should be treated quite differently from the PTE or PLC, which have outside shareholders.

We suggest a new form of incorporation which would emphasise the owner-manager status of the PTY. Anyone dealing with such an enterprise would know that the management was in the hands of those who both owned and ran the business.

Published reports and accounts, for the benefit of members would not be required: nor would an audit. Filing with the Registrar of Companies would be limited to an annual declaration of solvency, possibly confirmed by an independent accountant, for the protection of creditors.

Since members of the PTY are also the directors, formal meetings of members would not be required.

Thought could also be given to the limitation of liability – either with a minimum paid-up and authorised capital (500 and 1,000 respectively perhaps) or a partial limitation with a personal guarantee from the proprietor. In this way all creditors would benefit, rather than just a bank or other lessor who demanded a guarantee.

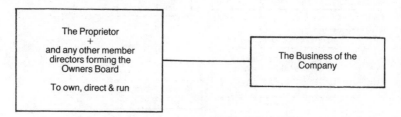

Fig. 5 Basis for governance in the PTY

Governance of the Subordinate Company (SUB) – and the role of the Accountable Business Activity (ABA)

With the subordinate company we are dealing with one company that is dominated by another. A SUB will be either a wholly-owned subsidiary, a subsidiary with other minority shareholders or an associate company over which the dominant company can exercise managerial control.

The theme behind these proposals for governance is that such relationships should be made explicit and the power base identified; moreover accountability should be along the lines of the business decision-making structures, introducing the idea of the accountable business activity to complement the SUB.

Classically, accountability and the limitation of liability are bounded by the corporate entity. This may be adequate for owners, because it is the entity that they own. It may not be adequate for creditors, employees or others, where results are influenced by decision takers, and power wielded, outside the entity with which they contracted. Thus, where business decisions, and therefore risks, are taken beyond the corporate veil, it is plainly wrong to rely on that cover as the basis for accountability and the limitation of liability. (Unless all parties so agreed at the outset.)

Firstly, on the question of limited liability, there is logic in the argument of the draft 9th directive that, since the directors of a dominant company can take decisions that could adversely affect the interests of minority shareholders and creditors in the SUB, such interests should have a right to pursue their debts with the dominant company and its directors. Whether such rights should be extended to employees in a SUB is a matter of labour relations, not governance and is not pursued here.

We would not go as far as personal liability (other than for fraud or misfeasance) for the dominant company directors: such a threat might inhibit proper business risk taking. But we do propose that subordinate companies may not shelter behind the protection of owners' limited liability. On the failure of a SUB, any minority shareholders or creditors whose financial interests have been damaged may take their claim to the dominant company, and pursue the assets of the group as a whole.

Such a proposal "pierces the corporate veil" and strikes at the heart of the concept of the autonomous legal entity with limited liability. But we are not dealing with an autonomous entity, in fact. Limited liability was a device originally offered to nineteenth-century dormant investors – not a mechanism for limiting exposure for decisions taken by directors in a group.

To facilitate such a proposal, it is suggested that the

ownership and organisation structure of groups of companies should be disclosed, as a statutory requirement. This would supplement existing requirements to list subsidiaries, and incidentally make them more useful.

Next, governance in a SUB, we suggest, should be by a management board consisting mainly of executive directors of the SUB; plus, possibly, non-executive directors employed by the dominant company, the ultimate holding company or elsewhere in the group; and, also, if desired, outside directors not employed either in the SUB or in other group companies.

Corporate direction would be by the management board, subject to the approval and consistent with the policies of the dominant company or group. Executive action would, clearly, be the task of the executive directors. Supervision would ultimately be in the hands of the dominant company board or the group, but of course, if the dominant company wanted to give considerable autonomy to their SUB there is nothing to prevent the appointment of independent non-executives of real substance to the board of the SUB. Where that company is overseas this may be highly desirable. Accountability would fall to the management board (see figure 6).

Where there were minority shareholders, members' meetings would be essential. Otherwise, in a wholly-owned

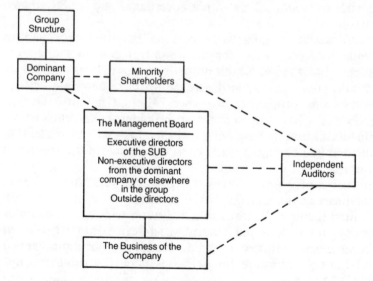

Fig. 6   Basis for governance in the SUB

subsidiary, they would be unnecessary.

Accounts would be audited, published and filed by all SUB's – as now. But, as already suggested, there would also be a requirement to produce audited accounts by accountable business activity.

Obviously, where the SUB's are the basis for the group's management decision-taking, the SUB's and the ABA's would be congruent. Where there was a mismatch between SUB's and ABA's, an additional and more realistic focus for governance – particularly for supervision and accountability – would be provided by the ABA.

The effect of such a requirement would probably be a tendency for SUB's and ABA's to converge – a coming together of the legal, corporate and the business management structures, which would be a beneficial reflection of business reality rather than an artificial perpetuation of legal and taxation bases.

Table 1 summarises the proposals for all the types of company.

Communication with Wider Constituencies

Consistent with the theme of this book that accountability is owed by a company only to those able to enforce the accountability contract, the proposals do not allow for participation in governance by workers as such (contrasting with the European Community's draft 5th directive) nor by representatives of other interest groups such as consumers, ethnic minorities, women or the public good (as favoured by some US commentators).

Nevertheless, the framework for corporate governance, by distinguishing the different types of entity and articulating the elements of the governance task, would enable those who are responsible for governance to consider whether there are practices they would like to adopt which would be helpful to relationships with such other interests.

For example, information about ABA's, in a complex group, would focus on organisational units which are likely to be of primary interest to employees, both the labour force and office staff and managers. What they are interested in is less likely to be the health of the group, as the standing and plans for the business entity for which they work. To be employed by a successful group is cold comfort if your activity has just been sold, without any advance notice, to a Japanese corporation, or is about to be closed.

Type of Company	PLC	PTE	PTY	SUB (ABA)
Limitation of shareholders' liability; authorised capital minimum paid-up	Minimum of 50% of net worth (with reserves)	£10,000 £5,000	No corporate shareholders £1,000 £500 (Plus personal guarantee)	Responsibility of the dominant company
Form of Governance	The Governing Body – Governors, Directors & the Company Chairman	The Board of Directors – separate Chairman & Chief Executive	The proprietor or the owner's board	The management board
Responsibility for:				
– Direction	The Board of Directors (with the Governing Body's approval)	The Board of Directors	The proprietor or the owner's board	The management board (with the dominant company's approval)
– Executive Action	The Board of Directors	The Executive Directors	The proprietor or the owner's board	The Executive Directors
– Supervision	The Governors	The Board of Directors (Non-executives & an audit committee recommended)	The proprietor or the owner's board	By the dominant company
– Accountability	The Governing Body	The Board of Directors	The proprietor or the owner's board	The management board
Methods of accountability:				
– Reports	A Governor's Report A Directors' Report	A Director's Report A Chairman's Report	No formal requirements	Director's Report
– Accounts	Published Accounts	Published Accounts	Filing of statutory statement of solvency	Published accounts by ABA
– Meetings	Members' Meetings	Members' Meetings	No formal requirement	Members' Meeting if minorities
– Audit	Independent Audit	Independent Audit	No formal requirement	Independent Audit

Table 1 Principal features of corporate governance proposed
(this table should be read in conjunction with table 1, chapter 6)

Special reports and accounts, related to each ABA, could be provided for employees in the units; and, possibly accompanied by briefing groups or explained through the processes of the works councils or committees. Such lines of communication, adapted to encourage good employee relations, and promoting identification with the business, commitment and participation, would parallel the lines adopted for governance. But the involvement in or codetermination of such governance is not proposed.

The idea of good communications could be broadened beyond employees. Any governance unit — PLC, PTE, PTY, SUB or ABA — which felt it had a significant effect on one or more of its constituent external groupings (customers, dealers, distributors, suppliers, bankers, employees, local or national interests, for example) could convene regular constituency meetings at which those responsible for governance could make a presentation, and be questioned, about the state of the company and its plans and aspirations.

Such meetings could have a considerable value for goodwill. They could enhance the relationships with suppliers, distributors, customers, employees and the societies in which the company operated: but they would not confuse the governance task with the ex-gratia disclosure of information and beneficial communication.

Another recent development, which might have considerable potential for enhancing two-way communication, is the international advisory council, created by some multinationals. Ostensibly a response to challenges of the exploitation of local resources, failing to transfer technology to developing countries and manipulating profits brought to tax in higher tax areas, these councils consist of a cadre of influential, international businessmen, independent of the company.

Such a forum is tangential to the Governing Body, but available to give advice, to take a local or international perspective and to demonstrate to constituents that the company does attempt to recognise the opinions and issues pertinent to operating in different countries.

Implications for the New Conceptual Framework

Finally we should consider some of the implications that might flow from these proposals for an alternative conceptual framework for corporate governance. Essentially they fall in two areas – implications for improving board level effectiveness and ideas for developing social policy about corporate affairs.

The identification of the four essential elements of corporate governance – direction, executive action, supervision and accountability – opens up, for the first time, a wide range of opportunities to assess board level competence and to improve directors' effectiveness.

The conceptual framework, by distinguishing the four fundamentally different types of company – PLC, PTE, PTY and SUB – enables a director to understand the basis of the governance in which he should be involved. Some of the potential confusion about the roles of executives and non-executives, independent outside directors, owner-directors and directors of subsidiaries, which arise because they are treated alike, will be resolved once their real differences are made explicit.

The way in which the ideas might affect the work of directors and change the processes of the boards on which they serve, is probably the most important aspect of our studies; and the one with the potential for immediate action.

In this book we can only intimate the range of possibilities for individual directors and for boards. Indeed, the opportunities for improving board effectiveness are such that a further book of practical briefings for directors, is being prepared within The Corporate Policy Group, based on the concepts of this study.

As for the implications for social policy, the proposals here basically provide a vehicle for further deliberation. Obviously much consultation and elaboration would be necessary before any legislative proposals could be drafted. What is offered here is a policy framework, which could form the foundation for business practices as we move into the twenty-first century, just as the present framework was inherited from the nineteenth.

Improving the Effectiveness of Governance

Starting from the proposition that corporate governance has four principal elements, we can use these to assess the work of directors in practice. Many questions come readily to mind.

The answers would have to be set in the appropriate context of the PLC, PTE, PTY or SUB and involve governors and directors where necessary.

1. *Corporate Direction*

The process of strategy formulation has three essential parts – the assessment of the strategic situation, strategic choice and implementation (see figure 7). Strategic assessment involves the exploration of the issues, opportunities and threats in the entire business environment, recognising the strengths and weaknesses of the available resources and reaffirming the company's mission and its objectives. Strategic choice is a matter of recognising alternative strategies, evaluating them and choosing the planned direction. Implementation, obviously, involves the establishment of appropriate policies and procedures for the fulfilment of the strategic projects and plans.

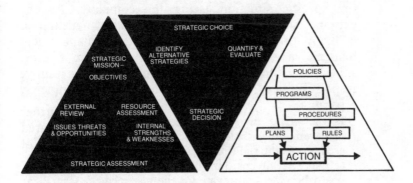

Fig. 7 Outline of strategy formulation

* How does the board go about setting corporate direction – by discussing and approving management plans, by stimulating strategic initiatives or by whole-heartedly accepting that the longer term direction of the business is in board hands?
* Is the board structure consistent with professional formulation of strategy? Do outside directors play a role? Would a board sub-committee be appropriate?
* Is sufficient time devoted to strategic issues, or does executive action and supervision tend to dominate with shorter term matters? Would a board meeting entirely devoted to corporate direction be worthwhile; or perhaps, a

two-day strategy seminar away from the formality of typical board discussion?

* Are directors adequately briefed on strategic issues: do they have the necessary information to play their part in setting direction? Are staff being used effectively? What other opportunities might there be for improving directors' knowledge about strategic matters?

* Are the members of the board well experienced and trained in strategic thinking? Are there opportunities for improving their effectiveness?

Overall, is the setting of direction for the company as a whole, and its member divisions, subsidiaries and businesses, done as well and as effectively as it could be? Has the board faced up to its responsibilities? Where are there opportunities for improvements?

2. *Executive Action*

The extent to which boards are involved in executive decision-making, as we have seen, is a matter of style and the specific situation facing the company. At one extreme the totally executive board or the owner-director is likely to be very much involved in management matters: at the other end of the scale the entirely supervisory board has, by definition, no executive responsibilities, the functions have been completely separated.

* Is the board involved in the most effective way with management activities taking the type of company into account? Is the right proportion of board time spent on this activity? Are all board members properly informed? Has the board become a surrogate for the management team, with individuals taking a functional role, rather than accepting a responsibility for running the business as a whole?

3. *Supervision*

The supervisory role of the board, monitoring and controlling management work is a well accepted role of the board. How it is carried out in practice raises many questions.

* Is the board appropriately structured? Is the balance between executive and non-executive members realistic? Are there needs to change the structure or membership?

* How is the supervisory activity carried out — by the board as a whole, by the non-executives or otherwise? Is there a need for an audit committee?

* How does the board interact with the external auditors? Do they meet the board as a whole?
* Are all directors sufficiently knowledgeable about the business to fulfil their supervisory responsibilities appropriately?
* How are board decisions about supervision of the executive followed up? How might supervision be improved?

4. *Accountability*

The board, and particularly its chairman we have argued, has a principal duty to be accountable on behalf of the company to all interests with a legitimate accountability relationship. This raises a multitude of questions.

* How does the board fulfil its accountability duty?
* Is the formal published set of accounts and related reports the only accountability link with many members? How are accounting standards pursued? Could the form or content of accounts be improved?
* How does the board use the annual meeting with the members? Could the interaction be improved? What about other ways of demonstrating accountability?
* Is there a case for constituency meetings or an independent advisory council? Are the links with the auditors appropriate?

On Audit of Board Level Processes and Practices

Such questions can only hint at the sort of issues and opportunities raised by examining corporate governance in practice, in the light of the new conceptual framework. Indeed it is feasible to consider a board level audit.

Again we can only illustrate the areas for examination here:—

1. *Board structure and membership*
    * Is the size of board relevant? — now and in relation to corporate strategy?
    * Does the board have an appropriate balance of executive and non-executive members?
    * Should the non-executives be independent?
    * Is there a good balance of expertise, interests, experience, ages, professional knowledge and so on?

Is there a succession plan for board structure and membership that is consistent with the overall strategy for the company? A board may be quite effective today, but due to retirements on the one hand and changes in the company's business on the other, may be quite inadequate in the future.

2. *Board processes and style*
   * Does the board work well together, to meet all four essential elements of corporate governance?
   * Are all members contributing to the full?
   * Is the balance of board time appropriate or could time be better spent? Are the right matters taking precedent; or are there important issues failing to reach the agenda?
   * Is the timing and location of board meetings appropriate? Could more imaginative use be made of directors? Should there be an audit committee, nominating committee, remuneration committee, or executive committee?
   * Could some outside directors be called on to give more time in an advisory capacity outside the board room?

3. *Board practice*
   * Are the board papers as informative as they could be? What do directors really need to know? Are there other ways of broadening and deepening the director's knowledge of the company and the businesses it is in?
   * Are newly appointed members properly briefed? Do they know the chairman's expectations of his board? Is there an induction programme, to enable them to learn more quickly – and thus be able to contribute earlier?
   * Are board members sufficiently well acquainted with the top management in the group's businesses and know enough about the business realities?

4. *Board development and director training*
   * Do some directors need further training or experience in certain areas?
   * How might the board as a whole be developed to play a more effective role in governance?

Such questions, though far from comprehensive, illustrate the range of issues that can be prompted by the conceptual framework. Reviewing the four elements of governance, in the context of the type of company concerned, has a significant potential for the analysis, evaluation and improvement of board level activities.

The other aspect of these proposals for corporate governance are the implications for social policy.

Implications for Social Policy on Corporate Governance

The first critical distinction, drawn in these proposals is between the four types of company. Being built on observed practice, such a typology could usefully form the basis for any future legislation designed to regulate companies in society. We have seen how each of the four types plays a quite different role in society and has distinctive needs for governance. Company law needs to reflect the role and facilitate such governance.

The PTY would encourage innovation and the further creation of new, small enterprises. This would be beneficial for economic well-being, as well as job creation, and is in line with government policy. The owner-director would have the benefits of incorporation without the absurdities of present day company regulation.

The PTE would formalise existing practices in the governance of private companies in which there was a degree of separation between management and owners. Wider use of venture capital and other external funding would be encouraged by the legitimisation of the supervisory and accountability functions.

The proposals for SUB's, and the related ABA's, face up, for the first time, to the complexity of modern groups of companies, particularly those operating internationally. The proposals provide a realistic means for their governance, encouraging effective business management whilst protecting the interests of those affected by those management decisions.

The most fundamental ideas for developing corporate governance are the proposals to create governors and a Governing Body for PLC's. This would clarify the present confusion of a duality of role for executive directors and enhance the work of non-executive directors.

More significantly these ideas, if incorporated into British company law and practice would provide a direct response to the proposals for two-tier boards and other demands for a separation of function between supervision and executive action – without losing anything of the flexibility and robustness of the present unitary board.

Implementing Policy on Corporate Governance

No fundamental shift in philosophy is involved in these proposals. Indeed they have been modelled on the basis of power in the different types of company in Britain today.

The suggestions are broadly in line with the socio-economic thinking of the present Conservative government. If, in the future, there was a desire to adjust the balance of power — for example by giving greater participation to workers — the conceptual model would enable the implications to be seen for corporate direction, executive management, supervision and accountability.

So, how might the ideas be pursued further? If discussion can be stimulated and, subsequently, specific proposals drafted, corporate thinking and practice could be taken to the next plane of experience.

Obviously some changes are being proposed for company law. But not all the proposals in this chapter need, necessarily, become mandatory. For example, the structures and duties could be optional: only to be required by law if the meeting of members or a Department of Trade Inspector so demanded when things were not going well. Transition provisions would also be necessary.

If the work is pursued energetically Britain has an opportunity to make a positive and fundamental contribution to European thinking on the governance of companies. The Anglo-Saxon mind has not taken readily to the prescriptive nature of most European proposals for company law harmonisation. Indeed there have been fears that the desire for social engineering and regulation has superseded the Treaty of Rome's prime emphasis on the encouragement of freer trade. Consequently the almost universal response of the British to draft directives has been negative — resisting the imposition of European style regulation and seeing even minor amendments in favour of UK practice as major achievements.

One has, of course, to appreciate the political reality: but Britain could be taking a far more proactive stance, and in the process contributing fundamentally to the ability of European business to succeed in the world in the long term. Instead of the search for order, regulation and neatness of the Napoleonic mind, we could offer ideas based on the experience of freedom, initiative and the opportunity to be flexible and to adapt. In conditions of change and stress, incidentally, it is the organic and adaptable that survive and grow, not the mechanistic and formal. The Government should affirm that British practice is not only relevant, but better for encouraging business initiative.

True, there are limitations to company law based on such traditions: but the British have always been prepared to accept the occasional buccaneer, as the price for freedom to trade. Indeed they tend to love them dearly. These proposals for rethinking the basics of corporate governance, though lacking such romantic imagery, do contain a vision of a future for companies that would both promote business and enhance society.

Of course, corporate effectiveness cannot be imposed by statute. If directors and management in a business are sound, they are likely to be successful — for themselves, the owners and everyone else involved with the enterprise: if not, no amount of exhortation or regulation will produce success. The role of the law is to facilitate and regulate: it is for the people to initiate and act.

The studies of The Corporate Policy Group have highlighted some fundamental and fascinating changes in the structure and financing of modern companies. The formality of corporate governance is in danger of being divorced from the reality of actual business activities.

The corporate strategies and organisation structures of the 50's, 60's and early '70's — with the comfortable management myths that accompanied them — seem less relevant to the business opportunities and needs of today. Then, the old acquisition strategies treating companies as commodities, the complex corporate groups with many layers of subsidiaries and large central staffs, innovation financed by ploughed-back profits and rights issues, now seem inappropriate to a world of technological revolution and the demise of the smoke-stack manufacturing industry.

As we face the loosening of the equity market — with new sources of venture capital, private investors encouraged by the business expansion scheme, the unlisted securities market, and new found power in the institutional investors — we are facing again the classical issues of corporate governance: the roles and responsibility for setting corporate direction, successfully running the business, and exercising supervision and accountability, with appropriate limitation of liability, legitimacy and regulation. It is almost as though the twenty or thirty years up to the mid-70's lulled us into a false sense of managerial security.

In this book we have not guaranteed to have found the right answers: but we do claim to be asking some of the right questions. Current practices of corporate governance in Britain do not readily encourage enthusiastic, committed and effective top level enterprise. They could: and it would be the better for everyone involved.

This book began with a telling quotation from a company chairman. It ends with wise words from a leading civil servant. Commenting on an early draft of the book, Philip Brown, then responsible for company affairs at the Department of Trade, wrote

> "On larger matters. Yes, I can see the value of this kind of attempted framework: but you will not be surprised if I say — again I am afraid — that for the administrator and I suspect the company director, the present framework is the one we shall have to live with for our working lives, and nothing will save us from having to argue in various contexts about alternative structures and procedures. Your efforts and considerations may — perhaps even desirably will — gradually change the way in which decision-makers view what they are doing and cause them to rethink some of their (our) current perceptions: but there is a long transitional period (and some tricky bridges to cross). This is not an argument against your doing your proper Socratic job but it is an argument for some pretty realistic view about the near and middle future.
>
> But then you would not expect a bureaucrat to say anything different."

Appendices

Appendix 1
Some Notes on the Research Method

The material on which the book has been based was derived in two main ways.

Firstly a desk analysis of published company data and individual company records was used to provide the background for our analysis of complexity in corporate structures. This was supported by confirmation, provided in correspondence and interview, with specific companies.

Secondly a programme of interviews with directors and company chairmen, in public and private companies, parent and subsidiaries, provided material on the processes of corporate governance.

It became apparent, from the analysis of early case notes, that expectations and perceptions in the minds of the principal actors in the corporate drama were as significant as any observed behaviour or analysis of board structures and procedures. Consequently an endeavour was made to explore the *ideas* of respondents about the nature of corporate governance, as well as obtaining *descriptions* of board practices.

Positioning papers on topics such as the role of the chairman, the nature of accountability, the role of the non-executive director and the responsibilities of subsidiary company boards were prepared and used as the basis for discussion in "roundtables" of invited directors. These roundtable discussions provided further valuable insights and evidence for the study.

The case notes are now voluminous; and in places have been quoted to enhance the text. However, the understanding with all respondents was that there would be no attribution and that their companies would not be identifiable. Accordingly the reader has to rely on the integrity of the researcher to present a balanced view.

The literature in the field has, of course, been studied; and discussions have been held with academics, professional advisers and regulators in the UK, continental Europe and

North America, including key figures in the European Commission, the Securities and Exchange Commission in Washington, the Department of Trade & Industry, The Stock Exchange, the Council for the Securities Industry, the American Institute of Certified Public Accountants, the Chartered Institutes of Accountants in England and Wales, Scotland and Canada, the Institute of Directors, and others.

Appendix 2

A Comparison of Forms of Legal Entity
– UK, France and Germany

The forms of legal entity available to business firms in France and Germany, with their nearest British equivalent, are: –

French Form	British Form
la société anonyme (SA)	the public limited company
la société à responsibilité limitée (SARL) (Minimum paid up capital 20,000 French francs)	the private limited company
la société en nom collectif (SNC)	the general (unlimited) partnership
la société en commandité par actions (SCA) ⎫ ⎬ (SC)	the limited company where directors have unlimited personal liability (section 202 of Companies Act 1948)
la société en commandité simple (SCS) ⎭	the limited partnership

German Form	British Form
Companies	
i. the Aktiengesellschaft-AG	the public limited company
ii. the Gesellschaft mit beschränkter Haftung-GmbH (Minimum paid up capital 5000 Deutsche Marks)	the private limited company
iii. the Kommanditgesellschaft auf Aktien-KGaA (a rarely used form of public company where *some* shareholders are personally liable)	the limited company where directors have unlimited personal liability (section 202 of Companies Act 1948)
Partnerships	
i. Gesellschaft des Burgerlichen Rechts (partnership governed by the Civil Code) ⎫ ⎬	the general partnership (all partners personally liable)
ii. the Offene Handelsgesellschaft-OHG ⎭	
iii. the Kommanditgesellschaft	limited partnership
iv. the Stille Gesellschaft	an undisclosed partnership which occurs when one person invests money in a sole traders business

Source: A New Form of Incorporation for Small Firms; Cmnd 8171 February 1981

Appendix 3

Size Classification of Companies and Concessions for Small Companies

The 4th directive on company law of the European Commission proposed a size classification for companies, and offered concessions on reporting, filing and audit. Only an abridged balance sheet, with no profit and loss account, would be required to be published in the small company: member states would also be permitted to exempt such companies from audit requirements. This provision was intended to help those countries with few qualified accountants.

The UK Green Paper "Company Accounting and Disclosure", Cmnd. 7654, September 1979, made proposals in response to the directive. A three tier classification was outlined:—

Top tier	all companies listed on the Stock Exchange and other companies which exceeded two of the following three criteria:—

Turnover	£5 million
Balance sheet total	£2.5 million
Average number of employees	250

Middle tier	all public companies not included in the top tier and all private companies which do not fall within either the top tier or the bottom tier.

Bottom tier	small private companies which do not exceed two of the following three criteria:—

Turnover	£1.3 million
Balance Sheet total	£650,000
Average number of employees	50

Additionally, a subsidiary of the public company would not be treated as a small private company and any company in a group which, taken as a whole, does not fall within the criteria for the bottom tier may not be treated. (See Table 1).

Size criteria	Public Company		Private Company	
	Stock Exchange Listed	Not Listed	Subsidiary of a public company	Not a Subsidiary of a public company
Large Company	Top tier	Top tier	Top tier	Top tier
Medium Company	Top tier	Middle tier	Middle tier	Middle tier
Small Company	Top tier*	Middle tier*	Middle tier	Bottom tier (Proprietary)

Table 1   Classification of companies in the UK, as proposed in the Green Paper, Cmnd. 7654

*in the unlikely event of there being public companies in this size range

The Green Paper proposed that small private companies, as defined above, should be called *proprietary companies* but there would be no requirement to indicate such status in their names. It further recommended that the existing legal requirements for drawing up full accounts for use by the company and for circulation to all shareholders should be maintained: but that full advantage should be taken of the concessions on the filing and publication of accounts. On the question of statutory audit, it was argued that the auditors of many small companies were unable to obtain adequate independent evidence with which to verify the transactions, and that consequently the statutory audit requirements should be removed.

In the event the Companies Act, 1981 did introduce size criteria (see chapter 2 reference 16), but did not recognise the proprietary company, nor remove the audit requirement from small companies.

An Anomaly in the Existing Typology

An interesting anomaly in the typology proposed in the Green Paper (and subsequently adopted in the Act) and the 4th directive, was pointed out in evidence given by The Corporate Policy Group to the Department of Trade in September 1979.

The classification of the 4th directive adopts a simple three tier structure by size criteria alone. The British model, however, introduces a three way classification by class, ownership and size. The effect is a potential mismatch between the UK tier category and that of the directive.

Appendix 4

The Corporate Policy Group and its Publications

The Corporate Policy Group is a non-profit, non-partisan charitable trust formed in 1979.

Its formal objectives are to advance public education in the field of corporate direction, control and governance by promoting study and research, and to disseminate the results. In practice it has been involved in the study of board level processes, formulation of strategy and the implications for organisation structure and management style at board level in companies in Britain, Europe and North America.

The Group provides a forum for the exchange of ideas and experience between company chairmen, executive and non-executive directors, and others in the professions, universities, government and the unions. It also provides a focus for research study and a library for relevant books and papers.

The Group operates as an independent unit, based at Nuffield College, Oxford.

Publications of The Corporate Policy Group

Two Tier Boards (PP1/80); Peter McGregor; Joint Anglo-German Foundation and Corporate Policy Group Conference; London, January 1980.

Control of the Corporation (PP2/80); Michael Shanks, Jeffrey Knight, Roy Grantham and Lord Croham; Joint Anglo-German Foundation and Corporate Policy Group Conference; London, January 1980.

Misdirected Directors (PP3/80); R.I. Tricker; Special University of London Lecture, London, November 1980.

Corporate Regulation (PP4/81); Harold Williams and Bill Thomson; Nuffield College, Oxford Conference, March 1980.

Corporate Accountability and the Role of the Audit Function (PP5/81); R.I. Tricker, Research Symposium, London Business School, December 1980.

Chairman of the Board (PP6/81); R.I. Tricker; November 1981.

Accountability of the Corporation (PP7/82); Robert Coleman, Bob Tricker, Jim Armstrong and Tom Watts: Nuffield College, Oxford Conference, December 1981.

The Context of Corporate Accountability (PP8/82); R.I. Tricker; Research Symposium, London Business School, January 1982.

Perspectives on Power (PP9/82); R.I. Tricker; September 1982.

The primary research focus has been on companies incorporated in Britain, but, given the effects of European and US regulatory activities, and the global activities of many companies, a wider perspective has been adopted. The conclusions reached and the new conceptual framework for the corporation in modern society will be pertinent to those interested in corporate governance in North America, continental Europe and elsewhere.

A study undertaken for the Institute of Chartered Accountants in England & Wales, during these researches, on the processes of governance in professional bodies has added further dimensions to the study of corporate governance (Tricker R.I.; Governing the Institute: ICAEW, London 1982).

Appendix 5
References

Chapter 1

1 In a personal interview with the author, in connection with this research, 1979.
2 Tricker, R.I.; The Independent Director; Tolley, 1978.
3 A description of The Corporate Policy Group and a list of discussion papers published under its aegis is given in Appendix 4.
4 Proposal for a 5th directive — "to coordinate the safeguards which, for the protection of the interests of members and others, are required by Member States of companies within the meaning of Article 58(2) of the Treaty of Rome, as regards the structure of sociétés anonymes and the powers and obligations of their organs." Original draft November 1972. Discussion paper from Legal Affairs Committee October 1974. Commission presents draft to European Parliament June 1978. Referred back September 1979. Further draft January 1980. Parliament adopts an opinion on the directive May 1982. Latest draft submitted August 1983 and published November 1983. (For a summary of present proposals see chapter 11).
5 Role of the Non-Executive Director: a booklet prepared for PRO NED — The Promotion of Non-Executive Directors, 30 Cursitor Street, London EC4A 1DS. February 1982.
6 Confederation of British Industry; The Responsibilities of the British Public Company: Company Affairs Committee; Lord Watkinson (Chairman), 1973.
7 Institute of Directors; A Code of Practice for the Non-Executive Director: Non-Executive Director Appointments Service, 116 Pall Mall, London SW1Y 5ED. 1982.
8 Sir Brandon Rhys Williams MP; Clauses dealing with non-executive directors, their candidature and their reports were proposed at the report stage of the Companies (No. 2) Bill 1981, but were not selected for debate.
9 For example Lonrho Ltd., Pergamon Press Ltd. and

London & County Securities Group Ltd. See also Inspectors Reports on:

Peak Foods Ltd., 1981
"G was able to operate (the company) in an unprincipled manner for his personal benefit, evading both external regulations and self-regulation alike."
".....the result of G's dominance and the failure of his co-directors to supervise his activities."

Court Line Ltd., 1978
".....none of the directors can be absolved from blame for allowing the continuation of a position where the board acted largely as a rubber stamp."

Roadships Ltd., 1976
"H ran the company as an autocrat, the board did not function as such and the tough atmosphere was livened by rumours and suspicions.....completely out of place in a public company."
See also:
Clarke, Michael; Fallen Idols: Junction, 1981.

10 The Conduct of Company Directors: White Paper, Cmnd. 7037, HMSO November 1977 and The Companies' Bill, 1977 (Bill 38); To Appoint Non-Executive Directors and Audit Committees in Major Public Companies. (Bill not pursued on change of government).

11 Report of the Committee of Inquiry on Industrial Democracy; Lord Bullock (Chairman): Cmnd 6706, HMSO, January 1977.

12 Proposal for a 5th directive, op. cit. chapter 1 ref. 4.

13 See Shanks, Michael (Chairman, National Consumer Council); The Role of Consumers: and Grantham, Roy (General Secretary, APEX); The Role of the Employee and the Trade Unions: in Control of the Corporation; Corporate Policy Group, Oxford, 1980.

14 The Conference Board; The Nominating Committee and the Director Selection Process: New York, 1981.

15 The accountancy standard setting process in the UK is discussed in chapter 8.
See also:
Solomons, D.; The Politicization of Accounting – the Impact of Politics on Accounting Standards: The Journal of Accountancy; No. 146, November 1978.

Williams, Harold (Chairman, Securities & Exchange Commission, Washington); The Role of the SEC in Overseeing the Accounting Profession – in Corporate Regulation: Corporate Policy Group, Oxford, 1981.

16 Accounting Standards (Steering) Committee; The Corporate Report: London, 1975.

17 Draft directive on procedures for informing and consulting with employees in complex groups of companies. Named after the Commissioner responsible – Commissioner Vredeling.

> "The original initiative was launched to protect the interests of employees in subsidiaries of multinational companies, forcing the disclosure of information to employees about general policy and specific information on decisions such as the closure or transfer of plants, major changes in business activity or organisation and the introduction or cessation of long term cooperation with other businesses.
> Employees would have a right to apply directly to the 'dominant' holding company where they were dissatisfied at the local level.
> Although focussed on multinationals the present draft would cover all groups of companies in which at least one subsidiary has 100 or more employees in a member state.
> The European Parliament amended the draft to exclude firms with less than 1000 employees, gave managers scope to declare information confidential, and would prevent workers from going straight to the controlling firm for information."

See "The Employee's Right to Know"; SEC/B24/83, 11th August 1983.

For details of the latest proposals see chapter 11.

18 Insolvency Law and Practice; Report of the Review Committee; Sir Kenneth Cork (Chairman): Cmnd 8558, HMSO, June 1982.

19 Draft 9th directive of the European Commission. Original draft circulated 1981, revision 1983.

> Concerns the protection of shareholders, employees and creditors in subsidiary companies. The draft distinguishes "dominant" undertakings, such as a parent company and "dependent" companies such as subsidiaries. Shareholders, employees and creditors of

dependent companies would have recourse to the dominant company for any loss suffered which resulted from the influence of the parent and were attributable to faults in management or to actions which were not in the dependent company's interests.
For full discussion see chapter 9.

20 A New Form of Incorporation for Small Firms; a consultative document: Cmnd. 8171, HMSO, February 1981.

21 See Coleman, Robert (a member of the office of the Director-General III, European Commission responsible for company law harmonisation); Corporate Accountability – A European Perspective: in Accountability of the Corporation: Corporate Policy Group, Oxford, 1982.

22 The case for a Corporate Democracy Act of 1980; Public Citizens Congress Watch, et al; Washington 1980.

23 See Child, John; The Business Enterprise in Modern Industrial Society: Collier-Macmillan, 1969.

24 Interestingly, Henri Fayol (1841-1925), one of the first writers acknowledged in the management field *did* seem to appreciate the significance of governance. Subsequent writers blurred the distinction.
Fayol was a French mining engineer who achieved recognition, late in life, for his paper on administration. In 1916 his "Administration Industrielle et Générale – Prévoyance, Organization, Commandement, Coordination, et Contrôle" was published. The English version appeared, translated by Constance Storrs, as "General and Industrial Management". As Pugh, Hickson & Hinings comment: "There has been some debate over the rendering of the title... in particular of expressing the French word 'administration' by the term 'management'. They argued that this would simply imply that Fayol was concerned only with industrial management, whereas his own preface claims that 'management' plays a very important part in the government of undertakings: of all undertakings, large or small, individual, commercial, political, religious or any other". Notice that Fayol recognised the concept of governance.
Fayol, Henri; Administration Industrielle et Générale – Prévoyance, Organization, Commandement, Coordination et Contrôle: in the Bulletin de la Société de l'Industrie

Minérale, 1916. Translated by Constance Storrs: General & Industrial Management, Pitman, 1949.
Pugh, D.S.; D.J. Hickson and C.R. Hinings; Writers on Organisations – Hutchinson, 1964; Penguin 1971.

25 Goldsmith, Walter (Director-General, Institute of Directors); The Role of the Company Director: Executive World; November/December 1980.

26 Eilon, Samuel; The Board – Functions and Structure: Management Decisions, Volume 12, No. 2, 1974.

27 Wilson, Harold; The Governance of Britain: Weidenfeld & Nicholson Ltd. and Michael Joseph Ltd., 1976; Sphere Books, 1977.

28 The Oxford English Dictionary; Oxford University Press.

29 Wiener, Norbert; Cybernetics: Wiley, 1948.

Chapter 2

1 U.S. Congress (House); Reform and Self-Regulation Efforts of the Accounting Profession (Hearings): 95th Cong. 2nd Sess (1978).

2 See Berle, Adolf A. and G.C. Means; The Modern Corporation and Private Property: Macmillan, 1932; revised edition Harcourt, Brace & World, 1968. A fuller discussion is provided in chapter 6.

3 Finance Act, 1981: HMSO.

4 Finance Act, 1982: HMSO.

5 Companies Act, 1948, (Ch. 38): HMSO.

6 Companies Act, 1967, (Ch. 81): HMSO.

7 Companies Act, 1976, (Ch. 69): HMSO.

8 The Institute of Chartered Accountants published a statement of intent on accounting standards in 1970, which aimed to narrow the variety of accounting practices, to disclose the bases of accounting and to disclose departures from definitive accounting standards.
See discussion in Zeff, Stephen A.; Forging Accounting Principles in Five Countries – A History and Analysis of Trends: University of Edinburgh, 1971.

9 Lonrho Ltd.; a report by inspectors appointed by the Department of Trade: HMSO, 1976 (paragraph 12.136).

10 Pergamon Press Ltd.; a report by inspectors appointed by the Department of Trade: HMSO, 1971.

11 London & County Securities Group Ltd.; a report by

inspectors appointed by the Department of Trade: HMSO, 1976 (paragraphs 15.09 and 15.10).

12 Companies Act, 1980, (Ch. 22): HMSO.

13 S.46, Part IV, Companies Act, 1980: HMSO.

14 Prudential Assurance Co. Ltd. v Newman Industries Ltd. and others: reported in The Times, 29th February 1980.

15 Companies Act, 1981, (Ch. 62): HMSO.

16 A company would qualify for the small company exclusions if it satisfied two of the following three criteria:
   1. turnover not exceeding £1,400,000.
   2. balance sheet total not exceeding £700,000.
   3. average number of people employed (determined on a weekly basis) not exceeding 50.

   A company would qualify as a medium sized company in a similar way with the limits increased to £5,750,000 turnover, £2,800,000 balance sheet total and 250 employees.

17 Exceptions to this general proposition can be found where debenture holders are given powers to nominate under the terms of the debenture deed.

Chapter 3

1 Postan, M.M.; The Medieval Economy and Society: Weidenfeld & Nicolson, 1972; Pelican, 1975.

2 Tawney, R.H.; Religion and the Rise of Capitalism: Holland Memorial Lectures, 1922; Pelican, 1938.
   See also:
   Tawney, R.H.; The Radical Tradition: Allen & Unwin, 1964.

3 Op. cit. ref. 1.

4 Postan references The English Farmers of the Customs 1343-52; Trans. Royal Historical Society, 5th ser. IX, 1959.

5 Trevelyan, G.M.; English Social History: Penguin, 1944.

6 Macfarlane, Alan; The Origins of English Individualism: Basil Blackwell, 1978.

7 ibid. chapter 7 page 165.

8 ibid. chapter 8 page 201.

9 ibid. chapter 8 page 202/3.

10 Wright, L.B.; Middle Class Culture in Elizabethan England: Chapel Hill, 1935.

11 Hill, Christopher; Intellectual Origins of the English Revolution: Oxford University Press, 1965; Panther, 1972.

12 Bacon, Works, xiv 22-28, 446, 460-5 (ibid. Hill, Christopher).

13/14 Bacon, Works, xii (ibid. Hill, Christopher).

15 Hill, Christopher; op. cit. reference 11.

16 Raleigh, Works, ii 31-32.

17 ibid. ii 135.

18 Quoted in F. Thompson; Magna Carta: Its Role in the Making of the English Constitution : p359 (ibid. Hill, Christopher).

19 Coke, E.; 2 Reports, p79; Commons Debates 1621, ed. W. Notestein, F.H. Relf and H. Simpson: Yale, 1935.

20 Op. cit. references 5 and 10.

21 Cottrell, P.L.; Industrial Finance, 1830-1914: Methuen, 1980.

22 ibid. chapter 1, page 8.

23 ibid. chapter 1, page 9.
   See also:
   Davies, R.; The Rise of the English Shipping Industry, 1962: and National Maritime Museum; Problems of Ship Management and Operation, 1870-1900: Monograph No. 5, 1972.

24 Cottrell, op. cit. chapter 3, page 43.

25 An act for the registration, incorporation and regulation of joint-stock companies. CAP.CX: 7 & 8 Victoriae: 5th September 1844.

26 See Shannon, H.A.; The First Five Thousand Limited Companies and their Duration: Economic History II, 1930.

27 Op. cit. reference 21.

28 Jeffreys, J.B.; Trends in Business Organisation in Great Britain, since 1856: University of London, Ph.D. thesis, 1938.

29 Society for Promoting the Amendment of the Law; Report of the Committee on the law of partnership on the liability of partners; 1849.

30 Report of the Royal Commission on Mercantile Laws; 1854.

31 An act for linking the liability of members of certain joint-stock companies. CAP.CXXXIII: 18 & 19 Victoriae:

14th August 1855.

32/33/34 The minor acts of 1857 and 1858 were consolidated into a major act, repealing Peel's Joint-Stock Bank Act. (Cottrell op. cit. page 53), under the title: —

An Act for the Incorporation, Regulation and Winding Up of Trading Companies and Other Associations: CAP. LXXXIX: 25 & 26 Victoriae: 7th August 1862.

35 Cottrell, op, cit. page 54 and 61.

36 The Joint-Stock Companies Arrangement Act, 1870, dealt with winding-up procedures.

37 The Companies Act, 1877, was very short and facilitated capital reductions.

38 Cottrell, op. cit. page 54.

39 ibid. page 55.

40 The Royal Commission on the Depression of Trade and Industry: First report, 1886; second report, 1886; third report, 1886; final report, 1886.

41 Cottrell, op. cit. page 66.

42 ibid. page 67.

43 Op. cit. reference 40.

44 ibid. First report.

45 Report of the Departmental Committee appointed by the Board of Trade; Lord Davey (Chairman): BPP.1895, LXXXVIII.

46 Companies Act, 1900.

47 The Company Law Amendment Committee; Loreburn (Chairman): BPP.1906, XCVIII.

48 Companies Act, 1907.

49 Op. cit. reference 21.

50 Cottrell, op. cit. page 164.

51 For a full discussion of the way in which today's large corporations superseded the small competing firms of the nineteenth-century, and of the mergers and concentration into groups, see:
Hannah, Leslie; The Rise of the Corporate Economy: Methuen, 1976.

52 Re: City Equitable Fire Insurance Co. Ltd.; 1925: Ch. 407.

53 For discussion see:
Loose, Peter; The Company Director: Jordan, 1953 and revisions; and Gower, L.C.B. et al; The Principles of Modern Company Law: Stevens & Son, 1979 (fourth edition).

54 For a fuller description of the evolution of the role of directors in British companies see:
Jervis, F.R.; Bosses in British Business: Routledge & Kegan Paul, 1974.
55 Companies Act, 1929.
56 Companies Act, 1948.

Chapter 4

1 Department of Trade & Industry; Companies in 1982 – Annual Report to 31st December 1982: HMSO, 1983.
2 Report of the Company Law Committee; Lord Jenkins (Chairman): Cmnd. 1749, HMSO, 1962.
3 Evidence given by the Board of Trade to the Jenkins Committee; op. cit. reference 2: quoted in Cmnd. 8171 op. cit. chapter 1, reference 20.
4 Limited Partnership Act, 1907. Failure to register will result in each limited partner being treated as a general partner and liable for unlimited debts (s.5).
5 A New Form of Incorporation for Small Firms; Cmnd. 8171, op. cit. chapter 1, reference 20.
6 Company Law Reform; Cmnd. 5391, HMSO, 1973.
7 Lowe, J.R.M.; The Incorporated Firm: Jordan, 1974. (An essay in a competition for the best draft bill for a new corporate structure for the small firm).
8 Cmnd. 1749, op. cit. reference 2.
9 In response to the Green Paper; Company Accounting & Disclosure: Cmnd. 7654, HMSO, 1979.
10 Cmnd. 8171, op. cit. reference 5.
11 Gower, L.C.B.; A Code for Incorporated Firms? A research paper in Cmnd. 8171, op. cit. reference 5. Professor Gower is Research Adviser on company law to the Department of Trade.
12 Memorandum, submitted in November 1981, to the Department of Trade by the Councils of the constituent members of the Consultative Committee of Accountancy Bodies.
13 Florence, P. Sargent; The Logic of Industrial Organisation: Routledge & Kegan Paul, 1933 and The Logic of British & American Industry: Routledge & Kegan Paul, 1953; revised 1961 and 1972.

14 Ulton, M.A.; Industrial Concentration: Penguin, 1970.
15 Report of the Committee on Industrial Democracy; Cmnd. 6706, op. cit. chapter 1 reference 11.
16 The Stock Exchange; The Stock Exchange Fact Book: London, June 1983.
17 Dunning, John H. and Robert D. Pearce; The World's Largest Industrial Enterprises: Gower, 1981.
18 Hannah, op. cit. chapter 3 reference 51, provides a lucid account of the shift from 1880-1970 of merger activity and the resultant concentration and corporate complexity of British companies.
19 Stopford, John, J.H. Dunning and K. Haverick; The World Directory of Multi-national Enterprises: Macmillan, 1980.
20 In December 1981 the EEC Draft Regulations were published which would create a new corporate entity to be known as the European Cooperation Grouping. This subsequently became the European Economic Grouping and is now the European Economic Interest Group (EEIG).

   An EEIG would provide services to support the businesses of its member companies but would not carry on a profit making business itself. The idea is to facilitate cooperations between companies in different member states.

Chapter 5

1 Mak, H. Johannes; Subsidiary Boards in Transition: unpublished research report for the Business Associates Program: International Management Institute (formerly Centre d'etudes industrielle) − Geneva, 1982.
2 Mueller, Joachim; Strategy and Structure in Transnational Government-Sponsored Joint Ventures: policy making in the European Space Satellite Programme: unpublished doctoral thesis; Nuffield College, Oxford 1983. Quoted with permission.

Chapter 6

1 Fifth directive, op. cit. chapter 1 reference 4.
2 Report of the Committee on Industrial Democracy; Cmnd.

6706, op. cit. chapter 1 reference 11.

3 S.46 Part IV Companies Act, 1980: but see also the 2nd Savoy Co. Ltd. investigation, which made the point that members present and potential were concerned.

4 A situation reported by many Department of Trade Inspectors in cases where public companies are effectively dominated by one man.

5 Smith, Adam; The Wealth of Nations; Book V, chapter 1, Part III, 1776.

6 Payne, P.L.; British Entrepreneurship in the Nineteenth-Century: Macmillan, 1974.
Payne, P.L.; The Emergence of the Large Scale Company in Great Britain: Economic History Review, 2nd Series XX, 1967.

7 Cottrell, P.L.; Industrial Finance, 1830-1914: Methuen, 1979.

8 Berle, Adolph A. and G.C. Means; op. cit. chapter 2 reference 2.

9 The Liberal Industrial Inquiry; Britain's Industrial Future: London, 1928.
This Inquiry, strongly influenced by Keynes, had misgivings about the upper echelons of British industry and wrote: —

> "The divorce between responsibility and ownership worked out by growth and development of Joint-Stock Companies.... provides one of the clues to the future. Private enterprise has been trying.... to solve for itself the essential problem.... of how to establish an efficient system of production in which management and responsibility are in different hands from those which provide the capital, run the risk and reap the profit."

10 See, for example:
Gerrison, F.C.; The History of the Royal Dutch: Brill, London, 4 volumes between 1953 and 1957.
Reader, W.J.; Imperial Chemical Industries: Oxford University Press, Vol. 1, 1970, Vol 2 1975.
Wilson, C.; The History of Unilever: Cassell, Vols. 1 & 2, 1954, Vol. 3, 1968.
The control of the giant American corporation is discussed in: —
Herman, Edward S.; Corporate Control, Corporate Power: Cambridge University Press, 1981.

The evolution of British business enterprise is covered
by: –
Hannah, Leslie; The Rise of the Corporate Economy:
Methuen, 1976
and the experience in the United States by: –
Chandler, A.D.; Strategy & Structure – chapters in the
history of the industrial enterprise: MIT Press, 1962.

11 Rubner, Alex; The Ensnared Shareholder: Macmillan,
1964; Penguin, 1965.

12 Midgley, Kenneth; Companies and their Shareholders –
the Uneasy Relationship: Institute of Chartered Secretaries
and Administrators, London, 1975.
See also:
Midgley, Kenneth; To Whom Should the Board be
Accountable and For What?: Institute of Chartered
Secretaries and Administrators: Discussion paper, un-
dated.

13 Securities & Exchange Commission, Division of Corporate
Finance; Staff Report on Corporate Accountability – a
re-examination of rules relating to shareholder communications and shareholder participation in the corporate
electoral process and corporate governance generally: for
the Committee on Banking, United States Senate, 4th
September 1980.
Other examples of action by dissident shareholders have
arisen in McGraw Hill (USA) when an unusually high
(12%) vote in the AGM dissented on the terms of the
American Express bid: also in AB Volvo (Sweden) forcing
the board to abandon a proposed sale of 40% of the equity
to the Norwegian government; and in Burmah Oil where
members sought better terms from the British government
for the company's stake in BP.

14 Berle, Adolf A.; Preface to The Modern Corporation &
Private Property; op. cit. chapter 2, reference 2: Property,
production and revolution, 1967.

15 Confederation of British Industry; Company Affairs Committee Report; The Responsibilities of the British Public
Company; Lord Watkinson (Chairman): 1973. See chapter
1 reference 6.

16 Burnham, James; The Managerial Revolution: John Day
Company, 1941: reprinted by Greenwood Press, 1972.
See also:

Marris, R.; The Economic Theory of Managerial Capitalism: Oxford University Press, 1964.

17 Crosland, C.A.R.; The Future of Socialism: Cape, 1956.
Crosland, C.A.R.; The Private & Public Corporation in Great Britain; in E.S. Mason (ed); The Corporation in Modern Society: Harvard University Press, 1959.

18 Pahl, R. and J. Winkler; The Economic Elite — Theory and Practice; in P. Stanworth & A. Giddens (eds); Elite and Power in British Society, 1974.
See also;
Nyman, S. and A. Silbertson; The Ownership and Control of Industry: Oxford Economic Papers, Vol. 30, No. 1, March 1978.

19 Dahrendorf, R.; Class & Class Conflict in Industrial Society: Routledge & Kegan Paul, 1959.
Alan Fox, in a research paper for the Royal Commission on Trade Unions & Employee Federations (HMSO 1966) contrasted the unitary view and the pluralistic as a reference frame for analysing companies.
Commenting on Dahrendorf's analysis, Nichols suggested that: —

"Dahrendorf.... entertains the possibility that conflict may develop both *within* the industrial enterprise and also *between* the ruling classes of business and the other ruling classes. Other writers, however, whilst they are eager to assert that businessmen may have their power delimited by other groups outside the enterprise are equally keen to imply that there is no conflict of interests *within* the enterprise itself. Such theories.... have a high degree of ideological potential. Large corporation directors often assert that their interests are identical with those of their employees which means that 'we must do away with this idea that there are two sides of industry'."

Nichols, Theo; Ownership, Control & Ideology: Allen & Unwin, 1969.

20 They are typically linked with major disputes between board factions or dominant shareholders. Cases current during the research study included: —
— Trusthouse Forte's attempt to appoint a director to

the board of the Savoy Hotel, in which it held two-thirds of the equity but only 40% of the votes.
- The appointment of two directors to represent the Lonrho investment in the House of Fraser, for which it had made a contested bid.
- British Sugar Corporation – the resignation of a director appointed to represent S & W Berisford's 40% investment – following his exclusion from discussions about profit because of Berisford's take-over bid.

The removal or resignation of directors, following policy disagreements is more usual. Directors can also be barred from office by the High Court; as with three directors of Gilgate Holdings Ltd. (The Times 14th March 1981).

But such evidence reinforces the view that contested elections, in any sense of shareholder democracy, are rare.

21 Ideas put forward by the SEC (see Staff Report on Corporate Accountability: op. cit. reference 13) include: –
.. rotation of the location of the annual meeting;
.. scheduling the annual meeting at a convenient time;
.. regional shareholder meetings to supplement the annual meeting;
.. post meeting reports;
.. surveys of shareholders to discover questions they might have and providing responses;
.. reports of questions and responses.   (P. 41 para 13)
.. the encouraging of shareholder nominations to boards. The Protection of Shareholders Rights Act of 1980 provided shareholder nominations by one half of one per cent of the shareholdings.
The Corporate Democracy Act of 1980 provided for cumulative voting for directors.
.. encouragement of the use of nominating committees.
(P.115-131/Para A53-A69)

22 S. 196 and 197 Part IV Companies Act, 1948.
S. 47, 48, 49 and 50 Part IV Companies Act, 1980.

23 9th schedule (S.162) Companies Act, 1948.

24 Cornhill Consolidated Group Ltd. (in liquidation); a report by inspectors appointed by the Department of Trade: HMSO, 1980.

25 Cornhill Consolidated Group Ltd. op. cit. See paragraphs 17.02 and 17.03 page 293.

26 Hayek, F.A.; The Corporation in a Democratic Society; in Ashen, M. and G.L. Bach; Management and the Corporation in 1984: McGraw Hill, 1960.

27 Galbraith, John Kenneth; The New Industrial State: Houghton Mifflin, 1967; third edition 1978.

28 Though Steel, writing in Accounting & Business Research has argued that, "despite their vagueness, such forecasts are not meaningless, since to a small extent, they reduce uncertainty..." Steel, A.; The Accuracy of Chairmen's Non-Qualified Forecasts − an exploratory study: Accounting and Business Research, No. 47, Summer 1982.

29 Sun Tze; The Art of War: c500 BC.

30 Financial Times, 16th October 1982; The Times, 1st July 1982.

31 Financial Times, 15th June 1982.

32 The Times, 29th September 1982.

33 The Times, 18th March 1983; Financial Times, 23rd February 1983.

34 Committee to Review the Functioning of the Financial Institutions; Sir Harold Wilson (Chairman): Cmnd. 7937, 2 volumes, HMSO, June 1980.

35 The Stock Exchange; Shareholders Analysis − a supplement to the Stock Exchange Fact Book: 31st December 1980.

36 See details in chapter 7.

37 Knight, Sir Arthur; Wilson Revisited: Industrialists and Financiers: Policy Studies Institute; Discussion Paper No. 5, January 1982.

38 Board of Trade Committee on Company Law Reform; Lord Davey (Chairman): 1896.
Companies Act, 1907.

39 S.1 and S.8(2) Companies Act, 1980.

40 The Act does not apply to directors' transactions with foreign subsidiaries, although such transactions may have to be disclosed.
In relevant companies loans, guarantees or the provision for security in connection with loans, for the benefit of a director of a company or its holding company, are prohibited. An exception to the general prohibition was given in the Companies Act 1981 where the total amount outstanding does not exceed £2,500.

In a relevant company quasi loans are also generally prohibited – that is transactions under which the company assumes liability for the debts of the director. A good example would be the use by the director of a credit card to obtain goods or services for his own use where the account is chargeable to the company. Again there is an exemption where the transaction is reimbursed within two months and the total amount outstanding does not exceed £1,000. Criminal penalties may be involved if a director of a relevant company knowingly participates in a prohibited transaction.

In non-relevant companies loans, guarantees or the provision of security to a director of a company or its holding company are also generally prohibited, with the exception when the total value of the loan does not exceed £2,500.

The prohibition which applies in relevant companies to quasi loans and credit transactions does not apply in the non-relevant company.

If a director in a non-relevant company enters into a prohibited transaction he is not liable to criminal penalties but the transaction will prime facie be voidable by the company. The development of statute law to regulate transactions by companies with their directors and officers is very detailed.

Similar distinctions are drawn elsewhere in the Companies Acts: for example in the case of dormant companies (S.5 and 12, Companies Act, 1981).

41 A New Form of Incorporation for Small Firms: Cmnd. 8171, HMSO, February 1981.

42 Evidence by the Consultative Committee of Accountancy Bodies advocating a proprietary company classification was given in response to the Green Paper on New Forms of Incorporation (see reference 41) and to the Green Paper on Company Accounting and Disclosure – a consultation document: Cmnd. 7654, HMSO, September 1979, which also advocated a proprietary form with limited disclosure and no audit under the provisions of the 4th directive of the European Commission.

43 S.150 Part IV Companies Act, 1948.
    S.1 Companies Act, 1976.   S.2 Companies Act, 1981.

44 Draft 9th directive; Section 2 Article 2.

45 Draft 9th directive; Section 2 Article 3.

Chapter 7

1 Nader, Ralph and Mark Green; Public Citizens Congress Watch: an opinion editorial in The New York Times, 28th December 1979. See also The Case for a Corporate Democracy Act of 1980; op. cit. chapter 1 reference 22.

2 Millstein, Ira M. and Salem M. Katsh; The Limits of Corporate Power — Existing Constraints on the Exercise of Corporate Discretion: Macmillan with Columbia School of Business & Collier Macmillan, 1981.

3 See for example: —
Copeman, George; The Managing Director: David & Charles, 1978.
Franks, John A.; The Company Director and the Law: Oyez, 1973, with the Law Society, revised 1981.
Institute of Directors; Guidelines for Directors: 1973, revised 1982.
Loose, Peter; The Company Director — Functions, Powers and Duties: Jordan, 1953, 5th edition 1975.
Mills, G.; On the Board: Gower with the Institute of Directors, 1981.
Parker, Hugh; Letters to a New Chairman: Director Publications, 1979.
Shackleton on the Law and Practice of Meetings: A. Harding Boulton (ed). Sweet & Maxwell, 1977.

4 Hadden, Tom; Company Law and Capitalism: Weidenfeld & Nicholson, 1972, second edition 1977.

5 Mace, Miles L.; Directors — Myth and Reality: Harvard University Press, 1971.

6 Pahl R. and J. Winkler; op. cit. chapter 6 reference 18.

7 Report of the Committee of Inquiry on Industrial Democracy; op. cit. chapter 1 reference 11.

8 Fidler, John; The British Business Elite — its Attitudes and Class, Status and Power; Routledge & Kegan Paul, 1981.

9 Gower, L.C.B. et al; The Principles of Modern Company Law: Stevens & Son, 1979 (fourth edition).

10 See for example: —
Brown, Courtney; Putting the Corporate Board to Work: Macmillan, 1976.
Copeman, George; The Managing Director: David & Charles, 1978.

Dill, William R.; Running the American Corporation: The American Assembly, Columbia University, 1978.

Juran, J.M. and J. Keith Louden; The Corporate Director: American Management Association, 1966.

McSweeney, Edward; Managing the Managers: Harper & Row, 1978.

Mills, Geoffrey; op. cit. reference 3.

Mueller, Robert K.; New Directions for Directors; Lexington, 1978.

Mueller, Robert K.; Board Compass — What it Means to be a Director in a Changing World; Lexington, 1979.

Mueller, Robert K.; The Incompleat Board — the Unfolding of Corporate Governance: Lexington, 1981.

Mueller, Robert K.; Board Score — How to Judge Board Worthiness: Lexington, 1982.

Vance, Stanley C.; Corporate Leadership — Boards, Directors and Strategy: McGraw Hill, 1983.

11 Op. cit. chapter 6 reference 10.

12 Sloan, Alfred P.; My Years with General Motors: Doubleday, 1963; Macfadden, 1965.

13 Drucker, Peter; Concept of the Corporation: John Day & Co., 1946, revised Mentor, 1972.

14 Wright, J. Patrick (with John Z. DeLorean); On a Clear Day You Can See General Motors: Avon Books, 1979.

15 Confederation of British Industry; op. cit. chapter 1 reference 6.

16 Smith, Adam; op. cit. chapter 6, reference 5.

17 Millstein, Ira M. and Salem M. Katsh; op. cit. reference 2.

18 Simon, H.A.; The New Science of Management Decision: Prentice Hall, 1965.

Simon, H.A.; The Science of the Artificial: MIT, 1969.

Simon, H.A. with J.G. March; Organisations: Wiley, 1958. And see, for discussion of satisficing behaviour: —

Simon, H.A.; On the Concept of Organisational Goals; in Etzioni, A.; A Sociological Reader in Complex Organisations: HRW, 1961.

19 Fox, Alan; Industrial Sociology and Industrial Relations: Royal Commission on Trade Unions and Employers Associations: Research paper 3, HMSO, 1969.

20 March, James G. and Herbert A. Simon; Organisations: Wiley, 1958.

21 Cyert R.M. and J.G. March; A Behavioural Theory of the

Firm: Prentice-Hall, 1963.

22 Weber, Max; The Theory of Social and Economic Organisation: Free Press, 1947.

23 Selznick, P.; Leadership in Administration – a Sociological Interpretation: Harper & Row, 1957.

24 Bagehot, Walter; The English Constitution: first published 1867; Longmans, 1915; Fontana 1963.

25 A matter confirmed by Corporate Policy Group studies – see chapter 10.

26 Ansoff, H. Igor; Corporate Strategy: McGraw Hill, 1965; Penguin, 1968.

27 Argenti, John; Systematic Corporate Planning: Nelson, 1974.

28 Andrews, K.R.; The Concept of Corporate Strategy: Irwin, 1971, revised 1980.

29 Peters, T.J. and R.H. Waterman Jr.; In Search of Excellence: Harper & Row, 1982.

30 Grinyer, P.H. and J.C. Spender; Turnaround – the Fall and Rise of the Newton Chambers Group – Managerial Recipes for Strategic Success: Associated Business Press, 1979.

See for example: –

Cole, Lord; The Future of the Board: seminar paper for Industrial Education & Research Foundation, 1969; in Taylor & Macmillan (eds); Top Management Strategy and Planning: Longman, 1973.

Ferguson, C.R. and R. Dickinson; Critical Success Factors for Directors in the Eighties: Business Horizons, May/June 1982.

Parker, Hugh; Letters to a New Chairman: The Director, August 1978.

Wommack, W.W.; Responsibility of the Board of Directors and Management in Corporate Strategy: Harvard Business Review, Sept/Oct. 1979.

31 Andrews, K.R.; Directors' Responsibility for Corporate Strategy: Harvard Business Review, Nov/Dec. 1980.

32 Chandler, A.D.; Strategy and Structure: MIT, 1962. cf. Charnon, D.F.; The Strategy and Structure of British Enterprise: Macmillan, 1973.

33 Burns, T. and G.M. Stalker; The Management of Innovation: Tavistock, 1961.

34 Mintzberg, H.; The Structuring of Organisations: Prentice Hall, 1979; and Power In and Around Organisations;

Prentice Hall, 1983.
35 Solomons, D.; Divisional Performance − Measurement and Control: Irwin, 1965.
36 Aguilar, Frank; Scanning the Business Environment: Harvard, 1962.
37 Pfeffer, Jeffrey; Power in Organisations: Pitman, 1981.
38 Selznick, op. cit. reference 23.
39 Pfeffer, op. cit. reference 37.
40 Accounting Standards (Steering) Committee; op. cit. chapter 1 reference 16.
41 See for example: −
Draft fifth directive, op. cit. chapter 1 reference 4.
Vredeling draft, op. cit. chapter 1 reference 17.
Royal Commission on Trade Unions and Employers Associations: research papers by George S. Bain, Alan Fox, A.I. Marsh, W.E.J. McCarthy; HMSO, 1966.
Bate, Paul and Iain Mangham; Exploring Participation: Wiley, 1981.
Bell, D. Wallace; Industrial Participation: Pitman, 1979.
Brannen, Peter, Eric Batstone, Derek Fatchett and Philip White; The Worker Director − A Sociology of Participation: Hutchinson, 1976.
Industrial Democracy in Europe; IDE Research Group, Oxford (Clarendon), 1981.
42 See chapter 1 reference 22.
43 Mitroff, Ian I.; Stakeholders of the Organisational Mind: Jossey-Bass, 1983.
44 Useem, M.; Corporations and the Corporate Elite: The Annual Review of Sociology, 6: 41-77, 1980.
45 Pennings, Johannes M.: Interlocking Directorates: Jossey-Bass, 1980.
46 Vogel, David; Coercian Versus Consultation: University of California, September 1980.
47 Companies Act, 1981: Deloitte Haskins & Sells; Tolley, London 1982.

> "It is important to appreciate that the concessions that are available relate to the financial statements and other documents in respect of an accounting reference period that must be delivered to the Registrar of Companies under Section 1(7)(a) of the Companies Act 1976. The concessions do not affect the information that must be provided to members of the company. Strictly speak-

ing, therefore, they are not concessions at all, since they permit small and medium-sized companies to do more work rather than less work. That is to say they may, if they so choose, prepare two sets of financial statements, rather than one set as now."

48 Op. cit. chapter 1 reference 11.
49 Thomas, R.E.; The Government of Business: Philip Allen, 1976 and 1981.
50 Crouch, Colin (ed); State and Economy in Contemporary Capitalism: Croom Helm, 1979.
51 The Council for the Securities Industry was set up in 1978 with the following aims: —
   a) to maintain the highest ethical standards in the conduct of business within the securities industry.
   b) to keep under constant review the evolution of the securities industry, market practice and related codes of conduct and to scrutinise the effectiveness of existing forms of regulation and the machinery for their administration.
   c) to maintain arrangements for the investigation of cases of alleged misconduct within the securities industry and breaches of codes of conduct or best practice and to keep these arrangements under review.
   d) to initiate new policies and codes as necessary concerning activities in the securities industry other than those properly within the domestic province of each individual constituent member.
   e) to resolve differences on matters of principle between constituent parts of the securities industry.
   f) to consider the need for changes in legislation affecting the activities of the securities industry and to examine any proposals for such legislation.
   g) to ensure liaison with the European Commission on securities industry matters and the implementation of the EEC Capital Markets Code of Conduct.
   See Rules and Regulations of The Stock Exchange, London; Admission of Securities to Listing: The Stock Exchange, London; The City Code on Take-Overs and Mergers: The Take-Over Panel; The Stock Exchange, London.
52 The Times, 15th November 1983: "No more private

investors after the year 2000?"
53 For further consideration see: —
Briston, R.J. and R. Dobbins; The Growth and Impact of
Institutional Investors: Institute of Chartered Accountants
(Research Committee), 1978.

Chapter 8

1 The argument in this chapter has previously appeared in
Tricker, R.I.; The context of Corporate Accountability;
paper to Deloitte Haskins & Sells/SSRC Research Symposium; London Business School, January 1982: The Corporate Policy Group 1982.
2 Chapter 4.
3 Chapter 5.
4 Chapter 6.
5 Op. cit. chapter 1 reference 9 and chapter 2 references 9,
10 and 11.
6 Chapter 1.
7 See Dahrendorf, R., op. cit. chapter 6 reference 19.
8 Op. cit. chapter 1, reference 11.
9 Op. cit. chapter 1, reference 10.
10 Flint, David; University of Glasgow; in private correspondence.
11 Op. cit. chapter 1, reference 17.
12 Op. cit. chapter 1, reference 6.
13 Company Accounting and Disclosure: a consultative
document: Cmnd. 7654, HMSO, 1979.
14 Op. cit. chapter 1 reference 16.
15 Which led to the Foreign Trades Corrupt Practices Act,
1980.
16 The SEC Staff Report (op. cit. chapter 6 reference 13)
commented that the issues "astonished the public, the
shareholders and, in many cases, the affected company's
directors themselves".
17/18 Op. cit. chapter 6 reference 13.
19 See Accountability of the Corporation: The Corporate
Policy Group, 1982.
20 Fidler, J.; Op. cit. chapter 7 reference 8.
Gower, L.C.B. et al; Op. cit. chapter 7 reference 9.
Spencer, A.C.; On the Edge of the Organisation: Wiley,
1983.

Spencer, A.C.; Some Lessons Arising from the Role Relationships of Non-Executive Directors: Ph.D. Dissertation; Sheffield Polytechnic 1980.

Spencer A.C.; Non-Executive Realities: Management Today, May 1983.

21 Principles of Corporate Governance and Structure – a restatement of recommendations: American Law Institute, 1982.

22 New York Times, 10th June 1982.

23 See for example: –
The Corporate Report, op. cit. chapter 1 reference 29.

24 Op. cit. chapter 6 reference 13.

25 Op. cit. chapter 1 reference 4.

26 Op. cit. chapter 1 reference 11.

27 Op. cit. chapter 2 reference 12.

28 Advisory, Conciliation and Arbitration Service; Code of Practice: Disclosure of Information to Trade Unions for Collective Bargaining; under S6(1) of the Employment Protection Act, 1975 and subsequent amendments.

29 Child, John; The Business Enterprise in Modern Industrial Society: Collier-Macmillan, 1969.

30 Shanks, Michael; Chairman, National Consumer Council, London; in private correspondence, 1980.

31 Op. cit. chapter 1 reference 16.

32 For example, a group representing the labour unions and other interests critical of managerial prerogative published proposals for a "Corporate Democracy Act" in 1980 (chapter 1 see reference 22). In it they called for a board with a majority of independent directors, with a "Constituency Board", with at leat nine members, who, in addition to their traditional fiduciary obligations, shall have special responsibilities to oversee, investigate, receive complaints about and address the board on matters affecting, respectively, 1) employee well-being, 2) consumer protection, 3) environmental protection, 4) community relations, 5) shareholder rights, 6) law compliance, 7) technology assessment, 8) anti-trust standards, and 9) political relations. Criticism has also been raised in the United States about the dangers of 'tokenism'; that is appointing directors with the appearance of appeasing interest group sensitivities.

33 For a fuller discussion see: —
Hickson, D.J. et al; Organisation as Power: Research into organisational behaviour; Vol. 3, 1981.
Scott, J.; Corporations, Classes and Capitalism: Hutchinson, 1979. (In chapter 2 refers to "constellations of interest").

34 Boston Consulting Group; Strategic Alternatives for the British Motor Cycle Industry: a report to the House of Commons, London, 1975.

35 Spurrell, Daniel J.; Business Strategy in the UK — the Challenge from Abroad: The National Westminster Bank Quarterly Review, August 1980.

36 The details of this proposal are developed in chapter 14, together with other normative suggestions.

37 Originally presented at a news conference on 12th December 1969 by the President of the Institute of Chartered Accountants in England and Wales, Ronald (now Sir Ronald) Leach. Published under the title "Statement of Intent on Accounting Standards in the 1970's"), London, 1970.

38 Zeff, Stephen A.; Forging Accounting Principles in Five Countries — a History of an Analysis of Trends: Arthur Andersen Lectures; The University of Edinburgh and Stipes Publishing, Illinois, 1971.

39 The Economist, 13th December 1969; Accountancy — Less of an Art.

40/41 Having failed to integrate the accountancy bodies in the UK and Ireland in 1969, the Consultative Committee of Accountancy Bodies was formed in 1974, to make public representations and pronouncements on accountancy matters for the benefit of the profession as a whole.
The original member bodies were: —
The Institute of Chartered Accountants in England & Wales
The Institute of Chartered Accountants of Scotland
The Institute of Chartered Accountants in Ireland
The Association of Certified Accountants
The Institute of Cost & Management Accountants
(The Chartered Institute of Public Finance & Accountancy joined later).
"The initial emphasis was political rather than technical. The profession was concerned to demonstrate the ability

to continue its tradition of professional self-regulation. However CCAB assumed responsibility for the Accounting Standards Steering Committee (now the Accounting Standards Committee) which existed before CCAB. This took it into the technical, and potentially contentious, areas.
Constitutionally the CCAB is a consultative body, lacking primary executive power. The sovereignty for major decisions lies with the Councils of the six individual bodies. Within the overriding authority of these bodies, the CCAB has power to organise joint committees, appoint their Chairmen and provide resources for them."
Tricker, R.I.; Governing the Institute: Institute of Chartered Accountants, 1983.

42 See, for detailed discussion: —
Institute of Chartered Accountants in England & Wales; Analysed Reporting; a research study by Coopers & Lybrand, published by the Institute, 1977.

43 Coleman, Robert; Corporate Accountability — a European Perspective: in proceedings of a conference on Corporate Accountability, Nuffield College, Oxford, December 1981. Published by The Corporate Policy Group, Oxford, 1982.

44 Op. cit. chapter 1 reference 15.

Chapter 9

1 Deloitte Haskins & Sells; Corporate Structure — Subsidiaries or Divisions?: August 1983.

2 Hadden, Tom; The Control of Corporate Groups: Institute of Advanced Legal Studies, University of London, 1982.

3 See Salomon v Salomon & Co., 1897 (AC22). The equivalent case in the United States is often referred to as the Deep Rock Case.
In a more recent judgement Templeton L.J. said (In re Southard & Co (1979) 1 WLR 1198): "English company law possesses some curious features which may generate curious results. A parent company may spawn a number of subsidiary companies, all controlled directly or indirectly by the shareholders of the parent company. If one of the subsidiary companies, to change the metaphor, turns out

to be the runt of the litter and declines into insolvency to the dismay of its creditors, the parent company and the other subsidiary companies may prosper to the joy of the shareholders without any liability for the debts in the insolvent subsidiary".

4   "Section 332 of the Companies Act 1948 provides criminal sanctions where it appears that any business of a company has been carried on either with the intention of defrauding the company's creditors or the creditors of any other person, or for any other fraudulent purposes. By virtue of the court's judgement in "Director of Public Prosecutions v Schildkamp (1971) AC1", however, these criminal sanctions for fraudulent trading applied only in circumstances in which the company was being wound up. The 1981 Act removes this restriction. In future, these sanctions will apply whether or not the company has been, or is in the course of being wound up. (CA 1948, s.332(3); Sec. 96)."
    Companies Act, 1981; Deloitte Haskins & Sells/Tolley, 1982.

5 Explanatory notes to the proposal for a 9th directive based on article 54(3) of the EEC Treaty on links between undertakings, and in particular on groups. European Community.

6 Proposal for a European Company statute: Original draft published 1975.

7 Writing on "The Group Problem and the Draft Ninth Directive" (May, 1981, CLP (81)10), Department of Trade), Professor L.C.B. Gower confirms the existing problem under UK law thus:—
    "As I see it, the problem under UK law (and to a greater or lesser extent under the laws of the other Member States) is as follows:—
    a)   We still accept the basic principle that each company in a Group 'is a separate legal entity possessed of separate legal rights and liability'. (Per Roskill, L.J. (1975) 3 W L R 491 at 521).
    b)   But, to an ever-increasing extent, inroads have been made into this principle both by the legislature (in the Companies Acts and in a vast array of tax, property, employment protection and other Acts) and by the judiciary, either by openly piercing the corporate veil or by the use or abuse

of various devices such as agency, trust or estoppel. (To the examples collected in my "Modern Company Law" (4th ed. and Supp), Chap 6 add "Amalgamated Investment & Property Co. v Texas Commerce Bank" (1981) 2 W L R 554."

8 The boundaries adopted in the existing Companies Acts (see chapter 2 reference 16) would probably suffice.
9 Hadden, op. cit. reference 2.
10 S.17 (1)(b); Companies Act, 1967.
11 Analysed Reporting – a background study: Coopers & Lybrand, for the Research Committee of the Institute of Chartered Accountants in England & Wales, 1977.
12 S.3 and 4; Companies Act, 1967.
13 S.4 (3); Companies Act, 1981.
14 The Corporate Report, op. cit. chapter 1 reference 16.
15 Securities & Exchange Commission; 10-K form pursuant to S.13 or S.15(d) of The Securities Exchange Act, 1934.
16 Welchman, Tony; Segment Reporting – Still a Long Way to Go: International Accounting Bulletin, November 1983.
17 Op. cit. reference 11.

Chapter 10

1 Op. cit. chapter 1 reference 10.
2 Op. cit. chapter 1 reference 8.
3 The suggestions about the role of the non-executive director promulgated by PRO NED (see chapter 1 reference 5) and the Institute of Directors (see chapter 1 reference 7) do provide a non-statutory set of insights.
4 Report of the Company Law Committee; Lord Jenkins (Chairman); Cmnd. 1749, HMSO, 1962.
5 Case law does indicate, however, a tendency for the courts, in both the UK and the United States, to take the status of directors into account when considering standards of care. In this context the position of executive directors, intimately concerned with day to day management of the enterprise, is likely to be different from that of an outside director. See discussion of Dorchester Finance v Stebbing in Boyle, A.J. and J. Birds (eds); Company Law, Jordon 1983.
6 The following summary of the American position is taken from Block, Dennis J. and Suzanne I. Tufts; The

Application of the Business Judgement Rule: American Bar Association; Conference on the dynamics of corporate control, December 1983: –

"The Business Judgement Rule In General

A. *Origin of the Rule – Fiduciary Duty of Directors to Corporation and its Shareholders:*

1. Directors have a duty to direct the management of the business and affairs of the corporation and are deemed to owe a fiduciary duty to the corporation and its shareholders. In discharging their duties, directors are expected to act with due care, in good faith and in a manner consistent with the proposition that a business corporation is organised and operated for the benefit of its shareholders. See Block & Miller, "The Responsibilities and Obligations of Corporate Directors in Takeover Contests", 11 Sec. Reg. L.J. 44, 46 (1983) ("Block & Miller"); Veasey, "Seeking a Safe Harbor from Judicial Scrutiny of Directors' Business Decisions – An Analysis of Framework for Litigation Strategy and Counselling Directors", 37 Bus. Law. 1247, 1250 (1982) ("Veasey").

2. *State Corporate Law* – matters relating to authority and responsibility of management and boards of directors are determined by reference to the law of the state of incorporation. Although most states rely on common law principles, at least twenty have codified these requirements.

   a. Delaware has not adopted any codification of the standard of care. Conduct of directors of Delaware corporations is measured against the standards set forth in Delaware case law. Veasey and Manning, "Codified Standard – Safe Harbor or Uncharted Reef? , 35 Bus. Law 919, 925 (198) ("Veasey and Manning").

   b. *N.Y. Business Corporate Law S 717* – requires that a director perform his duties in good faith and with the degree of care which an ordinarily prudent person in a like position would use under similar circumstances.

3. The Delaware Supreme Court has held that: "directors of a corporation in managing the corporate affairs are bound to use that amount of care which ordinarily careful and prudent men would use in similar circumstances," *"Graham v Allis-Chalmers Mfg. Co."*, 188 A.2d 125, 130 (Del. Super. Ct. 1963).

4. However, the *Graham* court went on to say that if a director:

> has recklessly reposed confidence in an obviously untrustworthy employee, has refused or neglected cavalierly to perform his duty as a director, or has ignored either willfully or through inattention obvious danger signs of employee wrongdoing, the law will cast the burden of liability upon him. *Id.*

5. The foregoing standards expected of directors are aspirational. A director who discharges his duties in accordance with these standards will not be held liable. See Section 35, Model Business Corporation Act ("35 MBCA"). That is not to say that, in all cases, if he or she fails to live up to those ideal standards, a director will be subject to liability. (Veasey & Manning). However, the converse is not necessarily true: failure to act in accordance with these standards does not automatically lead to liability. Here is where the business judgement rule comes in.

B. *The Business Judgement Rule — Definition and Concept*

1. In *Joy* v *North*, 692 F.2d 880, 885 (2d Cir. 1982), *cert. denied,* U.S. , 103, S.Ct. 1498, 75 L.Ed.2d 930, (1983), the Second Circuit noted that:

> Whereas an automobile driver who makes a mistake in judgement as to speed or distance injuring a pedestrian will likely be called upon to respond in damages, a corporate officer who makes a mistake in judgement as to economic conditions, consumer tastes or production line efficiency will rarely, if ever, be found liable for damages suffered by the corporation....

2. Thus, it has been noted that, "(t)he business judgement rule is a specific application of the directors' duty of care to the situation where, after reasonable investigation, the directors adopt a course of action which they honestly and reasonably believe will benefit the corporation, but which turns out to have been in error. Should the directors be sued because of their decision, the court — at least in theory — will not second-guess the merits of the decision but will examine only the directors' good faith and due care." Block and Prussin "The Good Judgement Rule and Shareholder Derivative Actions: Viva Zapata?", 37 Bus. Lawyer 27, 32 (1981) ("Block and Prussin")."

7 Op. cit chapter 7 reference 3.

8 Anthony, Robert N.; Planning & Control Systems – a Framework for Analysis: Harvard University, 1965.

9 Mace, Miles L.; Directors – Myth & Reality: Harvard University, 1971.

10 Spencer, A.C.; On the Edge of the Organisation – the Role of the Outside Director: Wiley, 1983.

11 Op. cit. chapter 1 reference 4.

Chapter 11

1 The New York Times (9th October 1983), reporting a study of board composition, concluded that the use of outside directors was widespread, that there was a greater use of board committees than previously, and a change in attitude by executive directors and others that the time for a strong, independent board had arrived.
Searching the files of 8.500 publicly held companies they found that no single person served on more than 11 boards, and that only 17 people had 8 or more public company directorships. In the top 17 were retired chairmen of companies, the Dean of a business school, the Chairman of the American Red Cross and one woman.
See also chapter 12 reference 8.

2 Juneval, Book 3.

3 Pearce, John A.; The Relationship of Internal versus External Orientations to Financial Measures of Strategic Performance: Strategic Management Journal, Vol. 4 297-306 (1983).

4 Bulletin of the European Community, Brussels, 1975.

5 Op. cit. reference 4.

6 See discussions in chapters 1 and 6.

7 Charkham, Jonathan; A New Way to Build Better Boards: PRO NED, 1983. (See chapter 1 reference 5).

8 Financial Times, 30th September 1983.

9 Henderson, Denys; The Large Company's View: Summer Conference, Institute of Chartered Accountants in England & Wales, 13-17th July 1982.

10 Op. cit. chapter 1 reference 6.

11 Op. cit. chapter 1 reference 10.

12 See for example: –
Bill 38, 1977. "A bill to amend the law relating to directors and auditors, to define their responsibilities; to make

provision with respect to the appointment and function of non-executive directors, auditors and audit committees; to require the preparation of certain data and estimates". House of Commons, 12th December 1977.

13 Op. cit. chapter 1 reference 8.

14 Hansard, 18th December 1977.

15 The Sponsors of PRO NED are: –
Accepting Houses Committee
Bank of England
British Institute of Management
The Committee of London Clearing Bankers
The Committee of the Scottish Clearing Bankers
Confederation of British Industry
Equity Capital for Industry Limited
Finance for Industry plc
The Institutional Shareholders' Committee
The Stock Exchange

16 The Role of the Non-Executive Director: PRO NED, February 1982. See chapter 1 reference 5.

17 Code of Practice for the Non-Executive Director; Institute of Directors. Undated. See chapter 1 reference 7.

18 Charkham, Jonathan; in a paper to a joint conference of The International Bar Association and The Institute of Chartered Accountants in England & Wales, London, 20th April 1983.

19 PRO NED – the Promotion of Non-Executive Directors: an organisation sponsored by a group of City of London and business institutions to promote the recognition of the importance of non-executive directors. Founded in 1982. Director – Jonathan Charkham, 30 Cursitor Street, London EC4A 1DS.

20 For further information see reports of: –
The Central Policy Review Staff – discussed in the Financial Times, 30th June 1981.
The Commons, Treasury and Civil Service Select Committee on the financing of nationalised industry, 1981.
The Nationalised Industries Chairmen's Group – including a joint study with the Treasury and a working party with the National Economic Development Council, CBI, TUC and others.

21 Partners of a private company's auditors used to be allowed to serve on the boards of such companies; but this

was prohibited by the 1967 Companies Act.

22 Op. cit. chapter 1 reference 7.

23 The Institute of Chartered Accountants in England & Wales: Progress Report of IMACE (ethical sub-committee), 12th July 1983.

24 New York Stock Exchange: White Paper 1983, with The American Institute of Certified Public Accountants (Executive Committee) statement on audit committees of boards of directors; 1967. The third payment for listing of a company; regulation 9th December 1976.
See also:—
Securities & Exchange Commission: Standing Audit Committees Composed of Outside Directors; Release 123 dated 23rd March 1972, SEC Accounting Rules.

25 Mautz, R.K. and F.L. Neumann; Corporate Audit Committees — Policies & Practices: Ernst & Ernst, 1977.

26 Op. cit. chapter 1 reference 10.

27 Op. cit. chapter 1 reference 10.

28 Bank of England Quarterly Bulletin, March 1983.
See also:—
Bank of England Quarterly Bulletin, December 1979.

29 Company Secretary's Review; Survey of Non-Executive Directors and Audit Committees: Tolley, 1981.

30 Korn/Ferry International; Boards of Directors Study 1980, 1981 and 1983: 2/4 King Street, St. James, London SW1Y 6QL.
Other studies include:—
Institute of Directors and Booz-Allen & Hamilton; The Responsibilities and Contribution of Non-Executive Directors on the Boards of UK Companies, October 1979.
The Director and The MSL Group; a Survey of Current Practices in the employment of non-executive directors: December 1969 (The Director) and October 1970 (MSL Group).
Corporate Consulting Group; The Non-Executive Director in the UK: based on discussions with chairmen and non-executive directors; undated: and the Survey of Non-Executive Directors Appointed in 1980; 24 Buckingham Gate, London SW1.

31 Tricker, R.I.; The Independent Director: Tolley, 1978.

32 Op. cit. reference 4.

33 Op. cit. chapter 1 reference 4.

34 Op. cit. chapter 1 reference 11.
35 Draft European Communities directive on procedures for informing and consulting employees; and draft fifth directive on the harmonisation of company law: Department of Employment and Department of Trade & Industry; consultative document, November 1983.
36 On 15th December 1983 the working group in Brussels examining the draft directive proposed a significant amendment; viz: that "The member states shall provide that the (public) company shall be organised either according to the two-tier system.... or according to the one-tier system. They may also permit the company to choose one of the two systems." In other words, the law would not necessarily have to permit companies to choose between the systems; it could legislate for a single tier or a two-tier system if thought appropriate: Department of Trade & Industry (Company Legislation Division) 19th December 1983.
37 Op. cit. chapter 1 reference 17.
38 For a discussion of a British alternative to the draft 5th directive and Vredeling proposals on employee participation see:
CBI: British Employee Involvement Today; The Practices and Experience of CBI Member Companies; December 1983.
39 Press notice issued jointly by The Department of Employment and the Department of Trade & Industry, 9th November 1983.
40 See discussion in chapters 7 and 8.

Chapter 12

1 Table A: Article 75; Companies Act, 1948.
The first directors may also be named in the Articles, appointed by the first meeting of the members or by special provision in the articles. (Loose, Peter; The Company Director: Jordans, 1953; Thomas R.E.; The Government of Business: Philip Allan, 1976 and 1981.)
2 Thomas, R.E.; op. cit. reference 1.
3 Loose, Peter; op. cit. reference 1.
4 See discussion in chapter 6.
5 Op. cit. chapter 1 reference 4.

6 Tricker, R.I.; The Independent Director — A Study of the Non-Executive Director and of the Audit Committee: a research study sponsored by Deloitte Haskins & Sells, London; Tolley, 1978.
7 Berle & Means; op. cit. chapter 2 reference 2.
8 The Conference Board; Corporate Directorship Practices — Membership and Committees of the Board (Jeremy Bacon), 1973.

This study, of 850 companies, reported that 86% of non-manufacturing companies and 71% of manufacturing companies had a majority of outside directors. The study also lists the principal title or positions of the outside director viz:—

	Number of Directors	%	Number of Directors	%
Manufacturing	653	22.4	424	17.2
Banking	428	14.6	357	14.5
Law	359	12.2	286	11.6
Retired	309	10.6	221	8.9
Investment	299	10.2	240	9.7
Education	162	6.0	108	4.4
Consulting	150	5.0	77	3.1
All Other	554	19.0	748	30.6
	2,914	100.0%	2,461	100.0%
Sample size	511 Manufacturing Companies		340 Non-Manufacturing Companies	

Principal affiliations of outside directors – USA companies

Whilst top executives of other, non-competing, companies are widely used, notice the representation of consultants and (under education) business school staff.
See also:—
Op. cit. chapter 11, reference 1.
The Conference Board; Corporate Directorship Practices — Role, Selection and Legal Status of the Board (Jeremy Bacon and James K. Brown), 1975.
More recently case examples have arisen of additional executive directors being appointed to American public company boards, but not in sufficient numbers to challenge the data in chapter 11 reference 1.
9 Murphy, Sir Leslie; Control and Financing of the Nationalised Industries: John Simons Lecture, The Institute of Administrative Management, 16th February 1981.
10 In the UK the taxation arguments in favour of incorporation become less attractive as the rate of Corporation Tax

in the small company approaches the marginal rate of tax paid by the proprietor.

The taxation rules for closed companies, basically PTY's, which seek to bring into tax charge sums reinvested in the business and which would otherwise bear a higher charge if distributed as proprietor's salary or dividend, were significantly changed in the Finance Act, 1982.

The principal benefit lies in the ability of the owner-director to invest any surplus profits through pension funds more tax beneficially than if trading independently. Pension schemes are now available which enable such pension fund investment to be reinvested in the business.

11 Emphasised, for example, in the following comment: —

> "It is the nature of capitalism. Nowhere in the world do people form companies and then guarantee that nobody will lose their money. This is the capitalist system."
> *Sir Freddie Laker in a 1983 BBC television programme, discussing his customers' losses on the collapse of the Skytrain service.*

12 Coyne, John and Mike Wright; Buy-Outs and British Industry: Lloyds Bank Review, October 1982.

The most dramatic example of an entire corporate buy-out was in the state owned National Freight Corporation sold to its directors and 28,000 employees. (For discussion see The Times, 7th September 1981).

13 The Telegraph, 24th October 1983.

Chapter 13

1 The numbers have been generalised to preserve the anonymity of the company, as agreed in the original research design.

2 Acknowledgement is given to David Brockhouse, then of IMR Consultants, Johannesburg, South Africa, for this idea, given in private correspondence following a presentation made by the author in May 1980 on the strategy, structure and styles of management in complex groups.

Chapter 14

1 Hofstede, G.; Culture and Organisation — a literature

review study: Journal of Enterprise Management, Vol. 1, 1978, Pergamon Press.

2 Macfarlane, Alan; The Origins of English Individualism – the Family, Property and Social Transition: Basil Blackwell, 1978.

The author challenges the Macaulay, Marx and Weberian analysis of a transition from peasant to capitalist society. He uses detailed studies of legal history, diaries and legal treatises to demonstrate that the current views on the nature of property, inheritance practices, household and kinship structures and industrial production (business) are misfounded: and shows that since the thirteenth-century

"England has been inhabited.... by a people whose social, economic and legal system was in essence different not only from that of peoples in Asia and Eastern Europe but also in all probability from the Celtic and Continental countries of the same period."

3 Tawney, R.H.; Religion and the Rise of Capitalism: The Holland Memorial Lectures, 1922, Penguin Books, 1938.

4 Smiles, Samuel; Self Help: first published 1859; Sphere Books, 1968.

5 Small firms; Report of the Committee of Inquiry on Small Firms; J.E. Bolton (Chairman): Cmnd. 4811, HMSO, November 1971.

6 Wiener, Martin J.; English Culture and the Decline of the Industrial Spirit – 1850-1980: Cambridge University Press, 1981.

7 Cole, G.D.H.; Studies in Class Structure: Routledge and Kegan Paul, 1955.

8 Jackson, J.B.H.; in a talk to the CBI in July 1983 on the implications of the draft 5th directive.

9 Collinge, Chris; Investing in the Local Economy: Business Finance and the Role of Local Government: Community Projects Foundation, London N5 2AG.

10 Rybczynski, T.M.; Structural Changes in the Financing of British Industry: National Westminster Bank Review, May 1982.

Index